79° West Longitude from 78° London

N I A   Portsmouth Norfolk
Suffolk   Dismal

ALBEMARLE SOUND

Currituck Inlet

Roanoke Inlet
nearfilled up

New Inlet

PAMLICO SOUND

Cape Hatteras

Ocracock Inlet

Cedar Inlet

Cape Lookout

Roanoke River

ATLANTIC OCEAN

Washington

Wilmington

Brunswick

Cape Fear

Frying Pan Shoal

Long Bay

Kingston

A T L A N T I C

hington 2°   1°   0   1°

The Kirklands
of Ayr Mount

William Kirkland (1768–1836). Portrait attributed to Jacob
Marling of Raleigh (d. 1833). Courtesy Richard H. Jenrette.

Jean Bradley Anderson

The Kirklands
of Ayr Mount

The University of North Carolina Press

Chapel Hill ❦ London

Library of Congress Cataloging-in-Publication Data

Anderson, Jean Bradley.
  The Kirklands of Ayr Mount / by Jean Bradley Anderson.
    p.   cm.
  Includes bibliographical references (p.   ).
  Includes index.
  ISBN 0-8078-1930-1 (alk. paper)
    1. Kirkland family.   2. Ayr Mount (N.C.)   3. Dwellings—
North Carolina—Orange County.   4. Plantations—North
Carolina—Orange County.   5. Orange County (N.C.)—
Biography.   6. Orange County (N.C.)—Genealogy.
7. Plantation owners—North Carolina—Orange County—
Biography.   I. Title.
CT274.K56A53   1990
975.6'565—dc20
[B]   90-12409
                                                          CIP

The paper in this book meets the guidelines for permanence
and durability of the Committee on Production Guidelines for
Book Longevity of the Council on Library Resources.

Manufactured in the United States of America

95 94 93 92 91   5 4 3 2 1

Endpapers: Map of North Carolina published by H. C. Carey
and I. Lea in *A Complete Historical, Chronological, and Geographical American Atlas, Being a Guide to the History of
North and South America and the West Indies* (Philadelphia,
1822). Courtesy North Carolina Collection, University of
North Carolina Library, Chapel Hill.

❧ *Contents* ❧

Contents

A section of photographs will be found
following page 73.

❦ *Preface* ❦

L ESS THAN A MILE outside the town of Hillsborough, North Carolina, stands Ayr Mount, an imposing mansion built in 1815. Situated on a rise above the Eno River, the house looks down on open
fields that gently slope away to the rich bottomlands below. In the period
of its construction, the house was almost alone in the region in being
brick, and it was clear testimony to the standing, ambition, and taste of
its owner and builder, William Kirkland. The "big house" of a southern
plantation shared many of the functions of the English country house as
described by Mark Girouard: "It was the headquarters from which land
was administered and power organized. It was a show-case, in which to
exhibit and entertain supporters and good connections. . . . It was an
image-maker, which projected an aura of glamour, mystery or success
around its owner. It was visible evidence of his wealth. It showed his
credentials."[1] William Kirkland's house filled these roles.

Ayr Mount remained in the Kirkland family for 170 years until the line
that held it died out. In 1985 it was purchased from Kirkland in-laws
and impeccably restored and renovated by Richard Hampton Jenrette.
Its impressive style and architectural distinction posed questions that
local lore and lateral descendants could not fully answer. Who was William Kirkland? Why did he settle in Hillsborough, and what was the
source of his wealth? Who composed his family, particularly those who
remained at Ayr Mount? Over the course of time, information about the
family's Scottish origins and the first generation in America had grown
fuzzy or had faded away entirely, even in the family itself. The house and
a few fine furnishings were the only tangible links with a past but dimly
remembered. Folklore began to fill the void that knowledge left blank.
By 1972 the last Kirkland at Ayr Mount had died, the original acreage
had drastically dwindled through piecemeal sales, and the house had
deteriorated from neglect.

The new owner, deeply committed to historic preservation, was determined to restore the house and grounds as they might have been in their
heyday and has spared no expense to fulfill that ambition. Today the
house speaks for itself. No building exists in a vacuum, however, and

beyond the image of wealth and respectability that William Kirkland wished to project, the house reveals nothing of the Kirklands themselves or the context of their lives in piedmont North Carolina. To restore the house and grounds without reconstructing the history of the life lived there, Richard Jenrette thought, was to leave the job half done. Thus the rationale for a history of the family: *The Kirklands of Ayr Mount*.

Unfortunately, no treasure trove of family papers has survived to supply ready answers to the questions the house posed. Two family Bibles, a bundle of letters, snapshots, miscellaneous recipes, and newspaper clippings remain as evidence of the Kirklands' one and three-quarter centuries at Ayr Mount. The dearth of family papers has been somewhat compensated for by two vast collections of in-laws' papers in the Southern Historical Collection of the University of North Carolina at Chapel Hill Library—those of the Ruffin and Cameron families—and by a variety of public documents in the North Carolina Division of Archives and History. Together with miscellaneous letters in other collections, these surviving records have yielded sufficient details to form a coherent family history.

Still, serious gaps mar its comprehensiveness. Almost nothing, for example, is revealed of either the Kirkland slaves or plantation operations. The basis for William Kirkland's wealth was unquestionably his commercial ventures, but his place in the planter elite depended on his ownership of numerous acres and slaves. Beyond the numbers of both, a few names of the more important servants, and a scattering of references to crops, the years of toil in the interaction of slaves and land remain a blank. Neither introspective nor inclined to epistolary discourse, the Kirklands left few clues to their feelings or considered opinions about the issues of their day and place—slavery, religion, politics—or of the pursuits that filled their leisure. Convention and fashion rather than individual preference and taste seem to have dictated their modus vivendi. Objective facts of their day-to-day existence are the primary content of their correspondence; nevertheless, these matter-of-fact and gossipy letters contribute significantly to the chronicle of their lives.

Besides the house itself, other family possessions have survived to fill out the picture of life at Ayr Mount, and whenever possible Jenrette has purchased them and returned them to Ayr Mount. The Broadwood fortepiano, the Sheraton dining table, two mahogany card tables, four mahogany side chairs, a tilt-top walnut table, a pine chest of drawers, table, and wash stand, a sleigh bed, three large crystal covered bowls, some flat silver and other silver items, and the portrait of William Kirkland are among the most important of the original furnishings now in the house. Additional pieces of crystal, an Empire sofa, a tallcase clock, a slant-front desk, a brass fender, and smaller items of furniture have been identified in other ownership.

The plantation culture of the Old South has been exhaustively studied, and its outlines are by now generally well understood. Behind a successful plantation family in North Carolina there generally stood an enterprising merchant, whose wealth became the basis for his status as planter, slaveowner, and member of the establishment. Ownership of land and slaves was often the only qualification for membership in the planter class, but it was frequently attended as well by inherited gentility and education, particularly in the professions—legal, clerical, medical—and affiliation with the Anglican, later the Episcopal, church. Class status in the early days of the nation was less rigid than it later became, and at a time when fluctuations in financial standing occurred quickly, kinship counted for more than wealth, and elasticity and openness characterized social structure.

The Kirklands of Ayr Mount represent more or less the usual pattern. William Kirkland's humble origins in Scotland did not stand in the way of his ambitions in the New World. After years of steady application to work and scrupulous integrity in business gained him wealth and respect, he won ready acceptance in the backcountry elite. The marriage of his daughters with other respectably established self-made men bound the Kirklands in a web of kinship that held the family securely in place even after its ticket of admittance—wealth—was lost.

William Kirkland is representative of a group of American settlers that needs more study—the Scottish merchants and their domination of commerce and trade in colonial and federal America. Note has often been taken of their presence, but no detailed or comprehensive analysis of their numbers and influence has been attempted. Of the hundreds of young men sent out from Scotland to represent Scottish mercantile firms, many established independent stores and remained to become American citizens. Besides William Kirkland, in this history Daniel Anderson and John Scott are examples of the pattern, and Hillsborough's annals could supply many other names to add to the list.

Besides the light thrown on this group of settlers, the Kirkland history reiterates the fragile financial basis underlying southern commerce. Because of being almost entirely dependent on credit, anyone involved in the market economy knew how uncertain his returns could be and how slippery was the ladder to financial success. Gentlemanly guaranteeing of notes for friends and relations, an expected and customary accommodation, frequently resulted in crippling losses from which there was no appeal. In this connection, Thomas Ruffin and George McNeill, Kirkland's sons-in-law, and Archibald Murphey, his brother-in-law, played vital roles in William Kirkland's life. The Kirklands' close relationship with these men and with other noteworthy North Carolina families such as the Camerons, Stranges, and MacRaes add interest to the family history.

A family with eight daughters could hardly fail to provide much information relating to women's roles in a plantation society. Most distinguishing about the Kirkland women, but not peculiar to them in that time and place, was a tendency to hysteria, and not a few letters relate their sufferings in unflinching detail. In addition, their letters give intimate glimpses of the social life of Hillsborough. The backcountry town, a center of commerce and schools and a summer resort for the coastal elite, is reanimated in their effusions.

In quoting from the letters, I have in some instances taken liberties with the original punctuation for the sake of clarity. Otherwise I have left the originals as found or have indicated in brackets supplied or emended words. In constructing the genealogical charts I have depended on a combination of sources: family Bibles, letters, gravestones, newspapers, family histories, and (particularly helpful) a record kept by Maggie McLester of family birthdays, marriages, and deaths. When sources disagreed about a date, I chose what seemed the most reliable source. Dates on gravestones are notoriously unreliable, and even Bible records, if entries were delayed, can be in error.

I T IS A PLEASURE to acknowledge the help of many people in piecing together the Kirkland history. The staffs of the Southern Historical Collection and the North Carolina Collection of the University of North Carolina and of the Duke University Manuscript Department did all in their power to make my research pleasant and easy. The Genealogical Library of the Church of Jesus Christ of Latter-Day Saints in Raleigh made available to me microfilm of the Ayr Parochial Registers without which the Kirkland family origins would have been impossible to discover. I am grateful to Donald Lennon of East Carolina University Manuscript Collection and to Norwich University Archivist Jacqueline Painter for help in obtaining materials from their collections.

Many Kirkland descendants or relations facilitated my research by their generous response to my requests for information or materials: Elizabeth Collins, Elizabeth Goode, Rosalie Kelly, May Kirkland Robertson Reynolds, William and Stella Roulhac, Rebecca Warren, and Isabelle Webb. Mrs. Warren put me on the track of Admiral Kirkland and his descendants and shared her findings with me. Mrs. Reynolds supplied letters crucial for relations in Scotland and the later days of John U. Kirkland. She also read and made helpful comments on the manuscript.

Paul Calloway, who landscaped the restored Ayr Mount, gave me a tour of the grounds, interpreting the few clues to once-existing outbuildings. Todd Dickinson, who did the restoration, gave me a tour of the house from basement to attic, explaining the original construction and its notable features. Bill Crowther was always accommodating in giving me access to the house and grounds.

Eleanor Bell introduced me to the collection of Kirkland papers at the Burwell School Records Room and, with Louise Clayton, to the Hillsborough Presbyterian Church records. Kenneth McFarland made those of Saint Matthew's Church available and spent much time at Ayr Mount and Fairntosh plantations photographing the paneling of the halls and stairs so that I could compare the craftsmanship. Laurie Sanford graciously opened Fairntosh to us for that purpose. Hillsborough natives Hilda Winecoff and Clarence Jones supplied information and local lore of the family. Marshall Bullock found a particularly elusive date. Jane Philpott interpreted botanical names. Ann B. Sanders volunteered to search for Kirkland landmarks in London. Charles M. Hale identified Schomberg House and provided its history and connection with Sir John Kirkland. David Southern helped solve some of the problems of turning tangled family trees into neat charts. Historians Catherine Bishir and Elizabeth Reid Murray contributed the results of their research on John Briggs, the master carpenter, and Charles H. Brewer, Jr., added facts about a house Briggs built in Oxford, North Carolina.

It would be difficult to describe the variety of assistance I have received from John Sanders, who was always ready to answer questions, suggest solutions, and give of his time and knowledge. Stephen B. Baxter gave sound advice on the Scottish chapters. John Sanders, Dick Jenrette, and Carl Anderson carefully scrutinized the manuscript and gave it the benefit of their expertise.

To one and all my sincere thanks.

The Kirklands
of Ayr Mount

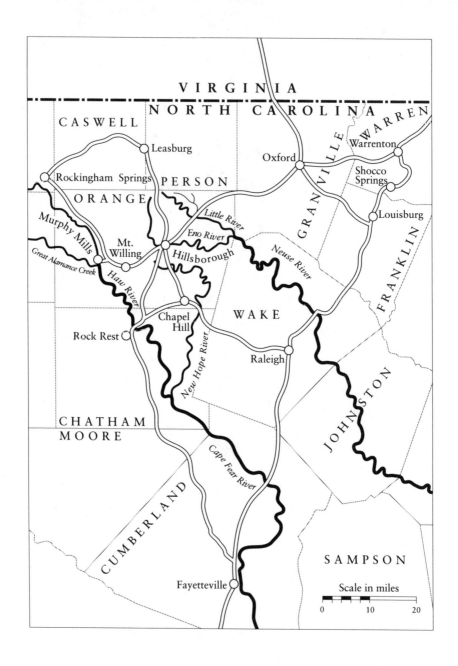

Adaptation of the MacRae-Brazier map (1833) by Michael Brady showing
places lived in or visited by the Kirkland family and their relations as well as
water courses and roads relevant to their history.

❧ 1 ❧

Eighteenth-Century Ayrshire

AYRSHIRE IN THE LOWLANDS of Scotland would not have seemed a promising place to be born at the beginning of the eighteenth century. On the west coast by the Irish Channel, far from the capital and cultural center of the country, the county was almost completely rural, and its people, yoked to relentless poverty, scrabbled little more than a bare subsistence from the barren hillsides. Sixty miles long and twenty-six broad, Ayrshire had a population of roughly fifty-nine thousand in 1755, the earliest year in which a reliable estimate was made. The county seat at the mouth of the river Ayr had an equally bleak prospect. Although it had been a thriving little port in the 1600s, the English civil wars had disrupted trade and demoralized the spirit of enterprise, and the economy had ebbed with the sea. Herring fishermen all along the coast still hauled in large harvests, which were brought to Ayr to be cured and for the oil from the offal to be thriftily processed and sold. A small woolen factory, started in 1670, gave employment to the jobless, vagrants, and orphans, who were in virtual bondage to it, as were the miners to the coal pits. But no coal was permitted to be exported. The small town (even at midcentury the population was little over twenty-five hundred persons) had a fort, a parish church and burgh school, a race course, and two principal streets, High and Sandgate. Heavy gales buffeted the exposed cluster of low thatch-roofed houses and shops of stone or clay and blew sand over the town from the dunes with such force as to uncover the graves in the churchyard. The Union of England and Scotland in 1707, bitterly opposed by the Scots of Ayrshire among others, brought a possibility for accelerated improvement. Progress, which had begun slowly in the seventeenth century with the end of the civil wars, had only inched ahead until the mideighteenth century, but thereafter change combined with intellectual vigor stimulated a cultural growth that would culminate in the golden age of Scotland.[1] At this time of awakening vitality and prosperity William Kirkland was born on

May 17, 1768. The second son and third child of John Kirkland, flesher, and his wife, Ann McNabb, William was baptized by the parish minister of the established Church of Scotland, the Presbyterian, three days later.[2]

William Kirkland's great-grandfather and grandfather, however, had had to endure life under the age-old conditions. The average man, a cottar, worked the land in return for a place to live. He rented only from year to year from the laird who owned the land (or from his tacksman) or worked for wages from a renter. William Kirkland's great-grandfather, another John Kirkland, was such a farmer, described in the parish records as a landlaborer.[3] Freeholders were few, rents were unreasonably high, and wages disproportionately low. Farmers worked in groups, tilling long strips of hillside land, from which they divided the produce among themselves, always paying a share to the laird; they were required as well to care for the land closest to the laird's dwelling for his benefit. Any fertilizer salvaged from the stock had to be used on the laird's land. Short leases, if there were any leases at all, gave neither cottar nor laird any reason to improve the land or its buildings. As a result, years of neglect showed in the wretched hovels that housed man and beast and in the eroded soil that produced meager crops primarily of oats and barley.[4]

Agriculture was in a desperate plight. The heavy wooden plows, one to a group of farmers, pulled by eight or ten starveling oxen on the run-rigs, the strips of hillside land separated by wide ditches, could work only one-half acre a day. The best land, in the valley bottoms, undrained and covered with trees and brush, still lay untouched. Because fields were not enclosed, animals had to be tethered at night. Married farmers generally lived in single-room cottages, which also sheltered the livestock at one end. Single laborers were satisfied with a loft. Because of insufficient feed, few cattle and sheep were kept over the long winter. So reduced by hunger were these poor animals by springtime that, too weak to walk, they had to be carried to the pastures, a time known as the "lifting."[5] The weather was always an uncertain factor in the yearly gamble. Late crippling frosts in spring or early sleet storms in autumn could blight the harvest. Thus the practice of agriculture in 1700 was antiquated and miserable beyond description. Into this hard existence in 1696 settled John Kirkland and his bride, Elizabeth Smith.[6]

Their third child and third son, David Kirkland, may have begun his adult life as a farmer, too, but he had moved to Ayr and was living at Castlehill when he married Jane (Jean) Hutchison in 1729. She was the daughter of George Hutchison and his wife, Jenet McLure.[7] Perhaps it was through his mother's family, the Smiths, or his in-laws, the McLures (McClures) and Hutchisons, that David Kirkland was able to escape the fate of his father and eventually become a flesher, or butcher. In the town a small group of artisans and tradesmen eked out a less marginal existence than did farmers. Small merchants, bonnetmakers, shoemakers, millers, hammermen (smiths), fleshers, and weavers supplied necessary services and goods and endured less physical stress and exposure. To be sure, farmers and tradesmen alike depended on a diet of oats, barley, kale greens, and some milk for survival; all wore homespun woolen clothes; few wore shoes and the children never.[8]

The lairds, through ownership of the land and the powers that adhered to their position, held complete civic control, but the quality of their lives was little better than that of the commonality. Their cold stone houses, often newer appendages to old fortified keeps, lacked architectural taste, comfort, or refinement. They had no paneling, pictures, or paper on the walls and no carpets on the floors. Whereas the English gentry had lawns, parks, and pleasing landscapes, these lairds had plowed fields, kitchen gardens, and depressing clusters of farm buildings crowding their dwellings. The children of the laird sat elbow to elbow in the parish school with children of all classes and knew them as friends. This common education, however, which was usually exacting and thorough, made for a homogeneous culture, shared and understood by all, and it created among the Scots a sense of unity that remained with them wherever they lived afterward. All knew, too, the pervasive control of their manners and morals by the Presbyterian church, although, strangely, the church made no effort to curb the common tendency to heavy drinking, which cost many young men a comfortable place in the social order and drove many families into indigence.[9]

Oppressed as Scots had always been by the dour existence that their geography and economy imposed, life on Castlehill must have seemed less harsh to David Kirkland than to his father, the landlaborer of Lochfergus. David was received as a freeman of the fleshers' corporation in 1748, almost twenty years after his marriage and when he was forty-seven years old. He had undoubtedly served some time as an apprentice in the craft, but what he had done during the previous years is not recorded. Once having been admitted to the guild, however, he possessed a measure of success and security. The corporation was an ancient organization; its dozen or more members maintained a slaughterhouse (after 1747) and meat market (after 1764) and controlled the slaughter of animals and sales of meat, primarily mutton and beef, in the town of Ayr. They sold the hides to tanners for leather goods and the dung to farmers for fertilizer. They articled apprentices and journeymen, whom they taught the skill of butchering and examined upon completion of their apprenticeships for admission as freemen to the guild. Dues, fees, and fines collected by the corporation went into a beneficial fund to aid widows of fleshers and other needy persons in the town. Although public charity was handled by the church, into whose mite boxes those who could contributed regularly, trade guilds took care of their own. The guild formed a cushion against adversity, and, despite an existence seen in hindsight as pinched, harsh, and bare of amenities, life probably seemed to David Kirkland and his family agreeably comfortable and much improved over the previous generation's.[10]

After midcentury change came more swiftly as agriculture and the general economy improved. The Society of Improvers of Knowledge of Agriculture, founded in 1723, had encouraged the use of new practices in farming, and a few enlightened lairds had brought English farmers to teach the locals innovative new methods being practiced profitably in England. They also changed the terms of land leasing and reapportioned the farms. They now gave nineteen-year leases instead of short-term (usually annual) leases and allotted individual possession of compact parcels of land instead of a dozen run-rigs scattered round the hillsides. Because each farmer was now responsible for the conduct and results of his own labor, he was spurred by ambition to greater energy and initiative, which improved his property and made it more productive. New and better tools and fertilizers had the same good effect. Smaller iron plows pulled by a few good horses proved more efficient, and enclosed fields and better-bred stock were managed more profitably than with the old methods. Equally important was the reforestation of the hilltops and the draining of the bottomlands, which produced abundant crops and yielded a surplus with which to fatten man and beast. The health of more than the animals improved; the people enjoyed a more varied and richer diet, which included cheese, potatoes, and other vegetables as well as the old staples, porridge and milk. Roads were built that carried farm produce to market towns and brought into the countryside wares that made life easier. They brought as well from Glasgow new wealth into Ayrshire and the other western Lowland counties, whose increasing crops earned profits to plow back into the land.[11]

The invigorating spirit of enterprise that invaded not only agriculture but also commerce and industry was fueled by Scotland's trade with the British colonies, which had been legalized after the Union. Glasgow, where illegal trade had long existed, particularly in tobacco from America, became during the eighteenth century the foremost tobacco importer of the United Kingdom. From the 1.5 million pounds yearly of contraband tobacco in pre-Union days, the figures rose to 6 million in 1722 and 47 million in 1771, the height of Glasgow's supremacy in the trade. Whether tobacco was manufactured in Glasgow or reexported to the Continent, it brought to the tobacco lords of the city a wealth undreamed of. They adopted an extravagance of dress and an opulence in living that expressed the power they possessed and wielded. Their scarlet cloaks symbolized not just a local superiority but a commercial domination of vast proportions in the tobacco colonies of America. They owned not only the ships that transported the tobacco but also chains of stores in America, from the seaports to the hinterland, which purchased tobacco from the farmers and shipped it to Glasgow to be processed or resold. From these stores colonial planters and yeoman farmers bought all manner of goods on credit at exorbitant rates, and, to pay for them, they ran up huge debts or mortgaged their farms and plantations to the Glasgow traders. In 1766 their debt to Glasgow merchants totaled £1 million sterling. To their stores in America, the tobacco lords sent managers and clerks from Scotland, who often became permanent residents in the colonies and gave to the emerging cultures a large Scottish mix.[12]

Preeminent among the tobacco lords were John Glassford, William Cunningham, the Hamiltons, Alexander and Daniel Campbell, and George Buchanan, represented in North Carolina by Buchanan, Hastie and Company, but many others, too, grew rich through the American weed. They also became imperious and arrogant. When the American Revolution suddenly cut off their source of income and the possibility of collecting their debts, some of them were ruined financially, but they had served a purpose. New, elegant buildings that they had built filled the town, and shops with international goods provided the populace with many new possessions and enlarged their knowledge, improved their taste, and helped remove the blinkers of provincialism. The lords had invested their surplus wealth in new industries. The halt of trade caused by the Revolution, moreover, was only temporary. Some farsighted traders, canny businessmen, who had managed neither their affairs so carelessly nor their money so lavishly, had stocked their warehouses and collected their debts and were able to weather the interruption in trade. When trade resumed, though it never regained more than a quarter of its former bulk, new investors came forward, new businessmen with sounder business practices took hold, and with the survivors continued the profitable trade.[13] There were other positive results. One historian wrote about postrevolutionary Glasgow:

> No sooner had the Virginia lords thrown aside their scarlet cloaks, gold-headed canes, cocked hats, and bushy wigs, and left the field open to the ambition and enterprise of the wider circle of merchants engaged in the growing commercial intercourse with the West Indian colonies and foreign countries, than a new order of things began to be developed. Business of all kinds became diffused among the citizens. The two great classes of society into which the city had been so long divided, gradually disappeared. The merchant and the manufacturer were now seen amalgamating; while the strict social barrier, which so long separated the tradesman from the foreign trader, was henceforth swept away. . . . Trade, in fact, was now regarded under a new and more universal phase; and society assumed a more cosmopolitan condition, under a happy amalgamation of all classes.[14]

Ayrshire was close enough to Glasgow to benefit from the new economic prosperity. A thriving trade in tobacco resulted, although it was dwarfed beside that of Glasgow, whose port and mercantile activity and overseas connections influenced the life of many an Ayrshireman. All through the century Scotsmen sailed from Glasgow's port of Greenock and even from the wharves of Ayr, a large number of Ayrshire families among them, to populate the New World.[15] After the Jacobite rebellions had finally been suppressed at Culloden in 1745 and many poor Highlanders were set adrift with the demise of the clan system, economic activity in the revitalized Lowlands attracted them and workers from other parts of Scotland and Ireland. New citizens flocked into Ayr in search of jobs and a better life for themselves and their families. Besides the curing of fish and weaving of wool, linen, and silk, other industry was carried on in the town or its vicinity—shipbuilding, tanning, shoe-making, and salt and coal mining. To these livelihoods the immigrants came. There came, as well, the occasional man of wealth, perhaps one who had returned with a fortune made overseas, to settle in the town and give his children the advantages of the burgh school. Education had been almost a tenet of the Scots' Presbyterian faith, a handmaiden to religious grace. Parish schools, established by law in the seventeenth century, had come into existence slowly but were more commonly available in the eighteenth century. The burgh schools, centuries older and better, provided not just good elementary education but preparation for the university as well.[16]

The Royal Burgh of Ayr took pride in its school as it did in its long history. A castle had once overlooked the town from the heights in medieval days, and there the Scottish parliament had met in 1315 and recognized Robert the Bruce as the legitimate claimant to the throne. A Saint John's Church had stood by the sea for centuries, first Roman Catholic, then Anglican, and finally Presbyterian. During the Cromwellian civil wars, a fort had been built near the old castle to quarter five hundred foot soldiers and one hundred mounted soldiers, the better to manage the unruly populace in those troubled years of both political and religious upheaval. From the struggle the zealous Covenanters had won the right to worship as they chose, according to the doctrine and rites of the Calvinist faith as tempered by John Knox.[17] In more recent times salutary changes had begun in the 1720s, when the Honorable Charles Cathcart and Captain Lawrence Nugent, the comptroller of customs, undertook to solve the problem of blowing sand. They were given long-term leases on a large tract of land on the south side of Ayr in return for leveling the dunes and stabilizing the soil. Their success in creating a usable beach and pastureland sown with grass and clover to replace the blowing sand became their monument.[18]

Monuments of a different sort soon followed. Out of the vitality and economic prosperity came renewed vigor of mind and spirit, the cultural enlightenment and intellectual distinction of Scotland's golden age. To it Ayrshire contributed the literary lights James Boswell, John Galt, and Robert Burns. Burns was born in Alloway (now part of Ayr) and baptized in Ayr only a few years before William Kirkland. Many of the places and people of his poems must have been familiar to Kirkland, for example, the Brig o' Doon and the original of the Tam o' Shanter Inn. Out of Ayrshire came, too, John L. McAdam, the road engineer, and William

McClure (undoubtedly a lateral relation of the Kirklands), who made the first geological map of the United States and helped to found the nation's first free public school at Robert Owen's model community at New Harmony, Indiana.[19] What the Union in 1707 had promised finally had come to pass. The influx of English culture and goods had stimulated the dormant Scots genius, which had begun to grow and flourish so luxuriantly that the cultural tide had turned. By 1800 Scots newspapers, literature, and education, and Scots engineers, doctors, and farmers would outdistance the English and become distinguished for learning throughout the Western world. With the agricultural, economic, and cultural promise already manifest, Ayrshire in 1768 was definitely a good place to be born.

❦ 2 ❦

A Sea Change

Auld Ayr, wham ne'er a town surpasses
For honest men and bonnie lasses—
—Robert Burns

AVID AND JANE KIRKLAND'S third child, John, was born at Castlehill in Ayr July 4, 1733.[1] John was educated in the burgh school and apprenticed in his father's craft. After passing an examination and paying twenty merks Scots money, he was admitted at the age of twenty-one as a freeman of the corporation, entitled to its full rights and privileges. The minutes of the fleshers' corporation record John's faithful attendance at meetings and increasing participation in the direction of the organization. Over the years he earned the respect of his fellow fleshers and was repeatedly elected to the various offices of the corporation: deacon or chairman, councillor, visitor, and box-master. On one occasion when a deacon could not host the regular meeeting of fleshers because "his wife was in childbed," they met at John Kirkland's house instead.[2]

A man did not marry early in those days; wages were so low that only after years of working and strict economizing could he save enough to support a wife and family. Therefore, John Kirkland waited until he was thirty years old before he married Ann McNab (variously written Anne and McNabb or McNabnie) and set up his own household in December 1763. That Ayr was not Ann's home is inferred from two facts in the records: the couple was married at Newfields in the Parish of Ayr, and in 1824, when Ann was fatally ill, she asked to be taken to Muirhouse to die.[3] For most of her life, however, she lived in the town of Ayr, where her children were born and baptized and these events were recorded in the parish register. Unfortunately, almost nothing else is known about her. From her, however, came the forename that was borne by so many of her descendants on both sides of the Atlantic. Only a single glimpse of her comes through a letter from Scotland, written by a granddaughter in 1822 to her American relations: "Grandmother I think is getting very frail, but what do you think of her dancing a reel at Captain Dowie's on Christmas night and repeating several verses of poetry?"[4] Ann McNabb Kirkland must then have been well into her seventies and perhaps even eighty.

During their life together she and her husband witnessed a massive transformation in Scottish life that was reflected in the fortunes of their children. Seven girls and six boys were born to them in Ayr between 1764 and John Kirkland's death in 1790 of "water in the breast," as the register recorded it. Although they lost their first child, a daughter, in her childhood, their next four children, all sons, survived to enjoy comfortable lives and some measure of success. These were Nugent, William, John, and David. Of the next five children, all girls, little is known; two married, two did not, and one dropped out of the records entirely. The last three children, two boys and a girl, lost out in life's race: one disappeared and probably died at sea, another died as a child, and the last died of tuberculosis a few months before her mother in 1824. Tuberculosis was common worldwide, but it was particularly tenacious in harsh climates. *The Statistical Account of Scotland* written in 1792 advised that "persons of a consumptive habit ought to dwell at a distance from the parish of Air. A sea voyage gives the best chance of recovery."[5]

With so large a family to feed and clothe, the John Kirklands can have had little if any money left over after the necessities were paid for. Like most housewives of that time and place Ann McNabb with her daughters' help undoubtedly spent the evening hours spinning and weaving. John Galt's *Annals of the Parish*, a fictional but historically accurate picture of social life in Ayrshire in that era, depicts the industrious housewife at work. Galt describes the "booming" of the large wheel to spin wool for the blankets and the "birring" of the little wheel to spin linen thread for sheets and napery; the house was as noisy as an organ loft with the "jangle and din" of wheels and looms.[6] The housewife who owned a cow could also make butter and cheese for market, but with so many mouths to feed the Kirklands would probably have used all they could make.

A year after William Kirkland's birth, Ayr's economy took another step forward with the establishment of a local bank, Douglas, Heron and Company, of which great things were expected. Four years later, however, financial havoc rocked the town when the bank collapsed. Its directors had mismanaged the business by irresponsibly endorsing each others' loans and through excessive lending on credit had incurred a debt of £700,000, more than half of it owed by the bank directors. Ironically, as in the collapse of the tobacco lords of Glasgow, besides ruin to those involved and short-term ills to the town's economy, the bank's failure left some long-term benefits. The money, though imprudently borrowed, had been judiciously spent on improvements of lasting value, land and buildings, roads, and industry.[7] The Ayrshire of William Kirkland now wore a different face.

Growing up almost at the head of the children in his large family, William Kirkland must have learned early to share the labor, take responsibility for his younger siblings, and begin to prepare himself for earning a livelihood. Although no details of his childhood are found in any surviving record, his letters indicate that he received a good education. They show a man at home with pen and paper, able to express himself with precision and ease. His education at the burgh school would have included literary, scientific, and commercial subjects, and if he had chosen less Latin and Greek and more bookkeeping and arithmetic in preparation for a career in business, he would still have been well grounded in basic skills. He might have chosen to follow his father in the flesher's trade or to become, as many others did, a sailor, or joined the army. In William's youth the Scots Greys were quartered in the town and with their fine uniforms must have offered to the patriotic youth a strong inducement to enlist in the army. William's brother David did just that. Another common choice, and the one William made, was to try one's luck in some American outpost of a mercantile company. To prepare for such a career, William's school years would have been immediately followed by an apprenticeship to a merchant. He may have been articled to a Glasgow firm, but he could just as well have started at home. The tobacco and other import trades had flourished in Ayr as well as in Glasgow, and though the American Revolution put an end to tobacco importing in Ayr, the export of coal, which had begun after the Union, became a thriving enterprise in the revived port town. In any case, William would have known from childhood of the great emigration to America and the opportunity open to any young man willing to seek his fortune overseas.[8]

Whatever the place from which he sailed, William Kirkland was in Warrenton, North Carolina, in 1789, when he was just twenty-one years old.[9] Warrenton was then a raw, new town, only a decade old, the county seat of the new county of Warren. The territory had earlier been within the county of Bute, but the Earl of Bute, first lord of the treasury under George III, aroused such anger during the Revolution that his name became odious and was obliterated by the division of Bute into two new counties: Franklin and Warren. The old Bute courthouse was abandoned. Around the new Warren County courthouse arose unpretentious clap-board houses and shops of tradesmen and the few professional men a court town attracted. Warrenton had not yet acquired the cultivated society and handsome buildings that would later make its reputation for gentility.

Already among its merchants, however, were two men who were to become lifelong friends of William Kirkland and with whom his mercantile career began in America. Although the evidence indicates that Kirkland could have been a clerk for either Daniel Anderson or John Scott, family tradition resolves the ambiguity. It says that Kirkland came to America in 1789 with a man named Anderson, with whom he went into business in Petersburg. Some of these details are inaccurate, but Kirkland's association with Anderson at the start of his career in America seems certain. Kirkland was apparently sent to Warrenton by a firm in Glasgow or Ayr with which Anderson had connections. John Scott first appeared in Bute County tax lists in 1771; in the earliest Warren County list, 1781, a time of notorious inflation, Scott was shown as worth £824. He owned no land, however, until 1788, when he listed five town lots and 260 acres of land. He owned one slave in 1784, two in 1785, and nine by 1790. In some years tax lists included the value of stock in trade, for example, in 1786 when Scott's goods were valued at £132/2/8 and 1787 when they were worth £147/15/9.[10]

Daniel Anderson, born in Glasgow in 1747, had come to America around 1768 and settled in Dumfries, Virginia, as a merchant. A newspaper listed him as a subscriber to William Blackstone's *Commentaries on the Laws of England* to be published in Philadelphia in 1771–72.[11] In the prerevolutionary era Dumfries was a thriving entrepôt for the tobacco trade. Many Scots merchants had settled there in 1749 after the town had been laid out on the land of John Graham and named for his birthplace in Scotland. The opening of a tobacco warehouse was the attraction, and the trade and town had developed together. Within a short time, Dumfries, like Ayr, began to suffer from a receding tide and silted-up harbor, which, together with the effects of the American Revolution, cut off the possibility of further trade, the town's lifeblood.[12] In 1785, Anderson moved his business to Warrenton, where others from Dumfries had already resettled. The Warren County tax list for that year listed his imported goods as worth £707. He bought three slaves in 1787 and four town lots the next year. In 1788 his investment in goods had increased to close to £2,000 in value, part of which represented large stores of rum and salt. He also owned four slaves. By 1789 his list included eighty-five gallons of wine and a large amount of western land as well. He had invested in 1,920 acres in Davidson and Sumner counties, at that time still North Carolina frontier land, now Tennessee, and owned other unidentified acreage. William Kirkland was a witness to several of Anderson's deeds of purchase, and once both Scott and Kirkland witnessed an Anderson document.[13]

The 1790 census did not include the name of William Kirkland, obviously because he did not head a household. He was probably living in the household of Daniel Anderson, which included five white males over sixteen years of age. Anderson had married in 1774 at Dumfries and by 1790 had four sons, but none was sixteen years old so that besides himself Anderson must have had Kirkland and three other clerks, or helpers, or boarders in his household. John Scott is also listed as the head of a household, which included himself, his son, four females, and nine slaves.[14] Despite Kirkland's apparent continued residence in Anderson's household, by 1790 he had already formed a partnership with Scott, for in April of that year a debtor deeded Scott and Kirkland two Main Street lots with their improvements in lieu of the £150 he owed them.[15] Perhaps Anderson had a larger house than Scott and could accommodate Kirkland more conveniently under his roof.

Daniel Anderson and Company, also known as Gracie and Anderson, continued in Warrenton until almost 1800, when Anderson moved to Petersburg, Virginia. In 1793 he had as a partner his son-in-law James Turner, who later became governor of North Carolina. For a few years the firm's name was James Turner and Company and included Anderson and Archibald Gracie, but Turner sold his interest to the firm of Gracie and Anderson when they moved to Petersburg, and the firm resumed its earlier name.[16] Soon after the move to Petersburg, Gracie moved to New York, where he later built for himself the house today known as Gracie Mansion, used as a residence for the mayor. Scott and Kirkland, however, remained in Warrenton only until 1792. At Christmas, Kirkland married Scott's daughter Margaret Blain Scott in Orange County and began a new phase of his life.[17]

Of Margaret's father's background nothing is known beyond the tradition that he was born in Scotland; of her mother's something more can be said. Elizabeth Machen Scott, or Betty, as she was called, had been born in or near Dumfries, Virginia, the third of six known children of Thomas and Letty Machen. Thomas Machen is first found in the records of Dettingen Parish, Prince William County, Virginia, in 1743. In 1751 he was clerk of the parish, as he was again in 1757 after an interim in which he served as reader. For his services in both capacities he received tobacco as wages, twelve hundred pounds as reader, only five hundred as clerk. Whatever his livelihood besides his parish duties, he seems to have gone into debt, for his possessions were sold at auction in 1765. At the sale, his household goods were bought by his son Thomas, Jr., who in 1769 deeded them back to his parents for life, with the exception of one bed that he gave to his sister Betty Machen, possibly anticipating her marriage; John Scott was a witness to the deed. Sometime between the sale in 1765 and the deed in 1769, the elder Machens, with Betty and perhaps other children still living at home, moved to Bute County, North Carolina, where Thomas Machen, Sr., was able to secure the job of clerk of the county court. After the formation of Warren County, Machen was appointed to the same post in the new county, a job he held until his death in 1782. His wife apparently died between 1774 and 1781, for she witnessed the marriage bond of Mary Armistead (possibly a relation) and George Tassie in 1774, but she is not mentioned in her husband's will, written in late 1781. Besides Betty and Thomas, Jr., the Machens' known children were George Wale, Henry, John, and a daughter, Mary McIntee, already married when her father wrote his will. Betty, too, was then married, for in it he refers to her as Betty Scott. He remembered a single grandchild with a pair of silver shoe buckles: Betty's daughter Margaret Blain Scott.[18]

❦ *3* ❦

Independent Merchant

T HE HILLSBOROUGH to which Kirkland and his bride moved was a very different town from the Warrenton they had left. The town had been laid out by William Churton and chosen as the county seat in 1754 by the county court of the recently formed Orange County. Almost from the start, lawyers, Scots merchants, craftsmen, and tradesmen of all sorts had been attracted to it. Situated on the Old Indian Trading Path, by then the wagon road from Petersburg, Virginia, the town had profited from a large share of transient custom as well as the permanent traffic of new settlers, who had come in a steady stream down the Valley of Virginia from the Middle Atlantic colonies or on the Trading Path from Virginia and the Chesapeake Bay area to take up land at the headwaters of the Cape Fear and Neuse river systems. Early residents of the town such as Nathaniel Rochester, who later founded the city with his name; Thomas Hart, James Hogg, Richard Henderson, and William Johnston, partners in the large land scheme known as the Transylvania Company; Francis Nash, clerk of the county court, representative of both the county and town in the General Assembly, and revolutionary war general; Edmund Fanning, the ringleader of the courthouse gang, Loyalist dandy, and, after his exile, general in the British army; Thomas Burke, member of the Continental Congress, a governor of the state during the Revolution, poet, and physician; William Churton, surveyor to Lord Granville and mapmaker; and William Hooper, a signer for North Carolina of the Declaration of Independence—these men had given it a reputation for both culture and enterprise, rivaled at that time by few others in the colony or state. By 1792, however, its colonial and revolutionary luster had faded, and its roster of citizens had changed. Men of comparable talents had not yet taken their places. Nor did the town's appearance substantiate its pretensions. A few small structures showing neglect dotted the grid of streets that Churton had laid out. A cluster of small shops, houses, taverns, the courthouse, market house, and jail made up the town and, with a few more widely scattered houses, still within town limits, made a total of fifty improved lots in the village.

William Kirkland seems to have begun his life in Hillsborough as an independent merchant, for already in 1793 invoices headed William Kirkland and Company were in use. His merchandise, like that of any general store, included everything from dry goods to hardware and from house furnishings to coffee and rum.[1] William Kirkland's name appeared on the town tax list for the first time in 1794. He owned no real estate, but he listed one "white poll" and two "black polls," and two "wheels of pleasure," undoubtedly the vehicle called a chaise or chair for one or two persons and pulled by a single horse. In 1795 he appeared on the list as the owner of a portion of lot 6, opposite the courthouse, with an improvement worth £400. A deed from the sheriff to Kirkland the following year reveals that the house and lot had belonged to John Allison, another Scots merchant. Lot 6 encompassed the whole block between Margaret Lane and King Street, an acre of land, so there was plenty of room for several structures. There were at least three other owners of portions of that lot in that year.[2] In 1795, too, Kirkland took a deed of trust on a tract in North Carolina's western lands, soon to be in Tennessee, from a debtor of William Duffy, a town lawyer. When the owner could not repay Kirkland, the land became his. In that year, too, Kirkland bought his first rural Orange County land from John Taylor, a tract of 346 acres for £346. Until the purchase of this land, the Kirklands lived in a house on lot 6, probably, as family tradition says, "over the store."[3]

Presumably Kirkland and his little family moved from their first home in the town to the farm tract, located close to Hillsborough, for he apparently improved the tract with a substantial structure: when he sold the tract to Duncan Cameron five years later, the price (£600) was almost double what he had paid for it. Further, a letter written by Kirkland in the 1790s, cited by an early local historian but subsequently lost, told of a house Kirkland had just built, for which he had been able to make brick from the earth dug for the foundation. Continuing to invest in land, in 1799 Kirkland bought from William Courtney the 385-acre tract then called Kinchen's old place, where he was to live for the rest of his life.[4]

This tract, lying along the Eno River and traversed by the Old Indian Trading Path, had first been part of a 560-acre land grant in 1760 from Earl Granville to Thomas Wiley (Wylie). In 1763 Wiley had sold 200 acres from the west end (a portion of the 385-acre tract later bought by Kirkland) to William Few, a recent settler from Maryland, and Few had built a house there and been granted a license by the county court to "keep tavern at his dwelling." The location was propitious, and the tavern soon became a landmark and magnet for travelers on the Trading Path (by then called the road to Halifax) and the alternate route (now approximately St. Mary's Road), which joined near the tavern. Sauthier's Map of Hillsborough (1768), showing the town and vicinity with the existing structures, includes what must have been Few's tavern and outbuildings just south of the junction. The Fews continued to live there until 1771, but William Few had already made plans to move to Georgia before his son James's involvement with the Regulators led to James's execution and the ravaging of the Few plantation by Governor William Tryon's militia following the Regulators' defeat at the Battle of Alamance. These events merely hastened the move.[5]

From Few's ownership the tract passed to John Butler and then to Ralph McNair, the Scots merchant who increased the tract to 824 acres through the purchase of two adjoining land parcels. McNair's occupancy was marked by his construction of a stone dam on the Eno River, probably with the intent of building a mill. The remains of the dam were still known in 1908 as McNair's Old Stone Dam. As a Loyalist during the Revolution, McNair wisely withdrew and sold off his property. The 824-acre plantation was sold to John Kinchen, a lawyer, who kept it only three years before selling it to William Courtney. Whether William Courtney the elder is meant, a justice of the county court, or his son, who died in 1794 (both of them were tavern keepers), is not clear. Kirkland's purchase of 385 acres of this land was not a direct one from Courtney but the result of a forced sale: Courtney and his partner Thomas Watts owed money to Kirkland and Company and to the Petersburg firm of Robert and Walter Colquhoun. Kirkland bought the land at a sheriff's sale for £486/10/0. Of additional interest in this transaction is the signature of a witness, James Kirkland, William's youngest brother. From 1799 through 1803 James witnessed other deeds for his brother; his signature is the only evidence of his residence in Hillsborough in these years, probably in the capacity of clerk in the Kirkland store. William Kirkland's next land purchase, six weeks later, was an adjoining tract of 118 acres, specifically designated as a part of the estate of William Courtney, Jr.[6]

Obviously Kirkland's business was going well. Daniel Anderson wrote to his brother-in-law Duncan Cameron in April 1798, "Kirkland has sent me home loaded with money both hard & soft, but I have contrived to get clear of 1000 Doll[ars] of it here [in Warrenton] for a draft of Mr. Walkers, which will make me go something lighter home."[7] Kirkland had so much surplus cash he was looking for ways to invest it with Anderson's help.

In 1800 Kirkland authorized Duncan Cameron, probably as an assist to the new young lawyer in town, to appear on his or his firm's behalf in any and all suits brought against them. In 1802 Kirkland made an agreement with Richard Bennehan and Catlett Campbell, also merchants, to import a stud horse from England, to be held by them jointly. Each contributed £180 and through the firm of Gracie, Anderson and Company engaged James Bell of 49 Saint Mary Axe, London, to buy the horse for them. The purchase of the horse would seem to be confirmed by Bennehan's 1803 tax list, which included a stud horse among his taxable properties.[8]

Another source of income for Kirkland was a new business partnership with James Yarbrough, but it is not clear what their business was. In 1802 they invested in two hundred acres of land, again purchased through a sheriff's sale. Two years later Kirkland bought Yarbrough's share and immediately sold the tract for more than double what they had paid for it. In 1802 as well Kirkland seems to have been in business under the firm name of Scott and Kirkland. The Scott was probably Thomas Scott, his brother-in-law. Again the nature of the business is unclear. By 1807 Kirkland had a partnership with James Phillips, the saddler, for a tanning operation, which was conducted on a portion of town lot 46, at the corner of present Cameron Avenue and King Street. In 1809 Kirkland bought from the firm of Robert Colquhoun of Petersburg two other town lots, numbers 2 and 44. They lay between Kirkland's tanyard lot and the courthouse, thus giving him ownership of prime sites in the town. At some time during his ownership, Kirkland located both blacksmith's and hatter's shops on lot 44.[9]

As Kirkland's ownership of land increased, so did his ownership of slaves. The 1800 census shows him with twelve slaves and the 1810 census with nineteen. The 1800 census also shows that Kirkland's household then consisted of eight persons; besides himself, his wife, and four little girls under ten years of age, there were a youth over sixteen and under twenty-four, probably his brother James, and a female in the same age bracket, possibly his sister-in-law Jane Armistead Scott. Ten years later the household included five daughters and two sons under ten years of age besides Kirkland and his wife.[10]

While Kirkland had been strengthening his business base in Hillsborough and investing in land and slaves, John Scott had pursued a different course. In 1795 and 1797 he had bought contiguous tracts of land on the Great Alamance Creek and Haw River, the approximate location of modern Swepsonville, amounting to just over 150 acres. He had undoubtedly been motivated to do so by the marriage in April 1795 of his daughter Letitia (Lettie) to Isaac Holt, a son of Michael Holt and his second wife, Jane Lockhart, who had settled on the Haw River much earlier. In 1800 Scott sold his landholdings to Archibald DeBow Murphey, who was to marry Scott's daughter Jane the following year. This sale and the marriage that followed would have far-reaching consequences not only for the Scotts but also for the Kirklands and whoever else was brought into Murphey's web of kin and friendship.[11]

Murphey was a native of Caswell County and a lawyer of exceptionally brilliant mind and engaging manners. His marriage into the family must have seemed to all his new relations a herald of good fortune. With charm and intellect that few could resist, Murphey later won a venerable place in North Carolina history for his direction and leadership through seven terms in the state legislature (1812–18). Although he was too far ahead of his time for his comprehensive program of reform to be accepted, he nevertheless gave to later statesmen a plan toward which to work. One historian has said that he "formulated an enlightened public policy or program which ultimately revolutionized the political and social thinking of North Carolina and laid the foundation of the present modern commonwealth."[12] Murphey had studied law under William Duffy, whose sister Maria married Thomas Scott just a year before Murphey married Jane Scott. Murphey felt an abiding affection for Duffy despite conflicting loyalties: Duffy challenged Duncan Cameron to a duel and received from him a lasting injury that shortened his life, and Cameron became Murphey's chosen successor to carry on the crusade for internal improvements in the state legislature. Many years later, in a speech praising Duffy, Murphey referred to him as "a child of misfortune," perhaps recognizing in Duffy's fate a kinship with his own.[13] In that small Orange County planter-mercantile-professional establish-

ment, it was inevitable that the lives of the members should be inextrica-
bly interwoven for good or ill.

Hillsborough at the time of the Kirklands' arrival and for many years
thereafter had no churches. The Anglican church, which had been provided by the colonial government, had lost its financial support and its
minister with the coming of the Revolution. When Methodist Bishop
Francis Asbury saw the old church on his visit to Hillsborough in 1783,
he described it as an impressive structure from a distance, but when
viewed closely it proved to be but a shell. After years of deterioration the
sanctuary was finally consumed by fire. Services by visiting clergymen of
various denominations had nevertheless been held in Hillsborough from
time to time. In 1780, for example, on his first visit to Hillsborough,
Bishop Asbury had preached at William Courtney's tavern to two hundred people. Four years later, on another visit, he found the snow deep,
"the street dirty, my horse sick, the people drinking and swearing," and
he was much discouraged by the moral tone of the village.[14] Other itiner-
ant preachers came too. James Meacham, also a Methodist, preached at
the courthouse in 1795. He wrote in his diary, "I had not much light nor
liberty in preaching in this poor place of wickedness; after I was done a
man who was intoxicated tryed to come to me saying that he wished to
talk with me, but the others kept him from me."[15] By 1796 the Reverend
George Micklejohn, who had served the three Anglican churches in Orange County before the Revolution, was intermittently visiting the vicinity to hold services in private houses.[16] Although there were Presbyterian churches in the countryside as early as 1755—the Eno Presbyterian
Church had been founded that year, followed by New Hope in 1758 and
Little River in 1761—there were not sufficient nominal Presbyterians in
the town to organize a congregation until 1816. The Kirklands may have
attended services at New Hope Presbyterian Church, not five miles away,
but their names do not appear in its few surviving records. By mere
coincidence, a Kirkland family, presumably from Ulster like the other
New Hope Church organizers, settled southeast of Hillsborough, and
its numerous members appear in the New Hope Church records as well
as the Orange County public records to the confusion of researchers.
There was, however, no interaction between the families and clearly no
connection.

Education attracted more support than religion in those years. By
1801 the Hillsborough Academy had been established in the town; Wal-

ter Alves, William Kirkland, William Whitted, William Cain, and Duncan Cameron were listed as its trustees. The following year these same men purchased five and a half acres just outside the town limits at the end of Queen and Tryon streets, probably with the intention of building a more commodious structure there. Five years later, however, the school was still in the town and they sold the tract for less than they had paid for it, an indication that nothing had ever been built on it. During its early years the school, which at first taught both boys and girls, was under the direction of the Reverend Andrew Flinn. The curriculum included Latin, Greek, English, reading, writing, arithmetic, geography, bookkeeping, and "the plainer branches of mathematics." The school benefited from a succession of unusually able teachers, including Richard Henderson, who had earlier taught at the university in Chapel Hill; William Bingham, who later established his own illustrious school; John Witherspoon, Presbyterian minister and grandson of the first president of the College of New Jersey; John Rogers, who had been educated for the priesthood but preferred teaching; and W. J. Bingham, later a successor of his father as head of the Bingham School.[17]

Despite the caliber of the Hillsborough Academy and Kirkland's connection with it, in 1804 he chose to send his two eldest daughters, Anne McNabb and Elizabeth Machen, to the Moravian boarding school, later Salem Academy. Perhaps the Hillsborough institution's plans to teach girls had been dropped for its later reputation was built as a school for boys. The Moravians had established schools for their own community in 1772. So widely respected had they become for their manner of conducting civic and business affairs and for the excellence of their moral principles and teaching that many outsiders had asked to place their children under the Moravians' tutelage. They finally acceded to the demand and opened the girls' school for boarders in 1804. The first outside students to arrive were Elizabeth Strudwick and the little Kirkland girls (accompanied from Hillsborough by William Kirkland), Polly Phillips, a ward of Duncan Cameron, and Anna and Felicia Norfleet of Halifax County. The Moravian community's Salem diary recorded that "Temporary arrangements have been completed for the Boarding School for Girls in Salem, which will occupy part of the *Gemein Haus* for the time being. The two school rooms of the little girls have been arranged for living rooms, and the sleeping hall prepared for their use."[18]

Few documents allow glimpses into the daily life of William Kirkland's family, but it is possible to reconstruct its general outline during those early years in Hillsborough and vicinity when the growth of his business and family went on apace. Besides Anne and Elizabeth, William and Margaret Kirkland were the parents of Margaret Scott born in 1797, William in 1799, who died the same year, Jane Rebecca in 1800, another William, whose life lasted a brief moment in 1801, John Umstead in 1802, Martha Shepperd in 1803, James in 1805, who followed his brothers to an early grave, Alexander McKenzie in 1807, Mary Anderson and Susannah Umstead (always called Susan) in 1809 and 1810 respectively, Phebe Bingham in 1811, and finally David in 1813.[19] To bear fourteen children within nineteen years was a heavy burden for Margaret Scott Kirkland, and the loss of four of their six little boys must have taken its toll on both parents and made their happiness seem very precarious. The officiating doctor for most if not all of these events is obvious from the names of two of the children. Dr. John Umstead, who lived at Mount Willing in present Bingham Township of Orange County, and his wife, Susannah Luttrell Umstead, had become respected friends of the Kirklands. Because of Umstead's distance from Hillsborough and the wide circuit of his practice, however, the Kirklands undoubtedly often called on a doctor nearer at hand, James Webb, who settled in Hillsborough in the late 1790s. A letter from Webb to Duncan Cameron reported after the birth of Martha Kirkland in 1803, "Mrs. Kirkland is mending slowly. But I fear much for her son [John Umstead] whom I think dangerously ill."[20] Childhood was perilous and parents were justifiably alarmed when their children were ill. Childbirth made life equally uncertain for women. In 1806 Rebecca Cameron, Duncan's wife, wrote to her brother, Thomas Bennehan, "Poor Mrs. Kirkland is thought to be a little better; she rode to town on Sunday."[21]

As well as duty, there was diversion to lighten the load and delight the spirit. In 1808 Daniel Anderson's family decided to go to the Rockingham Springs in Rockingham County, North Carolina, and to visit their Carolina friends and relations on the way. In turn the Camerons, the Kirklands, the Umsteads, and finally the Murpheys and Scotts, who lived on the same plantation, entertained the Petersburg family. When Duncan Cameron informed the Scotts of the Andersons' plans, Murphey replied, "Mr. Scott thanks you for the pleasing information of Mr. Andersons intended Journey. There is no Man in the World whom Mr. Scott would be more fond to see."[22] The Kirklands not only received visits from their friends but also went with them to the springs. In 1809 Murphey invited Thomas D. Bennehan, Richard Bennehan's son, to join him and his wife on their journey to the springs, adding that Thomas and Maria Duffy Scott and Anne Kirkland would also be in the party.[23]

That same year occurred the first of many weddings in the Kirkland family when in December Anne McNabb, fifteen years old, married Thomas Carter Ruffin. Ruffin had come to Hillsborough after graduation from the College of New Jersey (later Princeton University) to study law with Archibald Murphey and had been captivated by the eldest Miss Kirkland. Marrying so young a girl when he was hardly launched in his career was probably the only impulsive and apparently imprudent step Ruffin ever took in a long and demanding judicial career and is a tribute to the girl's charm. In what this charm consisted it is now impossible to know, for the only surviving picture of Anne Kirkland Ruffin was taken in her later years, after she had lost her teeth, and no portrait or miniature of her or her sisters in the bloom of youth has ever come to light. Beauty was certainly an element of it, as attested by the statement made many years later that her oldest daughter, an acknowledged beauty, was "just a homely likeness" of her mother.[24] Perhaps their charm lay not only in beauty but in their kindness and ability to create for those around them a sense of well-being and comfort. Certainly such traits are implied in Archibald Murphey's letter to Ruffin about the Kirkland ladies, whose qualities were probably very like those he admired in his wife: "Tell Anne and Mrs. Kirkland I wish to see them very much just now; to sit around the Table and feast upon some of their fine strawberries."[25] Anne Kirkland Ruffin never lost the power to enchant Ruffin. She had had little schooling beyond the good grounding of her two years at Salem. Afterward she had spent some time in Petersburg, probably at school while living at the Andersons' and studying music with John C. Pike. During this visit she and Mary Cameron Anderson had become fast friends despite the disparity in their ages. In 1809 Anne's newborn sister was named Mary Anderson, a mark of the Kirklands' affection and admiration for their old friend Daniel's young wife, and when the Ruffins welcomed their own first child the following year, they asked Mary Anderson to be her godmother.[26]

Concurrent with their friendship, the association of William Kirkland and Daniel Anderson continued on its original business footing as well, for Kirkland and Company from the start bought its merchandise from

Gracie, Anderson and Company, whose ships plied the transatlantic trade routes, delivering to Liverpool and Glasgow the raw materials from American plantations and bringing back the household luxuries the planters craved: fine china, glass, silver, fabrics, and furniture. One such item ordered through Anderson arrived for the Kirklands in 1806, a fortepiano. Presumably this was the instrument that was still in the Kirkland family in the 1980s, bearing the date 1797 and the name of the illustrious piano maker Broadwood. The name Scott (strangely, in Hebrew letters), written on the bottom of the harpsichord-shaped case, suggests that the instrument had been ordered by John Scott as a present for his daughter's family. The same ship that brought it carried another piano for Duncan Cameron's family.[27]

The frequent occurrence of Duncan Cameron's name in William Kirkland's affairs was a result of more than propinquity or clannishness, and, though informal, their association, like that of Anderson and Kirkland, had a basis in both business and friendship. It began in 1799 with Cameron's arrival in Hillsborough. By then Daniel Anderson had moved to Petersburg from Warrenton, where he had met and married as his second wife Cameron's sister Mary. When Duncan Cameron had finished his law training and was casting about for a place to practice law in North Carolina, his relations, among them his new brother-in-law, were eager for him to choose Hillsborough. Anderson wrote Duncan in 1798, "I much approve of your going to Hillsboro' court. I do not know whether I will be there or not, but if not Mr. [James] Turner [Anderson's son-in-law] can give you letters to Mr. Kirkland & his other friends there."[28] Although Cameron ignored this advice and settled in Martinsville, Guilford County, he quickly realized his mistake and moved to Hillsborough, where he began his long friendship with William Kirkland. Kirkland's wagons routinely made the journey to Petersburg to take produce for sale and to return with stock for his store, and Cameron's family just as routinely sent their letters to Cameron in the care of Kirkland or his wagons. Anderson's letters to Duncan Cameron frequently conveyed messages to Kirkland about the price of tobacco and other staples and news of investment opportunities for surplus cash. As their own friendship matured, Kirkland and Cameron took turns playing emissary between Anderson and his other Hillsborough connections.

Thus after two decades in Orange County, William Kirkland was securely established both as a merchant and a planter; owner of slaves and town and county land; investor in a variety of business ventures: a stud horse, a tanyard, hatter and blacksmith shops; trustee of an excellent school; friend and patron of the younger relation of an old friend and business associate; and father of a growing family. Despite the increasing hostility between the United States and Great Britain and the economic slump that affected both nations as a result of the Napoleonic Wars, William Kirkland must have felt that the promise held out by the New World to an ambitious but penniless Scot at the end of the eighteenth century had been fulfilled.

❦ 4 ❦

Ayr Again and Ayr Mount

A YEARNING TO SEE the old country and his family there had probably long been turning William Kirkland's thoughts homeward,
but until 1810 he had not been in a position to act upon them.
He was busy securing a foothold in the business of the town and with his
profits acquiring the requisite land and slaves to ensure his family a place
in the planter establishment. His ties to Scotland had therefore been
maintained only through correspondence. World events had lately slowed
the pace of his progress. In the first decade of the new century, the United
States had been caught between the opposing factions in the Napoleonic
Wars, and its economy had suffered by various embargoes enacted during Thomas Jefferson's administration to combat the depredations on
American shipping and the British impressment of American seamen. As
a consequence, Kirkland's business was much less brisk than it had been.
The lull gave him an opportunity to take time out to pay the longed-for
visit. It is not clear whether Kirkland left his able clerk, George McNeill,
in charge of what business there was or whether he closed the store
entirely.[1] He left any family crises that might arise in his new son-in-law
Thomas Ruffin's capable hands. Undoubtedly Kirkland had an overseer
who could be trusted to keep plantation matters in trim.[2] If he meant to
see his mother once more before she died, the time had obviously come
to go abroad, for she was probably seventy years or more, an age much
above the life expectancy of that time.

Letters of William Kirkland's sister Elizabeth and his brother John in
1810 refer to William's projected visit, indicating that his plans were at
last materializing. They also wrote of conditions in Scotland, of the
economy, and of the family. "I regret sincerely," Elizabeth wrote, "that
times have been so bad in America; indeed it is not to be wondered at
considering everything. We feel it here very much, trade at present is very
low, never was more so. We want consumption & confidence."[3] John
echoed her remarks in his letter. He also commented wistfully on their

brother Nugent's successful business: "I wish he would share it with me and I would leave old reeky tomorrow, for the Grocery line in which I have been so long employed is by no means what it once was—the profits are reduced to an old song, chiefly owing to the opposition [it] has met with which I can assure you will not suit a man with a rising family as I have."[4]

But though business was temporarily affected, the family prospects had decidedly improved over what they had been at the time of William's emigration. The alteration seems to have stemmed from his brother John's marriage to Sybilla Mackenzie in 1795, for her brother Alexander had become a national hero. In 1774, after their mother's death, Alexander Mackenzie had been taken to New York, where an uncle, John "Ready Money" McIver, was well established in business and agreeable to training his young nephew. When the American Revolution routed the Loyalists, Alexander went with many others to Canada, where at the age of fifteen he began a clerkship in the counting house of Finlay, Gregory & Co., a firm of fur merchants. He remained a clerk for five years and acquired both book and practical knowledge. Particularly influential in shaping Alexander's career was James Finlay, who had long experience in the trade and had himself ventured into the Northwest, preempting the Hudson's Bay Company agents by outdistancing them in gathering furs from the Indians.[5]

Mackenzie eventually left the Montreal office and became a "wintering partner" in the informal conglomeration of Montreal firms and independent fur traders known as the North West Company. Intrepid, bold, and inured to the hardships of terrain and climate through this experience, Mackenzie was sent by the company on two expeditions to search for a northwest passage, which might open trade on the Pacific coast and reduce the high costs of transporting men and skins so far across the frozen wastes. On his first voyage of exploration (1789), which led west and north into the Arctic, he discovered the river that now bears his name. On his second expedition (1793), he discovered the Fraser River and actually reached the mouth of the Bella Coola River, an outlet to the Pacific, after long and difficult passages by canoe and on foot over extraordinarily rugged terrain, and he thereby became the first person to make the overland journey to the Pacific Ocean north of Mexico.[6]

His published accounts of these explorations won him a hero's welcome in England, where he was lionized in the highest circles. The Duke of Kent, the father of the future Queen Victoria, became a friend, as did many other high-placed members of British society and government. He was knighted in 1802. Wealth won in Canada through his part-ownership in the North West Company and in another of his own formation allowed him thereafter to pursue an entirely different way of life. He maintained a house in London, enjoying his fame and fortune, and in 1812, at the age of forty-two, married the daughter of a Scots merchant resident in London. His marriage brought him an estate in Scotland and three children.[7]

Undoubtedly through Sir Alexander Mackenzie's influence, Nugent Kirkland obtained the business that his brother John described as "a very safe and a very snug one." Nugent was general agent for the recruiting service of the British army. Having made his own fortunate marriage to Phoebe Bingham, by whom he had a daughter, another Ann, Nugent was ready to help his brother's children in very practical ways. John's oldest son, another John Kirkland, was taken to London in 1810, where his uncle entered him in a military school, probably to groom him as his successor in the job of general agent. Another son of John's, another Nugent, was sent to Haileybury College in 1820–21 to prepare for a career in the East India Company. Later, in India, he worked up the ladder to become magistrate and collector of Kaira. John's daughter Isabella, eight years old in 1810, was taken to London to live with Nugent's family and to be educated by a private governess along with Nugent's daughter. John's next son, Alexander Mackenzie, went into his father's business. Only John's youngest son, Kenneth William, failed to benefit from the general good fortune.[8]

John Kirkland was planning a change in his own affairs in 1810. In Ayr he had won a respectable position both as a grocer and as a magistrate, an office to which he had been elected four times, and had refused a fifth term only because he was preparing to move to Glasgow, where he would have better business prospects. He did move there before William's visit. Their mother, Ann McNabb Kirkland, was already living in Glasgow with her daughters Elizabeth, Ann, and Nancy so that Glasgow served as the family base from then on.[9]

The letters from Scotland contained both good and bad news. More good news concerned another brother of William Kirkland, David, who was in the army, stationed at Goa on the Malabar Coast of India. He had bought a house and lacked only a wife to make him completely

28

happy. The bad news was the death of their sister Jean (Jane) Kirkwood from tuberculosis shortly after the birth of a second child. Her husband, who had worked in the customhouse at Ayr, was so despondent that he gave up his job and went to Edinburgh to live with his father. His little daughter Anne, two years old, was living with William Kirkland's mother. Also disturbing was the lack of news from William's youngest surviving brother, James. Apparently he had left Hillsborough early in the century, for his name does not appear in the records after 1803, and he was last heard of by his family in Scotland through a school friend who had accidentally met him in Baltimore in 1806. At that time James was a seaman on a vessel then in port, but he had not communicated his whereabouts to his family for many years before or since. They wondered whether he was still alive and were hurt by his silence.[10]

With all these changes in the family fortunes to see for himself, in the summer of 1811 William Kirkland made preparations for his long absence. He gave a power of attorney to McNeill and Ruffin to sell, if necessary, any of his property not devised in his will to his wife or sons, and he paid a farewell visit to the Murpheys and Scotts. Murphey wrote to Ruffin, "He views his intended trip with great calmness, having made up his mind to undertake it & having settled his business, his ardour seems to increase as the time draws nigh. Comfort Anne at his departure; for I anticipate much grief in the family when he bids them farewell."[11]

In mid-August he set out with his son John Umstead, then nine years old, for London, where he arrived on September 25. He visited Nugent and his family at 8 Bennett Street, St. James's, for several weeks before continuing to Edinburgh for a week, thence to Ayr, and finally to Glasgow. Young John Kirkland was immediately entered in school in Glasgow, and his father probably spent most of the time with the family, reestablishing ties with his kin and revisiting the scenes of his youth. But he also took occasion to buy some household furnishings, probably as presents for his wife, who cannot have entirely enjoyed staying at home with her seven daughters and little son Alexander McKenzie, named for his famous relation. A single invoice has survived of William's purchase of a set of china and a set of castors from William Proudfoot and Company of Glasgow for £13/10. After a visit of seven months, he sailed for home from Greenoch in mid-April 1812, leaving behind young John, who was to be educated in Scotland. John Umstead spent the next six years living with his uncle John's family, forging ties of affection as he absorbed a Scottish education and the strict Presbyterian code of his ancestors, and acquiring a polish of thought and manner that character- ized him as a man. He also made a close and lasting friend of Robert Strang, who continued to correspond with him in later years.[12]

During William's absence from home, Margaret Scott Kirkland gave birth to her eighth daughter, who was named Phebe Bingham for Nugent Kirkland's wife. The name was chosen at the instance of Elizabeth Kirkland, who had made the request as early as September 1810 that William's next child be named for either Nugent or Phoebe Bingham Kirkland. Although the child born in December 1810 was named for Susannah Umstead, Dr. Umstead's wife, William and Margaret Kirkland gratified Elizabeth's whim the following year. After Phebe's birth another son was born to them in 1813, whom they named David for William's brother, but he did not live, so that Phebe proved to be their last surviv- ing child.[13]

At home again in the spring of 1812, just before the eruption of open warfare between Britain and the United States, Kirkland found some changes in his family. He met his new daughter Phebe, and he discovered that George McNeill had been attending to more than business. He and Elizabeth Machen, sixteen years old in May, wanted to marry. In June, McNeill and Kirkland signed an agreement for a partnership in business, to be called McNeill and Kirkland, to operate a dry-goods and grocery store in Fayetteville, North Carolina. Kirkland agreed to invest $10,000 while McNeill contributed $560 and would add $1,440 later. They would share the rent for the store, the wages for a clerk or clerks, and all other expenses. Neither partner would receive a salary, but they would divide the profits or losses.[14]

The importance of Fayetteville as a trade center stemmed from its location at the head of the Cape Fear River. From earliest days it had served as a collection and distribution center in the backcountry for those engaged in the market economy. Merchants abounded there, if they did not all flourish, and most of them were Scots. Among the many firms were the various partnerships of John and James Hogg, who had stores in Wilmington, Fayetteville, and Hillsborough. There were also Robert Donaldson, Sr., Robert Adam (an Ayrshireman representing the firm of Archibald Fleming and Company), William Meng, Duncan Mc- Leran, and William McKenzie. Although Fayetteville, like Cumberland County as a whole, was primarily a Highland Scot settlement and contained many McNeill families, George McNeill had no connection with any of them. He was the grandson of Thomas McNeill of Caswell County, an immigrant from Ulster. George's father, John McNeill, had married Anness Lea of Leasburg and ran a thriving store near the town. Nonetheless George and Elizabeth Kirkland McNeill quickly made themselves at home in Fayetteville. He soon became a respected member of the community where he was to live out his long life. McNeill had, in fact, already established himself in Fayetteville in 1812 in a firm called McNeill, Cain and Company, for the agreement with Kirkland described McNeill as "of Fayetteville," and the mercantile books of Nott and Johnson in Fayetteville listed the firm of McNeill, Cain and Company as a customer in 1812.[15]

William Kirkland's large outlay of money to establish George McNeill in business and the further decline of trade during the War of 1812 must have postponed any private plans he had for further investment in real estate. The records show few land transactions between his arrival home and the end of the war in 1814. He bought from Thomas Scott a lot in Chapel Hill that Scott had bought from Murphey and that Kirkland resold six months later; he accommodated a friend in Tennessee by bidding on a relative's land at an auction sale and reselling it to him; and he bought the 431¼-acre McKerall tract, also from the sheriff.[16] He was probably saving and planning for the project he intended to undertake when the opportunity offered of building a family house to match his now assured status of planter, prosperous merchant, and patriarch of a large family. He had ten living children, of whom two were married daughters with their own families coming along. His recent visit to Scotland and the pride and satisfaction he felt in seeing the Kirkland family's comfortable position in the Old World must have influenced his perception of himself and his place in the New. These factors unquestionably shaped his vision of the house he would build. When the war was over and the economy began to boom, William Kirkland began his mansion.

Since no surviving family papers mention its construction, it is impossible to know exactly who drew up the plans for the house, when it was begun, and under whose direction it was built. By the end of 1815, however, there had arisen on the same tract on which the family had been living an imposing mansion to which William Kirkland gave the name Ayr Mount. (He always spelled it Airmount, but Ayr, too, in the old records had been spelled Air.) It was common practice for Americans

31

to commemorate their European origins in the names of their new homes; Kirkland had Duncan Cameron's recent example, Fairntosh, close at hand. A high-style brick house with a central section forty feet square, flanked by two wings, each twenty-four feet square, Ayr Mount represented a popular architectural style of Southside Virginia and North Carolina houses of the late eighteenth and early nineteenth centuries. Construction features, such as Flemish bond walls with modillioned cornices, molded windowsills, dressed brick window arches, and high-molded water table, gave Ayr Mount architectural details characteristic of the best construction in the state. To build entirely of brick, moreover, was unusual anyplace in North Carolina at that time. In the vicinity of Hillsborough, Judge Alfred Moore's Moorefields was an eighteenth-century example of the tripartite house, which may have been based on an illustration in Robert Morris's pattern book *Select Architecture*, published in 1757, or the more modest examples of William Halfpenny's *Useful Architecture* of 1752; but Moorefields was built of the customary wood.

Two letters from Kirkland to Ruffin in December 1815 approximately date Ayr Mount's construction. In the first he wrote:

> Mr. Collier has presented me with an Acct of the Brick work done on my house. I think he charges me with laying a great many more brick than there is in the house counting sollid walls. He also charges one Dollar for every Arch in the house, that is cutting the brick for them, amounting to $51; he also charges for Pencilling and repairing joints, $35. [The walls had been painted red and the joints white.] As I am perfectly unacquainted with the usual mode of settling for work of that kind, I should be much obliged to you, if you will apply to Mr. Parish & know of him whether he paid such charges; in fact if you could get a copy of Mr. Colliers account against him, it would be better & forward by Mail or otherwise. Should Mr. Parish have lost the account & not remember how he settled, it is probable you may be able to get information from some person in Raleigh. Be so good also as [to] enquire the price of Laths by the thousand and delivered in Raleigh.[17]

Apparently Ruffin did not answer this letter immediately, and ten days later Kirkland wrote again:

I have again to request your attention to that business as I think Mr. Collier charges me with the laying of a great many more Brick than he ought to do counting all the Walls solid, that is making no allowance for Doors & Windows besides one Dollar for cutting the bricks for each Door & Window. He measures the Walls from outside to outside which I think unreasonable. I calculate in this way which I think must be right. You know the main body is 40 feet square & the Wing[s] 24 feet. I measure two walls of the Main body 40 feet long each, the end walls are of course shorter than those by the thickness of those two Walls which I take off & the same in the wings; for to pay him in the way he measures I give him for all the space in the corners 4 Dollars pr thousand instead of two. I wish also to be informed how many Bricks were counted to the foot in his settlement with Mr. Parish, as when Mr. Collier & I agreed I understood he was to do the work on the same terms he did his.[18]

The importance of these letters is obvious. Kirkland not only refers to the walls of the house as just recently built, thus supplying a close date for its construction, but by specifying its dimensions he makes incontrovertible the particular house in question.

The house is majestic in scale: a forty-foot lateral hall across the front, which faces south, gives access to the large room in each wing. One large and one small room lie behind the hall in the center section, facing the back (or river) side of the house. In the upper stories are four rooms on the second floor (two of them originally unheated attics over the wings), on the same plan as the first floor, and two more finished rooms and under-eaves storage space on the third. The full English basement originally corresponded exactly with the floor plan above it. In the large room beneath the dining room, large fieldstones laid on the earth supplied a rough paving. There, too, was an open fireplace, now long since stoned over. A separate entrance under the east wing gave access to the unpaved, unsheathed, unceiled areas under the wings and hall. The scale of the structure eclipses in size any other of its time in the Hillsborough vicinity.

One craftsman's name is known besides that of William Collier. He was John Joyner Briggs (1770–1856), a carpenter, who was responsible at least for the stairs and possibly the paneling of the halls at Ayr Mount. Briggs lived in Raleigh from about 1792 to the end of his life, but he frequently worked elsewhere. His most noteworthy job was the capitol on which he worked from 1833 until its completion in 1840. Several times he served as head carpenter on the project and was afterward particularly proud of the work he had done on the ribs and purlins of the dome and on the arches in the senate chamber. Briggs was also responsible for building the stairs of both sections of Duncan Cameron's Fairntosh plantation house and for those of Thomas B. Littlejohn's house in Oxford. A James Briggs, who supplied laths for the Fairntosh house, was probably a brother of John and seems therefore to have been the originator of the business associated with John's son Thomas H. Briggs: a construction company and hardware store in Raleigh. Kirkland's question about the price of laths in Raleigh suggests that possibly James Briggs had supplied the laths for Ayr Mount too.[19]

The Cameron family papers disclose the names of most of the Fairntosh craftsmen. Since two of the workmen involved in the building of Ayr Mount are known to have worked on Fairntosh, it seems likely that Kirkland might also have employed the man who made all the mantels and overmantels in the 1810 section of Fairntosh, Elhannon Nutt. Nutt was the third son of William Nutt of Wake County, and, like Briggs, was located in Raleigh. He is known to have worked on the houses of Captain William Jones and John Haywood as well as on Fairntosh. A comparison of a mantel at Ayr Mount and one at Fairntosh shows similarities in design and decoration. Two decorative features characterize the mantels in all four houses: an elongated guilloche, used sometimes as a frame for the central panel in the overmantel and sometimes as a decorative ribbon on the mantelpiece, and a linked series of concentric circles running across the mantel under the molding of the shelf. Perhaps these may be taken as Nutt's signature. Unique to Ayr Mount, however, is the molding around the cornice in both west parlor and the dining room. Nothing like it exists at Fairntosh or in any house in the vicinity of Hillsborough. It is impossible to guess who the carpenter might have been for the cornices if he was not Nutt. It should be remembered, moreover, that working on all the structures along with the craftsmen whose names are known were slaves and apprentices, black as well as white, whose names are not known and whose work is also represented in these houses.[20]

Although some of the outbuildings originally at Ayr Mount were standing well into the present century, all are now gone. Those that are remembered include a two-room kitchen, icehouse, well, another out-building (possibly a slave house), and a massive stone barn, which was demolished in this century and the stone sold. A stable and carriage house were located to the east at the end of the carriage drive. The road to Halifax, still identifiable, passes the house just north of and parallel with the present picket fence. Stones found at the northeast corner of the fence are thought to identify the site of Few's dwelling, where he "kept tavern," but the last Kirkland at Ayr Mount believed that Few's tavern stood on a line with the house and to its west, close to an old dug well in a field, the same area in which the stone barn was said to have been located. Since the Kirklands presumably inhabited the Few house until William Kirkland built his own, it is reasonable to suppose that it, too, had a collection of outbuildings around it, which continued to be used after the move to the new house.[21] Sauthier's map of 1768 shows what is probably the cluster of Few's buildings.

Patterns of depression in the ground and rudimentary remains of stone foundations here and there in the yard suggest the original disposition of the outbuildings at Ayr Mount. Clustered behind the main house at the east end and running south in a line and then west, creating in the backyard a work area surrounded by buildings on three sides, would have stood the kitchen, dairy, smokehouse, corncrib, a slave house or two for house servants, and small barns for poultry and milch cows. The daily work conducted in these buildings and the yard and the continual passage of servants to and from the big house would have made the backyard the busiest place at Ayr Mount. The house, its dependencies, and the yard must by necessity have been enclosed by a fence to prevent the encroachment of farm animals and shaded by trees to alleviate the summer heat. Within the fence, too, must have been the vegetable garden and whatever flowerbeds Margaret Kirkland, who was fond of flowers, found agreeable to cultivate. Phebe, writing in 1825 to her niece Catherine Ruffin, reported that the rose Catherine had sent her grandmother was growing and that Catherine was not to forget another flower she had promised to send her.[22]

Until the 1840s, little if any serious attention was paid to horticulture in piedmont North Carolina, even by the wealthiest planters, so that oral traditions of terraces at Ayr Mount running to the river and elaborate parterres around the house must date to a later period than William Kirkland's, or, more likely, represent wishful fantasies about a vanished era. In front of the house, however, was a large, flat expanse of lawn called the green, which set off the size and lines of the house. Only the brick and stone rubble carriage drive, which ran from the entrance to the porch steps, interrupted the otherwise grassy glade. Beyond the fence, however, cleared fields spread out in all directions for pasture and crops. The landscape would have been open, even more than it has been made today, giving long vistas of lovely rolling and well-tended land.

The furnishings of this imposing house are known from inventories of 1836 and 1839.[23] Undoubtedly most of the items were in the house almost from the start, for very soon after its completion, Kirkland's fortunes began to decline. In general, the inventories listed the contents room by room, beginning with the dining room, where a massive built-in cupboard of walnut, left unpainted, still stands to the north of the fireplace to hold the china and glass. Among the listed items are eleven cut-glass decanters and eighteen cut-class tumblers. Next came the silver: tablespoons, dessert spoons, and teaspoons, ladles, and sugar tongs. Dozens of cut-glass wine, water, and jelly glasses and other containers such as cut-glass pitchers, salt cellars, bowls, and dishes followed. Pieces of this glassware, still in descendants' hands, are described as Waterford crystal. The dishes consisted of large bowls, a tureen, four dozen cups and three dozen saucers, two steak platters, five dozen plates, and odd pieces of other china. Eight blue-edged plates, a common variety of china now often found in the soil at old house sites, were probably the remains of a much larger set. Sixteen knives and forks, a carving set, two cream pots, and a sugar dish completed the serving utensils. The furniture consisted of a walnut leaf table, two sets of mahogany dining tables, mahogany sideboard, fourteen Windsor chairs, plate warmer, six mahogany wash stands, four small walnut tables, two mahogany card tables, and twenty-two flag bottom chairs. A "carpet rug" is listed as well as one "ingrain carpet," two gilt frame mirrors, and a pair of brass andirons, shovel, and tongs. Dozens of other furnishings from the main house and outbuildings were also listed, including twelve beds.

Not everything known to have been in the house was included in the inventories, for example, the Broadwood piano, pictures for the walls, including the oil portrait of William Kirkland (unsigned but identified as Jacob Marling's work), an Empire sofa, a desk-box (one was mentioned in a family letter), and more personal articles such as brushes, hand mirrors, and jewelry.[24] The descriptions in the inventory are tantalizingly spare; quality and style of the listed items are left to the imagination. It is safe to conjecture, however, that although the furnishings were in no sense ever lavish, the house included everything then considered indispensable to the comfort of a prosperous planter and his family. Ayr Mount was not just a handsome house, sufficiently large and aesthetically pleasing to house fittingly a man of Kirkland's status. In conception and execution, it was among the first rank of plantation houses in the state, the masterwork of William Kirkland's career—an expression of personal fulfillment and a monument to his aspirations.

❦ 5 ❦

In the Sun

THE SECOND DECADE of the nineteenth century encouraged growth and expansion, for the economy began to recover after the war, and agriculture shared in the improvement. Having just built an impressive house for himself, William Kirkland was in an exhilarated mood, poised and prepared to be generous to his marriageable daughters, eager to extend his landholdings and business at the same time as his family was extending its relationships.

In 1814 Kirkland's management of the tanyard underwent changes. James Webb and Ruffin were added to the partnership, and Phillips's share was bought out. The new firm became Kirkland, Webb and Company and employed Peter L. Ray as clerk. John Holloway, the tanner, managed the work with the help of a slave, Phil. When Ruffin's father, Sterling Ruffin, gave up his own tanning operation in Rockingham County in 1818, he offered to sell Kirkland the services of a good apprentice whose term of service was not yet up. Holloway agreed to take him on and train him. To increase the tanyard's productivity, Kirkland purchased an adjoining section of lot 46. To supply the tanyard with its raw materials, Kirkland's store in Fayetteville bought animal hides and probably accepted them as well in exchange for its wares. It advertised highest prices for hides and deer skins. The tanyard regularly sold hair in bulk to be used to reinforce plaster, as well as leather for shoes, harness, saddles, and the like.[1]

The emphasis on the tanyard and its expansion was to compensate for the closing of his Hillsborough store, which occurred in 1815 or 1816. Perhaps the tanyard's greater profits had persuaded William Kirkland to concentrate his efforts there. He discharged both his store clerks and did not try to replace them. Instead, in 1818 he extended his business interests to an entirely new area through the formation of a partnership with Henry Y. Houze of Louisburg, Franklin County. They agreed to operate a store there opposite the town square. Besides the purchase of real estate in Louisburg for this purpose, Kirkland added other Franklin County land to his holdings. He also began to invest in Cumberland County real estate; from 1818 until 1828 he made close to a dozen purchases of town lots in Fayetteville and larger tracts in the county. He also bought land for his home plantations, adding more than twelve hundred acres to his holdings on or near the Eno River, as well as land on New Hope Creek.[2]

Commerce was in his blood, however, and the Hillsborough store did not stay closed long. An advertisement in the *Hillsborough Recorder* in 1820 announced a new Kirkland enterprise, a "cash store" in his former store building with new dry goods and imported fabrics to sell; the ad also requested the services of a sober, steady clerk, qualified to keep accounts.[3]

Anne's marriage to Thomas Ruffin had further entrenched the Kirklands in the southern planter establishment and proved a kind of keystone in Kirkland affairs. Not only was Ruffin well connected and well educated and destined to rise in his profession, but he was also a thoroughly reliable person, fiscally responsible and tireless in attention to duty. His marriage into the family added solidity to the Kirkland name, marking it as a desirable one with which to be connected. This was no mean advantage to a man with seven other soon-to-be-marriageable daughters. Ruffin's relationship to William Kirkland was an instance of the familiar pattern of mercantile-legal alliances, which underlay so many successful families in the South, of which the Bennehan-Cameron example was the most notable in Orange County. The Cain-Mangum, Hogg-Norwood, and Scott-Murphey relationships followed the same principle.

Despite his social standing, Ruffin had to make his way in the world. Security for his family through ownership of land and slaves sufficient to sustain a comfortable style of life and, should his own life be cut short, to support a widow and children became a driving necessity for Ruffin. Advancement in his profession and wise investment of any money he could spare were his only means to achieve it. In 1811 he bought forty-three acres of land previously owned by Cullen Pollock on the eastern boundary of the Hillsborough town limits where he and Anne set up housekeeping in the old Cullen Pollock house.[4] The house had been built by James Hogg, from whom Pollock had purchased the acreage, and has been identified as the site of the founding of the Society of the Cincinnati in North Carolina. The story-and-a-half structure with a central chimney had "three rooms and a garret." In the same year Sterling Ruffin, Thomas's father, gave him seven slaves, two of whom Ruffin immediately sold. Those he kept were Cupid, Henry, Molly, Parmy, and Dick. Kirkland, too, helped with a gift of a woman Milly and her two children, all of whom Ruffin sold within a year or so.[5]

Anne Kirkland Ruffin, as prolific as her mother, bore fourteen children over the next three decades, of whom only one died as a child. The establishment of the Ruffin household so close to his own was both a practical help to Kirkland and a joy. In a letter to her husband, Anne wrote teasingly about her father's spending all his time with her, taking his meals with her, and in fact proving a formidable rival to Ruffin in her affections.[6]

The Ruffins were always hospitable to a fault and could find room for visitors no matter how large their family grew. They had three little children in 1815 when they offered to have Ruffin's brother James live with them while he attended the Hillsborough Academy. Sterling Ruffin wrote to his daughter-in-law about the arrangement: "I can't find out in your small house & large family where you can possibly stow him; I don't recollect one hole or corner that can be conveniently spar'd for him; I would therefore advise you to make an exchange with us, which would operate to our mutual advantage. Unless you do this, when I come down, if I find my chap at all in your way, I shall look out for some other place to fix him where there is more room & fewer carcases."[7]

In 1818 Ruffin added a law office to his homestead. Kirkland reported the progress of the project to him because Ruffin, as frequently happened, was away on law business. Local workmen were employed to build the office under the supervision of Captain James Phillips. "Hancock has commenced underpinning your office," Kirkland wrote, "& yesterday finished working up all the rock & it is not yet nigh done notwithstanding Henry hawled some for a day or two last week. Captain Phillips informs me Mr. Neals Brick are so badly burnt, they will not answer for the Chimney; he has therefore concluded to have it built with rock up to the funnell, & he can then pick out enough of good Brick to finish that."[8] The law office is still standing in good condition on its original site.

In 1818, too, Ruffin sold William Cain, Jr., almost two acres of his home tract, on which Cain immediately built a modest house for himself and his bride, Ruffin's sister Mary, whom he married early in 1819.[9]

This marriage extended, if somewhat tenuously, Kirkland's ties with the planter ascendancy in Orange County. The Cain family had been early settlers in the area and owned vast tracts of land, a mill, and other commercial enterprises; and Hardscrabble, the house of William Cain, Sr., was almost as large as Ayr Mount.

Like other professional men with money to invest, Ruffin formed partnerships in trade. The first of these was with Paul Kinnion (Paul Kinnion and Company), begun in 1814 and dissolved at the end of the year when Ruffin found a new partner in J. H. Bland to carry on the business: the making and selling of hats. He also participated in an unidentified business with George Williamson. Like Kirkland, he was meanwhile adding to his landholdings, taking deeds of trust, and trying to help his younger brothers get started in life. James H. Ruffin was sent to Fayetteville to learn the mercantile business in McNeill and Kirkland's store, but McNeill had to report that James was lazy and uninterested in his work. Ruffin next sent him to the university, from which he was temporarily suspended in 1816 for taking part in the student riot that year. William Frederick Ruffin, another younger brother, was sent to the university in 1824, but he died while still a student.[10]

In Hillsborough townspeople were banding together to obtain services that until then they had been unable to afford. The Presbyterians, who had been holding church services in the courthouse whenever a visiting minister would conduct them, organized formally in 1816 and in 1817 were able to pay the salary of a regular minister. Kirkland's name is on the subscription list for the Reverend John Witherspoon's salary. Although Kirkland and his wife were never members of the Hillsborough Presbyterian Church, Kirkland seems to have contributed to its support from time to time. His name is not on the sole surviving list of subscribers for the building of the Presbyterian church in 1819, but it is likely that he did donate to the cause. John Umstead Kirkland became a member in 1825 and along with his wife and sisters Mary and Susan, who joined in the early 1830s, was a communicant for the rest of his life.[11]

Although in Scotland the Presbyterian church was recognized as the state church by 1560 and had become securely established by the late seventeenth century, there were few differences in the form of worship of the Presbyterian and Episcopal churches at the time of the Union of England and Scotland in 1707. The Episcopal church gave its members more latitude to enjoy life, but it was as intrusive as the Presbyterian in matters of manners and morals. "Nearly all Scottish families of the early eighteenth century, especially those of the gentry," the historian George Trevelyan wrote, "regularly attended either the Parish Church or the Episcopal Meeting House, where they received much the same spiritual medicine, diluted with different quantities of water."[12] Perhaps this historical situation had something to do with the apparent impartiality that William Kirkland felt, sometimes attending services at the Episcopal Saint Mary's Chapel, which was resurrected in 1818 with Duncan Cameron's help, or, after 1824, at Saint Matthew's, for which Ruffin donated acreage, or at the Presbyterian Church, yet never becoming a member of any. One inhabitant of Ayr Mount was, however, a member of the Hillsborough Presbyterian Church at its inception: Sam, a slave.[13]

When Elizabeth Machen Kirkland, known as Betsy, and George McNeill married in 1812, she established a precedent followed by her next three sisters. Each married and settled in Fayetteville. First came Margaret Scott Kirkland (1797–1820), who married John MacRae (1793–1880) in 1814. He was the grandson of a Scot from Invernesshire who had emigrated to Wilmington, North Carolina, before the American Revolution and the son of Duncan and Rhoda Young MacRae. John MacRae spent his life as a general factotum in Fayetteville—postmaster for almost forty years, mayor for thirty-five, and a leader of many of the civic undertakings in his lifetime. He was librarian for the Bible Society, secretary for the Committee of Arrangements for the reception of General Lafayette, secretary of the school committee of Fayetteville Academy, captain of the volunteer Phoenix Fire Company, president of the Presbyterian Church Board of Trustees, and warden of the poor. For a short time he was the publisher of the Fayetteville newspaper, the *Carolina Observer*. Besides his post office job, his means of livelihood may have been as a coppersmith, for he was proprietor of such a shop. His name will survive, however, not because of his important civic contributions but because he was the prime mover in the production and publication of the MacRae-Brazier Map of North Carolina (1833). As mayor of Fayetteville he had earlier been responsible for bringing out a town map (1825) and had been associated with Robert H. B. Brazier, the surveyor, since 1821, when Brazier had laid out the streets for the town. The state map, however, was a much more difficult and costly undertaking. After an initial grant from the legislature for the project, repeated delays and obstacles forced MacRae to borrow to support the effort, for example, in

1827 a $10,000 loan for which Kirkland went bond, and he raised other money through advance sales.[14]

MacRae's marriage to Margaret was short-lived, for she died in 1820, four months after the birth of their fourth and only surviving child, Duncan Kirkland MacRae. Like her sister Betsy, who died two years later, Peggy was afflicted with tuberculosis, which she passed on to her infant. Although threatened throughout his life by recurrences of the disease, Duncan fortunately survived it to enjoy a long and productive life. The "motherless babe," as MacRae called his new son, became a member of the Ruffin family, for Anne and her husband quickly helped MacRae by assuming care of the infant, and after his father remarried, Duncan still spent much of his time in their home or at Ayr Mount when he was in school in Hillsborough, where he had maiden aunts to dote on him. In his letters written during his school years and later, he frequently addressed Ruffin as "Dear Father." Ruffin, who was not easy to please, said of Duncan that he was "one of the finest & cleverest boys I ever knew."[15]

Obviously, John MacRae was not only a versatile and capable man but an amiable person. A second marriage, which brought to him six more sons and three daughters, did not efface the charm of his earlier happiness or memories of Hillsborough. In a letter to Ruffin just before the Civil War he reminisced about visits to Hillsborough and the Ruffins' cottage:

> I have long had an earnest desire and it is daily increasing to walk on the old familiar grounds of Hillsboro and its vicinity and to greet again those to whom I feel so deeply indebted for so many acts of kindness—My recollections go back to the ford of the Muddy Eno, Thompson's Tavern, the little Market House, & King George's clock, the strong red Jail, the store, the Tanyard, the Locust Hedge, the Hospitable Mansion on the hill with three rooms and a garret but never too small to accommodate any amount of company, although it might be necessary to make a shakedown in the Library, but above all the cheerful, always cheerful faces of its inmates. These are things to be remembered—and there is the Barn in the grove which has been supplemented I learn by a steeple and the path through, as we used to say, instead of the Road round—[16]

Jane Rebecca Kirkland, who married Robert Strange (1796–1854), was the next to follow her sisters to Fayetteville. Ruffin was responsible for introducing Strange to his sister-in-law, an act that Strange still remembered with gratitude many years later. Born in Manchester, Virginia, Strange was the son of a Glasgow Scot, James Strange. After finishing his education at Hampden-Sydney College, Strange wished to settle and practice law in North Carolina. On the advice of many people, including Ruffin and possibly a cousin, William F. Strange, who lived there, he decided on Fayetteville as the place to study law. He also seems to have finished up his studies with Ruffin in Hillsborough. Strange's connection with Glasgow must have immediately recommended him to the Kirklands because John Umstead, still in school there, had formed a friendship with Robert Strange's cousin, another Robert and a brother of William F. Strange. Robert Strange married the seventeen-year-old Jane Kirkland in October 1817. He became in time a respected lawyer and judge of the Superior Court (1827–36); he also represented Fayetteville in the legislature (1821–23) and North Carolina in the United States Senate (1836–40). Eager to supplement his income, which was never large, he became in 1823 president of the Cape Fear Navigation Company and in 1832 a commissioner of the Cape Fear and Yadkin Railroad. He also tried industry, joining William L. McNeill, George's brother, in the construction of the Cool Spring textile factory on Cross Creek in 1827. It failed soon after, and again under Henry A. Donaldson's ownership; but it finally succeeded as the Cross Creek Manufacturing Company in 1838, long after Strange's connection with it had terminated.[17]

Strange was not inclined to ingratiate himself with others and, on the contrary, frequently found himself the center of controversy. The infamous Robert Potter sued him for his handling of Potter's trial for assault and mutilation of the Reverend Lewis Taylor in 1832. In 1840, as a Democrat representing North Carolina in the Senate, Strange lost his seat because he refused to vote as instructed by the Whig state legislature. At that time senators, who were elected by the legislature, were expected to vote as directed.[18]

A more general disaffection with Strange came about because of his novel *Eoneguski* (1839), which he probably wrote not only to while away lonely hours in his Washington boardinghouse but also to expose what he saw as a cruel and misguided government policy. The first novel with a North Carolina setting written by a North Carolinian, it told of the clash of Indian and white cultures and sympathetically depicted the Cherokees as having been exploited by whites. Strange's choice of topic was no doubt dictated by a fascination with Indian lore and history, which he had heard during his experience on the western court circuit, and their relevance to the government's impending removal of the Indians to Oklahoma, the infamous "trail of tears," in order to expropriate their lands. Based on historical events, his book presented only thinly disguised portraits of prominent North Carolina citizens, whose roles in the novel were anything but admirable. Although Strange's name did not appear on the book, it was common knowledge that he had written it. He wisely withdrew it from circulation but not before it had stirred up a tempest.[19]

Though Strange the writer was heard from no more, his attraction to literature was genuine, and if he had had the time he would happily have indulged his talent and predilection for writing. It was a family interest. William F. Strange with his partner, Thomas L. Hybart, became the publisher in Fayetteville of the *North Carolina Journal* until the fire of 1831 wiped out the business. John Strang (as the name was spelled in Scotland), a brother of John Kirkland's friend Robert, was probably the same man who wrote *Glasgow and Its Clubs*, a social history, published in London in 1856.[20]

The last daughter to move to Fayetteville was Martha Shepperd Kirkland (1803–77), known in the family as Patsy, who married Dr. Edwin Louis de Graffenriedt (1798–1871) in 1820. He was a great-great-grandson of the Landgrave Christoph von Graffenried, who had founded the Swiss colony at New Bern. The sixth and youngest son in a large family, Edwin was born in Lunenburg County, Virginia, and undoubtedly studied medicine with an older brother, two of whom were physicians. It was probably John de Graffenriedt who taught Edwin, for John was in practice in Chatham County, and from there to Fayetteville to establish his own practice might have been a logical next step for Edwin. Ruffin may have been again responsible for introducing a prospective husband to a sister-in-law, for John A. Cameron of Fayetteville supplied Edwin with a letter of introduction to Ruffin.[21] Before that, however, de Graffenriedt seems to have been acquainted with Polly Burke, the daughter of the revolutionary war governor, who had supported herself by running a school in Hillsborough. In a letter to a former pupil and classmate of Patsy Kirkland in early 1820, she warned her of placing confidence in the doctor as an escort from Fayetteville to Hillsborough. "Don't depend on Dr. De G—— tho' he should appoint the next morning—it may be next year before he comes," she wrote.[22] Edwin and Patsy were married in November 1820, less than five months after de Graffenriedt had appeared with his letter of introduction. The de Graffenriedts did not remain long in Fayetteville. By 1823 they were in Greensborough, Georgia, and by 1829 in the new town of Columbus, Georgia, of which Dr. de Graffenriedt was a town commissioner empowered to lay off and sell lots, thus a founder of the town. Like her mother and sister Anne, Patsy became the mother of a large family, twelve children, of whom eight survived to adulthood. The eldest was another William Kirkland.[23]

It is evident that the years after William Kirkland's return from Scotland were eventful and happy, with much to engross the family's interest and energies. A tradition in Fayetteville asserts that William Kirkland built houses for Betsy and Jane in 1817 around the corner from each other so that the sisters might remain close. If the story is true, he would certainly have built one for Peggy, too, but that is not part of the tradition. Whether or not Kirkland paid for their houses, he undoubtedly contributed something to their construction, if only advice. In later years McNeill told Ruffin that Kirkland was visiting him in Fayetteville when the plans for his own house were decided on. The five-bay house on Hale Street with a sandstone foundation and a handsome winding staircase was the result. The only evidence that bears on its building is found in a letter from George McNeill to Ruffin when McNeill's finances were a shambles. He regretted having built so fine a house. He had wanted to build something small, he told Ruffin, to which he could have added as his circumstances permitted; instead, Kirkland had urged him to build a large, two-story house.[24]

Around the corner from where the McNeill house stood is the other house identified as having been built by Kirkland in 1817—for his daughter Jane. The house in its present form was certainly not built that early. The Stranges' town house was damaged by the fire of 1831, and the house there now is probably the one reconstructed at that time. Alternatively, the house reputedly built in 1817 for the Stranges may have been their plantation house, Myrtle Hill. A story-and-a-half three-bay structure above a high English basement of brown stone, it became the favorite home of the Stranges. In 1849 Patsy's son Robert wrote to his only sister, "You would find Myrtle Hill robed in her freshest and loveliest livery to welcome you back, the trees and flowers are beginning to recover from the effects of the snow and to look green and fresh again—and you know in the month of May Myrtle Hill is a pretty and pleasant place."[25]

One other happy event for the Kirklands took place near the close of the decade. John Umstead Kirkland came home from Scotland at the end of December 1817. How small and backward, how isolated, even benighted, Hillsborough must have seemed to him after the bustle and pace of Glasgow, which was becoming a major industrial city. Yet he can but have felt approval of and pride in the house his father had built and the changes in his sisters' situations. He was far better schooled than any of his siblings and needed scope to practice his skills and develop his business abilities. Fayetteville was chosen as the place to begin his mercantile career, probably in the McNeill and Kirkland firm. He was at hand, therefore, when the first of many clouds began to form over the family members in that place. It became his task to break the news to Anne Ruffin of their sister Peggy's death in early December 1820.[26] His letter's curiously pious and unnaturally impersonal tone contrasts markedly with that of a similar letter he wrote twenty years later when maturity and experience had refined his style as a man and a letter writer.

By 1819, a year of economic panic in world affairs, the Kirklands had completed much vital building. Kirkland had a magnificent new house, many acres of plantation, three commercial businesses in which he was sole or part owner, four daughters married and presumably established in life, his oldest son well educated and already making his way in the business world. Patsy had not yet married, but she soon would, and his four younger children, from eight to twelve years of age, were being educated in local schools and enjoying new amenities in the little village. In 1820 Kirkland along with William Cain, Jr., and John Taylor, clerk of the Orange County Superior Court, contracted with a teacher for dancing classes to be held at William Clifton's Traveller's Inn. Perhaps the Reverend Mr. Witherspoon's strenuous and outspoken objections to the classes were the cause of Kirkland's disinclination for a closer connection with the church.[27]

Without unforeseen catastrophes Kirkland's younger children might be expected to assume equally satisfactory places in society. The distress in the economy, however, was so widespread that it did not fail to have an effect on local affairs. A letter to John Umstead Kirkland from Robert

Strang paints a vivid picture of the situation in Glasgow, of labor upris-
ings, threatened riots, soup kitchens, business and industrial failures, and
soldiers in the streets: "The times are truly alarming and you are well
away from this place."[28] But even in the isolated and miniature world of
Hillsborough, winds from the storm were about to disturb any compla-
cency the Kirklands may have felt.

❦ 6 ❦

The Plantation

THE SOUTHERN plantation system was unlike anything William Kirkland had known in Scotland. His immediate forebears had dealt with an end product of Scottish agriculture—animals for slaughter and the preparation of the meat for sale—but they had had no part in crop farming. The corn, tobacco, and cotton of the American South were, in any case, a far cry from Scotland's barley and oats. On his entrance into agriculture in the late 1790s, therefore, Kirkland by necessity would have depended entirely on an overseer to manage his farming. Unfortunately, no clues survive to identify that key person. Mention by Kirkland of the burning down of his overseer's house in 1817 is the only reference to an overseer in his correspondence.[1]

In Orange County, overseers were usually local farmers or their sons with a reputation for familiarity with plantation routines and capability to manage land and slaves. Often they were landless or had inherited portions of their fathers' estates too small for subsistence. Managing other men's plantations gave them a living. The only Kirkland overseer whose name is known, John Miller, was such a man. He was a son of James Miller, whose land lay northeast of Hillsborough. The patriarch of the family had been George Miller, one of the original Orange County settlers. Although possibly Quakers originally, over the years the Millers had married into the Rountree and Hall families, members of Little River Presbyterian Church, and themselves had become Presbyterians.[2]

In 1800 William Kirkland owned twelve slaves; a couple of them would have been house servants, one or two handymen in the store, and the rest field hands. By 1810 their number had increased to nineteen and by 1830 to twenty-six. This was not a large work force for the amount of land Kirkland owned. Much of it was uncleared, however, and some of the cleared land supported sheep and cattle, requiring little attention. His herds yielded some of the sheepskins and cowhides needed at the tanyard as well as dairy products and wool used on the plantation. Kirkland's

49

views on chattel slavery, another aspect of southern agriculture foreign to his experience, were nowhere expressed in his letters. Because he was a naturally kind, gentle, and just man, it seems fair to presume that he was a conscientious and even indulgent master. This supposition is supported by a letter from his daughter Phebe to her niece Catherine Ruffin in which she mentions the ailing slaves Dick and Collin. "Papa just to gratify them sent for a black Doctor that lives in Chatham to attend them; poor things! they put a great deal of confidence in him. He thinks he can cure Dick but for Collin he has no hopes." Perhaps the doctor was right; a Dick was listed among Kirkland's slaves in the inventory of his estate, but no Collin.[3]

The estate inventory, taken in 1836 after Kirkland's death, listed twenty-two slaves.[4] Ten were sold to Dr. Edmund Strudwick: Harry, aged about sixty-five and lame; Betsy, aged about fifty; Joe, a blacksmith, aged about forty-five; Duncan, aged about twenty-five; Glasgow (one eye), about seventeen; Henry, aged about fifteen; William, aged about ten; Jeany, aged about sixteen; Patsy (scrofulous), about fourteen; and Ritta, aged about ten.

From their descriptions and ages, it is obvious that Strudwick was motivated by more than self-interest in his purchase, which cost him $8,196. Charity to his friend's family or to known slaves, who might otherwise have ended up on the Deep South slave auction blocks or in unsympathetic hands, may have influenced his action. The young woman with scrofula, a form of tuberculosis particularly associated with poor nutrition and unhygienic living conditions, would not have been useful to him for long. Of two past their prime, one was probably not able to do much work. The blacksmith, however, was a clearly valuable acquisition. The twelve slaves remaining to the Kirklands were Milley, Judy, Dilcey, Chany, another Jeany, Suckey, Osborn, Henry, Lewis, Dick, Charity, and her child. Chany and Suckey were taken to Alabama by a local slave dealer, George Laws, to be sold because they were unruly and insolent. They were provided with new shawls, shoes, blankets, and clothing before being sent. In Alabama their sale brought $884. Osborn was probably the most valuable and trusted of the Kirkland slaves. He was mentioned repeatedly in letters, acting in a variety of capacities. Among his many skills was that of shoemaker.[5]

In the wake of Nat Turner's rebellion in Southampton, Virginia, in 1831, irrational fear took possession of many North Carolinians. The

Kirklands, for the most part, did not share the widespread panic. Alexander McKenzie Kirkland had nothing but scorn and derision for those who did, attitudes displayed in a letter to Catherine Ruffin.

> Christmas we had, such as it was—all in arms and parading the streets in consequence of a supposed insurrection among the slaves, stuffing notions into the poor creatures heads they never would have had. They, the blacks, were highly amused and kept up during the holidays an incessant gigling in their sleeves at our fears—it was more than diverting to witness the powerful effect produced among our gentry. The Town divided itself into patroll companies—one company to perform duty every night—that is, shoot with mustard seed all negroes seen in the streets after the ringing of the bell—a signal for retireing. The Masonic Hall was appointed as a place of general rendezvous for the women in case of an actual attack—Your humble servant was appointed to the high and mighty office of Capt of the 9th Patroll. Nothing occurred during the night to distinguish me save a few fires given by the Company upon a parcel of trees, blindly taken by those Don Quixots for negroes—I presume from the orders my company received they would have kept up a constant fire till this late period, had not daylight fortunately interceded—it would be almost as difficult a task to describe this ludicrous seen [*sic*] as your fears—in my grandmothers house on a certain occasion. The Principal actors however were Messrs Will: J. Bingham, Will: Norwood & Stephen Moore. It is questionable whether the former gentleman will be able to resume his station as teacher in our Academy this season, as he is at present mentally deranged; facts speak for themselves: ... The boys say he walks backwards to & from school for fear a negro might creep up behind him and knock him in the head.[6]

Alexander Kirkland's sister Susan also had little sympathy with the general reaction. Writing to Catherine many months after her brother, she expressed the hope that Catherine's mother's fears of Negro rebellion were groundless. "I have never felt an uneasiness I think I can safely say with regard to myself though I have felt much for those who were more likely to be exposed to insurrections as well as for the poor negroes who I doubt not in many instances will be, if they have not already been, driven to desperation." She adds, "Your dear Mother's situation [pregnancy] prevents her from taking the view which she would take were it otherwise, though she is pretty much of a coward at any time."[7]

Anne Kirkland Ruffin may have been a coward, but as the wife of Thomas Ruffin she was in a more vulnerable position than her sister realized and had cause for alarm. Ruffin's views of slavery were not only uncompromisingly callous; they were instrumental in shaping North Carolina law. He was responsible for the landmark decision of *State* v. *Mann* in 1829, which declared that "the master is not liable to an indictment for battery committed upon a slave. The power of the master must be absolute to render the submission of the slave perfect."[8] Ruffin had the grace to add that he recognized the harshness of the dictum, but his private actions show that he had little compassion for slaves' human condition. In 1821, when his financial affairs were in precarious shape, he resorted to a solution that most men of his standing would have found repugnant—slave trading. He formed a partnership with Benjamin Chambers "to carry on together and as copartners the purchasing of slaves and selling the same." Chambers would do the actual dirty work while Ruffin would put up the initial $4,000 to get the operation started. When their original contract expired, it was renewed, presumably because it had proved profitable. It was terminated only by Chambers's death in 1826. By the terms of his will Chambers liberated his own slave Dick "if possible."[9]

Ruffin's heartlessness to slaves was evidenced not only at a distance; he could be equally merciless to his own servants. In 1824 Archibald Murphey felt constrained to write Ruffin a carefully worded, tactful, but clearly urgent letter about the treatment of Ruffin's slaves by his overseer, Cephus Hudson. Murphey told Ruffin that his character was at stake; all his neighbors were complaining. To convince Ruffin that the allegations of cruelty were true, Murphey added that he had seen the slaves' backs himself.[10] Nor was Murphey the only one to broach the subject with Ruffin. Earlier Dr. Webb had written of a Ruffin slave who complained to him of Ruffin's treatment; and even Anne K. Ruffin, who seldom wrote letters, even to her husband, wrote to him of a woman and child who could no longer endure their treatment and were planning to leave. Not surprisingly, Ruffin was plagued by cases of runaway slaves.[11]

His attitude never softened. In 1852 a neighbor, General Allison, inquired whether Ruffin would be willing to sell Noah, a longtime Ruffin slave, for $150. The price was high for a slave past his working days.

Ruffin told his daughter to consult Noah about his wishes in the matter. Although he learned from his daughter that Noah was anxious to spend the "remnant of his pilgrimage here on earth in the society of his beloved better half," Ruffin was unmoved and took the $150.[12] "Old Uncle Noah," Sally wrote her father, "left here this morning according to your directions; he disliked parting very much."[13]

It is hardly surprising, therefore, that Anne Ruffin privately feared her slaves or that in 1835 the Ruffin house was set on fire by an unhappy house servant. Twice in one day she attempted to start a fire by placing a live coal first under the bricks in the hearth and next in a rat hole behind a cupboard. Anne Ruffin had her removed to another plantation until she heard from Ruffin what he wished done with her. Catherine Ruffin wrote about the terrifying incident with compassion. "Poor creatures," she ended her account, "I wish they were in Africa."[14]

William Kirkland's participation in slavery was a concomitant of his participation in southern agriculture as a whole and in the market economy in particular. Many small North Carolina farmers, subsistence farmers, for example, farmed without the use of slaves, depending on the help of family members, but for any large-scale agriculture slaves were a necessity. In addition to foodstuffs needed for his own and his black family's use, Kirkland grew staple crops such as corn, wheat, and cotton, as well as Irish and sweet potatoes and some oats. His low grounds along the Eno River offered prime land for his corn crop. The only complete account of what was grown on the plantation is found in the 1850 census many years after William Kirkland's death. As John Umstead Kirkland had undoubtedly continued the farming routines established by his father, however, the census report probably approximated the kind of farming carried on in William Kirkland's day. The main difference would have been in its extent: a much smaller quantity of land was under cultivation in 1850 because of the sale of plantation land after the elder Kirkland's death. The 1850 report showed the following:

Improved Land 250 acres
Unimproved 262 acres
Cash Value of Farm $6,000
Value of Farming Implements and Machinery $400
Horses 8
Asses and Mules [none]

Milch Cows 13
Working Oxen 1
Other Cattle 17
Sheep 45
Swine 75
Value of Live Stock $830
Wheat, bushels of 400
Rye [none]
Indian corn, bushels of 1,750
Oats, bushels of 1,000
Ginned Cotton [none]
Wool, lbs. of 75
Peas and Beans, bush. of [none]
Irish Potatoes, bush. of 200
Sweet Potatoes, bush. of 150
Barley, bushels of [none]
Buckwheat, bushels of [none]
Value of Orchard Products in dollars [none]
Wine, gallons of [none]
Value of produce of Market Gardens [none]
Butter, lbs. of 200
Cheese, lbs. of [none]
Hay, tons of 15
Value of Home-made Manufactures $50
Value of Animals slaughtered $200[15]

It is impossible to reconstruct any comprehensive picture of William Kirkland's agriculture because only scattered references to his plantation affairs occur in his surviving correspondence. A letter written in 1815, for example, reveals that he sent sixty-one bushels of wheat to Petersburg to be sold and received $48.80 in payment. At the same time he contributed $50 to the victims of a devastating fire in that city so the profit from the sale of wheat must have represented only a small portion of his annual farm income. Another letter tells of Kirkland's planting clover, an excellent forage and field fertilizer, the seed for which he ordered from New York. He bought cottonseed from Thomas D. Bennehan, who also supplied him with threshing machines like those used at Stagville, also ordered from the North. Kirkland had his mares bred at

Stagville, too, for Bennehan continued to keep stud horses there from time to time. His correspondence with Ruffin and Bennehan shows that Kirkland frequently exchanged seeds and produce with them and other friends and relations.[16]

With the hope of making cotton a more profitable crop, James Webb and William Kirkland procured a cotton gin and went into business together in 1822, setting up the machinery on a Hillsborough lot that Kirkland had purchased from William Cain and encouraging local farmers to bring in their cotton. By 1825 the business was operated as Yarbrough and Kirkland, but expenses for the gin's building, hauling, repairing, and supplies were charged to the firm of Kirkland and Webb, the owners. They seem to have had some trouble with the gin at first. In 1830, however, Kirkland wrote to Ruffin, "The gin picks finely now and [I] have sent 37 lb cotton by Walton."[17]

Typically, Kirkland's main interest in agriculture was in the processing and manufacture of its products, not only because his predilection and training were for business but also because he knew so little about farming. But he was conscientious in all his endeavors and did all in his power to make his planting profitable. Besides rising early to look over the work on the plantation before leaving for work in his store each day, he tried to improve his acquaintance with scientific agriculture by subscribing to the *American Farmer*, a periodical published in Baltimore by J. L. Skinner from 1819 until 1872.[18] It is ironic that tobacco, the golden weed of Glasgow's prosperity and foundation of the Scottish mercantile domination in America, was not grown by Kirkland. The soil of his Orange County plantation was unsuitable for its cultivation.

❦ 7 ❦

Family Life

ACCOMPANYING THE MAIN themes of commerce and farming ran the counterpoint of family life with its ups and downs, its accelerandos and diminuendos, its harmonies and dissonances. For the Kirklands, the education of the children was of central importance. With the establishment of Mary (Polly) Burke's school, William Kirkland's younger daughters could be educated in Hillsborough rather than being sent to Salem. Polly, the only child of Governor Thomas Burke, set up her school beside Dr. Webb's house on Queen Street, probably at his request, so that his daughters and those of other strict Presbyterian families might have the good instruction she was well equipped to offer.

Alexander Kirkland, however, and the older Ruffin children, his contemporaries, were given special educational advantages. Catherine Ruffin, after her years with Miss Burke, was sent for a few months to a school in Fayetteville to acquire polish in the society of her aunts Jane Strange and Minerva Ruffin McNeill and after that to Mrs. Edward Jones's boarding school at Rock Rest Plantation in Chatham County to finish her education. Catherine's brother William Kirkland Ruffin, on the recommendation of William Gaston, was sent to Saint Mary's College in Baltimore, run by the Jesuits. There William Ruffin lived under exacting mental and physical discipline, feeling lonely away from his family and, as a Protestant, alien, but neither he nor the school's principal relayed any complaints to Ruffin. To his aunt Mary Ruffin Cain, however, William Ruffin expressed some of his misery, particularly with the school diet. Alexander Kirkland wrote to his niece Catherine Ruffin, whom he always called Kate, that William was not permitted to eat "shortened bread, butter, meat, nor sweet things, but lives upon codfish, Butter-milk, and unions [sic], a sweet composition upon my word to enter a wind mill."[1] Perhaps it was this Spartan regimen that later propelled William into excesses that gave his parents years of anguish and anxiety. Cards, alcohol, and debt were his demons. In one drunken debauch in South Carolina he shot a man and was injured himself. The voluminous Ruffin family papers do not disclose how he later lost a leg.[2]

Alexander Kirkland, like most Hillsborough boys, probably attended the Hillsborough Academy. Upon completion, in the natural course of events, he was sent to the university at Chapel Hill. Soon after his matriculation in August 1823, he was elected to the Dialectic Society, whose president, William A. Graham, was soon to become a permanent resident of Hillsborough and friend of the younger Kirklands. Up to October 1824, when he was no longer listed on its rolls, Alexander was conspicuous at Dialectic Society meetings by his absence. He would attend one meeting, then miss several in a row, turn up once more, pay the fine for his absences, and then disappear again. If his attendance at classes was equally lackadaisical, it is easy to understand why he did not continue past the summer of 1824.[3] No record of any disciplinary action by the university against him was recorded so his withdrawal was either voluntary or the result of failure in his courses.

From October through December 1824 Alexander worked in the store while his father pondered what should be done with him. He was obviously unhappy in Hillsborough, and his father wanted him educated for some useful occupation and away from the flirtations and idleness he had been prone to in Chapel Hill. "The longer I remain the more disagreeable and dull I find Hillsborough to be," he wrote to Kate. "Daddy has not mentioned north to me in a month. I suppose he has declined. I expect to join Mr. Hooper as a private student as soon as he arrives in this place."[4]

It is not clear what future course had been contemplated for Alexander, but in January 1825, he was sent to Captain Alden Partridge's American Literary, Scientific, and Military Academy in Middletown, Connecticut. Duncan Cameron had inaugurated the fashion by sending his older son to the school a year or two previously when it had been located in Norwich, Vermont. In 1825 Alexander would have had the company of plenty of friends from home: Tom and Paul Cameron, Henry Webb, William Strudwick (a ward of Henry's father, Dr. James Webb), and Thomas Bond.[5] Captain Partridge, a graduate of West Point, believed that mathematics and science should receive as much emphasis in the curriculum as classical studies, not only as preparation for a military career but also for engineering and scientific pursuits. The prospect of going away to school was attractive to Alexander Kirkland but distressing to his adoring sisters. Mary Kirkland wrote on the eve of his departure: "I am sorry dear Catherine to tell you that brother is so soon to leave us and can assure [you] it will be very painful to me to be parted from him so very long and I know it will be no less so to you. He is very anxious to go and I am in hopes it will be of great service to him."[6] Her sister Susan wrote several months later: "You cannot tell how sensibly I feel his loss & my anxiety to see him increases every day. Poor fellow, two long years & perhaps three before we see him but if he returns improved which I fervently hope he will that will be ample compensation for so long a separation. Sometimes I think of him until I get so low spirited that I am obliged to go into my room to give vent to my feelings & after taking a hearty cry I feel greatly relieved."[7]

His sisters were no doubt overjoyed to see him at Christmas 1826, even though the reason for his return was his dismissal from school for having struck a fellow cadet. He nevertheless returned to Connecticut with the other boys in January 1827 and seems to have finished the course in the summer of that year.[8] Catherine Ruffin informed her father: "Uncle Alexander has returned at last—a week today since he arrived—he is thought by all his friends to have improved a great deal. His exterior I can answer for myself as being one of the handsomest and most genteel looking young men I know of. He thinks I believe of studying medicine. He is much more sedate than he used to be and I am in hopes will make quite a steady young man."[9]

Even Thomas Ruffin acknowledged to his wife that her younger brother was a fine, gallant-looking person with the mental powers to distinguish himself by "diligent study and persevering steadiness." No doubt thinking of himself, Ruffin remarked that ambition and necessity were indispensable to young men who wished to acquire eminence. Wryly and somewhat tactlessly he added, "The latter he has ready to his hand in the poverty, of which his father's various misfortunes and large family can give him abundant assurance."[10] He hoped the boy would go to college and prepare for a profession. Possibly Alexander tried once more to study at the university, for his name occurs in a directory under the year 1827, but this second experiment did not last long; he was soon back in his father's store.[11]

Although William and Catherine Ruffin, Alexander Kirkland, and his fellow cadets were removed from the Hillsborough scene, there were plenty of young people left behind to enjoy each other's society. Catherine heard from her aunts Phebe, Mary, and Susan, and other former schoolmates who kept in touch with her and with each other through lively correspondence relating the diversions of Hillsborough life. To them the scene had its charms, particularly in summer, when families from eastern North Carolina fled the annual agues for the airy purlieus of Hillsborough. The Simpson, Burgwin, and Devereaux families, all with daughters of similar ages, added to the general gaiety. Teenage teasing and frivolity filled their letters; " 'sweethearts' and all such stuff," as Catherine phrased it to her father—Hillsborough was the place for them. "Well really," said Fanny Yarbrough, as she glanced out the window, "the street is alive with beaux."[12]

Eliza Bond, a niece of Polly Burke, received the following playful letter from her cousin in Raleigh:

> You say you have three beaux—which of them do you claim? but I beg pardon—Mr. Kirkland will be sufficient under present circumstances—do I pray tell me when I shall have a bidding in time to have my go-to-meeting frock in order—above all things at present I should like to be at a wedding—Lucy Plummer is married by this time I guess to Mr. Battle a Lawyer. . . . There's Wm. Plummer. Cousin Eliza I should like to have him for a Cousin—Throw away John [Kirkland], and aspire to him, for unless you do or [unless] he'll wait for Eliza I shall be deprived of any connection with him— Beaux are a scarce commodity here—and altho' a young lady ought to have a beau, just like a reticule, *for show*, I'm entirely destitute of this necessary requisite to female bliss.[13]

John Kirkland was among the young men-about-town, primarily merchants or lawyers, who were eligible bachelors, having finished their education and either about to begin or already earning their livelihoods. In 1824 John Kirkland had moved back to Hillsborough to work with his father after finding the climate in Fayetteville too debilitating. Also in his group were William and Walker Anderson, sons of Mary and Daniel Anderson, who had lived in the town first as boarding students at the academy and then as permanent residents when their widowed mother moved to Hillsborough in 1817 to be near her brother Duncan Cameron and the Kirklands. There were also Henry K. Nash, the young Norwoods, George Johnston, the older Webb boys, and various other scions of established local families. A letter from Fanny Yarbrough to Eliza

Bond described John Kirkland's situation in 1825: "William Branch says he is going to court Miss Mary Ashe if she is not engaged to Mr. John Kirkland which I rather believe she is by his going to Aunt Burkes [where she was a boarding student] every night and sitting up there untill nearly eleven o'clock." Fanny's letter writing was interrupted, and she continued a week later: "Jno K came to see me a few moments ago and told me that your Aunt Burke frightened him last night very much, by insinuating that it was not absolutely certain M—— would have him; he told me that from what has passed between them he considered her as engaged provided her parents had no objection."[14]

Two days later Fanny was reporting again: "M—— has discarded JK and it would excite your pity to see how melancholy he is; his face as long as your arm."[15] John was not easily discouraged. Two years later, his continued courting of Mary Ashe was still town gossip. David M. Saunders wrote to his former classmate William A. Graham, who was then studying law with Thomas Ruffin in Hillsborough: "Tell Jno Kirkland if he courts that girl any more he will make a Cad of himself—and that all the good or harm that I can wish him is that she will not have him."[16]

The end of the romance prompted John's sister Mary to write to Eliza Bond, who was visiting her cousin Mary Ashe:

> I had heard of the defeat before receiving your letter and bore it like a hero. I scarcely ever think of it now, *never* indeed without it is mentioned and then I take very little interest in it. As the old saying is that all things turn out for the best, it is a true saying, I believe in this case, for Mary Ashe's heart has too much of the flirt in it to suit brother's. I never hear *him* say anything about the matter, appears quite indifferent upon the subject. And for my part I console myself *under the firm belief* that there is as good fish in the sea as ever came out and that if he will only exercise a little prudence he will be able I have no doubt in a little time to take unto himself a wife—one which will suit him better.[17]

And so it later proved. Town sentiment was all in his favor and Mary was criticized for her behavior, but John defended her and held no grudges. His good nature and good company made him a particular favorite. Paul Cameron, six years John's junior, while away at college wrote to his sister, "I would give anything if I could but see him; his society is allways a source of great pleasure. His lively disposition, his affectionate and free intercourse give him no ordinary rank in the social circle."[18]

Soon John was his usual self, calling on the Nashes, where he "kept the girls in a roar of laughter."[19] These were Ann, Maria, Susan, and Sarah, daughters of Frederick Nash. They too wrote Catherine about their days as belles; for example, this from Sarah Nash: "Mr. London is now serenading very delightfully so you must excuse a few mistakes though I wish he would stop for he puts me in a fever: I never heard serenading by whistling before but I believe they are trying it now."[20]

Mary Kirkland also had admirers. She had formed a close friendship with Maria Simpson, whose family always summered in Hillsborough. When Maria expressed hope that Mary would visit her in New Bern soon again she teased, "I will indulge myself with the hope that you will be induced to visit us again before very long, but I fear that hope will not be realized if *the ever true and constant* Mr. Bennehan continues to engage so much of your attention; don't forget Mary that you are to supply me with wool."[21]

Mr. Bennehan was, of course, the perennial bachelor Thomas D. Bennehan, son of Richard Bennehan and brother-in-law of Duncan Cameron. Maria Simpson's curious reference to wool was a metaphor for news or gossip, apparently current among Hillsborough girls. In a letter to Eliza Bond from another Hillsborough young lady, Caroline Heartt, the same usage occurs: "Susan Kirkland has referred you to me for the news, but I am afraid she has sent you to a goat's house to get wool."[22]

These letters from apparently empty-headed and idle-handed young women are deceptive, however, for moments of leisure were few, and the girls were mostly confined to their studies, as a rare letter from Susan Kirkland to Catherine makes clear: "I will tell you how I spend my time I rise prety early study deffinitions & geography until breakfast I have a most elegant atlas cost 25 dollars after breakfast I work & study my french until five in the afternoon & then Thomas McNeill & myself revise our english grammer & read history until dark & after dark I read some interesting book or amuse myself with the children."[23]

The children Susan referred to were Kirkland grandchildren, the Mc-Neills, the Stranges, or Duncan MacRae. The boys in these families were sent to school in Hillsborough and lived at Ayr Mount so that the house was usually alive with a few grandchildren. Visits from friends varied the routine. In June 1823 the leisurely summer pace must have quickened considerably with the prospect of a visit from Andrew Smith and his family. Andrew Smith of Richmond, a friend of both William Kirkland and Thomas Ruffin, prepared to escort his wife and three daughters to Ayr Mount for an extended visit. He wished to set a time, he wrote William Kirkland, when he would find Ruffin at home:

> I should also anxiously desire to meet my estimable young friends Mr. & Mrs. Strange, Mr. McNeill, and your son John, as I shall not have time to go to Fayetteville then, and only a day or two with you.

> Some conditions on the part of Mrs. Smith remain to be stated before undertaking the journey: it must be expressly understood that she and her three girls are to be considered as members of your family, no extra trouble whatever to be taken on their account, except perhaps an additional quantity of *Porridge and milk*. One chamber with two beds only necessary. Your daughters to join mine, at such hours as may be found most convenient, in taking lessons of Music—Painting—French—Geography etc. provided they are not already furnished with better means of acquiring these branches, seeing that Mrs. Smith devotes a portion of each day to that employment. Miss Ruffin may probably find it convenient to join them. I should think 'twould be too severe upon them to attend school in Hillsbro' during the hot season. You must try to have the piano in order, and tell Misses Mary & Susan I still calculate on hearing them both perform on it, and *sing charmingly*, when they accompany our girls in some of my favourite duets and Scotch songs. Have you plenty of Music, or shall the Girls bring theirs? If it is the wish of Mrs. Kirkland and Mrs. Ruffin that the young Ladies should take lessons in painting, can you get furnished with good water-colours and drawing paper, and brushes at Hillsbro'? Painting on velveteen is also a beautiful accomplishment. I presume the proper paints are not to be had with you. Is it desirable that we should procure the necessaries and bring on with us? The cost of the materials will be small compared to the value and beauty of the accomplishment to every young Lady of Taste. A Box of colours etc. complete may be had here for $9 or $10 and is sufficient, I believe, to give a learner a good knowledge of the Art.

Agreeable to Mrs. Kirklands friendly wish, my second daughter sketched a small piece for her which was sent to Messrs T. & R. Dunns at Petersburg to be forwarded to you, 'twas secured between two square pieces of strong Pasteboard. Rachel begs her acceptance of it as a small token of esteem with a promise of trying to produce something of more interest at Ayr Mount.

The two Legnumvita R[h]eum were sent to Messrs T. & R. Dunns. My friend at Phila wrote me they were the best that could be found there. I hope they gave satisfaction.[24]

At the time of this visit the three youngest Kirkland girls would have been twelve, thirteen, and fourteen years old, probably about the same ages as the Smith daughters. The six girls no doubt enjoyed chatter over their busywork during the hot summer days of the visit.

In 1827, when James Strange was staying at Ayr Mount, he fell into mill machinery and his legs were nearly severed from his body. During his long recuperation only his Aunt Anne Ruffin's ministrations could soothe his pain.[25] She had a way with children and they, like everyone else, loved her. Phebe Kirkland told her niece Alice Ruffin that Anne was her favorite sister because of her gentleness and humility; Alice had confided to Phebe at Rockingham Springs the previous summer that she wished to be like her Aunt Jane Strange.[26]

Although the younger Kirkland girls admired their older sisters, they felt very competitive with, even jealous of, each other. Mary Kirkland, sixteen years old, wrote to her sister Phebe, fourteen, how tired she was of their sister Susan, fifteen, who was always so sober and solemn. She signed her letter, "your favorite sister, Mary A. Kirkland."[27] The rivalries, tiffs, teasing, and jockeying in that trio kept the household lively. They vied for the attention of their niece Catherine Ruffin, fourteen, who was told by her sister Anne that "Aunt Phebe says she will not write to you untill you send your love to her; she says you send your love to every person but her."[28] On another occasion Susan wrote to Catherine "reluctantly because I fear it will not be acceptable; if you had manifested the least desire to have heard from me, I would not in the least have doubted but what it would be received with pleasure, but when I hear of a letter from you to Sarah, Elizabeth, Charlotte, and Sally & not one for me what reason have I but to believe you have forgotten me?"

Such epistolary pouting alternated with playful banter in their essentially unruffled existences. Having vented her annoyance, Susan proceeded to give Catherine the news. Her sister Mary was taking piano lessons from Mr. Aykroyd, apparently a tutor in both French and music.

He generally ties up her fingers with his handkerchief. They have a dispute every day but I never go in the room. Caroline Heartt is taking lessons also, the most ridiculous thing I ever heard: she had much better stay at home & attend to the family. But I have nearly finished my letter & have told you nothing about my french. I said my vingtième lesson last Tuesday & am just conjugating the troisième verb; he pursues quite a different plan with me from what Mrs. Smith did. I do not get two or three verbs of a day, but I find it quite a difficult task to get one & get it as I ought & I am confident that I know three times as much french as I did after I finished with the above mentioned lady. I understand Miss Julia Burgwin speaks french very fluently. Maria Simpson has joined our class & I see her quite often. She is quite a fine little girl. She goes to Miss Brainerd & expects to spend the winter here.[29]

Susan went on to speak of a letter from their Uncle John in Scotland to her brother John. At this time the two families were in closer contact than usual because the president of the university, the Reverend Joseph Caldwell, had visited Scotland in 1824 and spent some time with the Kirklands in Glasgow. He was able to give the Scottish family detailed accounts of their American relations, and, presumably, had brought back to Hillsborough the latest news from Scotland. At the time of his visit the family abroad was very melancholy because of the recent deaths of both Ann McNabb Kirkland and her daughter Nancy, who had finally succumbed to tuberculosis. While Caldwell was still in Glasgow, the family learned of the death of Augusta Vesey Kirkland, the young wife of John Kirkland's son John, and of her sister Charlotte, both from tuberculosis. Of this news Susan wrote the puzzling comment, "Well may he mourn the loss of Augusta for she was truly an amiable woman. I knew her from her infancy."[30] Perhaps she was quoting the letter or John Umstead Kirkland. He would have known Augusta during his years in Scotland, whereas Susan could not possibly have met her.

Thus the Kirklands' family life proceeded through the 1820s while the younger children were completing their educations. Their dalliance with

French and music, like that with learning in general, probably did not go very far, in any case not far enough to beget solid results. High spirits, however, matched high hopes, and daily existence was still unaffected, at least on the surface, by any shock waves of the financial disaster that had already overtaken them.

❦ 8 ❦

Illness

WHILE THE YOUNGER family members went their lighthearted ways, their married sisters were enduring the stresses of frequent childbearing and ill health. Over the years Anne Ruffin bore fourteen children, Jane Strange seven, and Patsy de Graffenriedt twelve. Betsy Kirkland McNeill had had five children in ten years of marriage and Margaret Kirkland MacRae four children in six years. Tuberculosis, which had cost the lives of three family members in Scotland in 1824, was equally common in the New World. Margaret Kirkland MacRae had died of it in 1820 and probably her sister Betsy, as well, in 1822. Duncan Cameron would lose four of his six daughters to it, and Jane Strange also would eventually succumb to it.

Although Jane died of tuberculosis, she suffered for many years from periods of illness similar to that which plagued Patsy, Anne, and Phebe. In 1825 Patsy de Graffenriedt described her symptoms to Anne Ruffin as palpitations of the heart, icy hands and feet, and a sensation of numbness gradually rising from the feet to the heart. Phebe Kirkland wrote of her sister Jane Strange's illness in 1838 that she had lost weight and looked wretched and that neither Dr. Webb nor Dr. Strudwick knew what was wrong with her. Jane suffered attacks in which she lost the power of speech and had heart palpitations, pain in her back, and violent convulsions. Alice and Catherine Ruffin described their mother's symptoms as palpitations, numbness in tongue and stiffness of jaws, melancholy, and a diseased mind. Doctors Webb and Strudwick pronounced Anne's illness hysterical, a diagnosis that provides the clue to all the others' as well.[1]

Hysteria was an ancient name for a well-recognized syndrome of symptoms attributed to malfunction or malposition of the uterus. It was not until the latter part of the nineteenth century that it became recognized as a psychogenic disorder or neurosis related to mental or physical stress, anxiety, repression, or poor health and associated with excessive sensibility. Although all through the ages some men had suffered from the same malady, in which cases it was identified as hypochondriasis, hysteria was predominantly a female affliction. After World War I, however, when thousands of soldiers were diagnosed as suffering from shell-shock and exhibited the same or similar symptoms, interest in the problem soared and understanding of its nature and treatment developed.[2]

The reason for hysteria's frequency in women, particularly upper-class and idle women, is only now beginning to be understood as related to the stresses and constraints of their lives. The cultural expectations to which they were required to conform, particularly confining in the nineteenth century, consigned them to almost passive existences. Many wives and daughters were virtual prisoners in domestic cages, like canaries kept for their pretty plumage and song. Limited education and legal disabilities, together with society's demands that they be pure and innocent as well as dutiful and selfless, augmented their personal helplessness and vulnerability to neuroses. Increasing frustration with these limitations heightened their tendency to nervous afflictions, often referred to as "the vapors." A very high incidence of hysteria in nineteenth-century women was the inevitable result.

Religion and illness provided two acceptable outlets or safety valves for emotional repression in the nineteenth century. It is not surprising that large numbers of women, consciously or subconsciously, found relief in both. Expression of anger, aggression, desires, or opinions was unacceptable. Suffocated spirits found no relief in interesting or challenging work for respectability countenanced no careers for women outside the home except as teachers or governesses and then only for spinsters. Religious enthusiasm allowed them to give vent to their feelings, and as invalids they could doff their emotional straitjackets and win sympathy and attention. Tight corsets were truly symbols of their total restraint.

Some of the Kirkland sisters, more than usually conscientious, sensitive, dutiful, and physically debilitated from pregnancy and childbearing, broke down from time to time and manifested their stress in hysteria. Ruffin understood his wife and her burdens very well, and when Anne Kirkland Ruffin was enduring one of her attacks, he urged her to get away from home, visit her sisters and parents, and even shirk her responsibilities entirely and come to Raleigh with him. At another time he advised Catherine to encourage her mother to spend as much time as possible in her garden, "sowing her seeds & training her flowers & admiring them. There is nothing that contributes more to a sound body & a cheerful mind than that delightful occupation."[3]

Hysteria was often an illness of young, unmarried women and widows as well. In the latter cases the doctors blamed sexual repression for the condition. In young girls they were more likely to blame menstrual irregularities, a diagnosis Strudwick and Webb immediately jumped to, along with the classic diagnosis, misplacement of the uterus, when Phebe Kirkland began to manifest symptoms of hysteria in late 1829. Her troubles, however, were not physical. In Phebe the illness presented with casebook clarity the most severe and long-lasting symptoms. Because it began in late 1829, her illness may have been related to her father's financial troubles, which culminated in that year and must have made the family feel that an abyss had suddenly opened before them. She was almost eighteen years old at the end of November when her father wrote to Ruffin, "The family are all well, excepting Phebe who is still complaining, but I think is getting better; she is not confined, but has not been well for some time past."[4]

The following month she developed the alarming symptom that characterized her illness at its worst—spasms. This term could be used to describe muscular cramps, paralysis, or convulsions, but Phebe Kirkland seems to have suffered from all three. Although her family was much encouraged in mid-January by her improvement, return of appetite, and ability to sit up or walk short distances in her room, late in the month the spasms returned and caused the family grave concern. Ruffin learned that her nerves were influenced by the slightest noise, and she had violent paroxysms without intermission for three days. The doctors, Webb and Edmund Strudwick, now said her problem was an internal injury, which would be hard to cure, and they applied blisters, which made her bleed freely. She had not eaten for six days. When she did not improve, the doctors called in Dr. James S. Smith as a consultant, and they all stayed by her bedside. Her mind was affected; she did not know her brother John even though she had asked to see him.[5]

Suddenly, for no reason the doctors could assign, she began to improve: she asked to see her minister, William Mercer Green, who administered the sacrament to her, and from that moment she had begun to feel better. Her father was happy to tell Ruffin that in March she was in as good health as she had ever been. Plans were made for a visit to Jane Strange. Anne Ruffin, the second Ruffin daughter, went with Mary, Susan, and Phebe to Fayetteville, Mary riding a pony borrowed from Walker Anderson. It was a long visit, and Phebe began to seem herself again.[6] Some six weeks after their arrival at Myrtle Hill, Anne Ruffin wrote to Catherine about the sudden renewal of Phebe's illness:

Last Saturday Phebe was very cheerful and appeared to be nearly well all day and eat [sic] heartily (I am afraid too much so) and went to bed and slept soundly for about two hours. Mary and myself were awakened by a noise which she was making in her sleep and arose and went to her bed immediately. She was crying and appeared to be very much agitated. We were frightened but thought it was a frightful dream. We called her and told her it was a dream she had had. She then began to repeat some lines of a hymn. With that we called up Aunt and Uncle S. The doctor was sent for. Her head was very much affected. She said she was at home and called Uncle S "Grandpa" and Doctor C "Dr. W." She knew Mary and myself. *All* the time talked about home and said not one of her relatives were glad to see her but Susan and Uncle J. She was very much disappointed when the letter came [saying William Kirkland would be delayed in coming to fetch them home]. She said she believed if she could get home it would cure her. She had several spasms and about one o'clock she had a very severe one. Her teeth were clenched and we suppose they were from that time until 3 o'clock yesterday as she made several efforts to speak and drink but could not. We discovered it just after day. She made signs to Dr. C by putting her hand on his mouth and then on hers. He examined and found she had the Lock Jaw and put blisters on her head and jaws, ankles and wrists. They all drew well which relaxed her system so much that he could get his fingers between her teeth. We were all surprised that she could not swallow after her mouth was open and the doctor discovered her tongue paralyzed which she did not get over for some time. She was very sick at her stomach last night about 11 o'clock and threw up after which she was able to speak and swallow. She spent a very comfortable night considering all things and she has been better all this morning until now she is laboring under a sick stomach produced by a dose of calomel, which is the only medicine she has taken since Saturday night. She took a pill which she does every night. She was very much distressed at her condition and thought she was dying (which she was very near doing). She sent for the Rev. Mr. Jones to see her and appeared quite composed while he was talking to her. She is prepared. She makes us understand her by spelling on her fingers. She asked the doctor if he thought she would recover. He told [her] she was very sick, that she might recover but that he did not want to flatter her. I don't think she ever can get over it but even if she were to die, my dear sister, we ought not to mourn her loss when we know how well she is prepared and see how patiently she bears her sufferings.[7]

When William Kirkland went down to Fayetteville to bring the girls home ten days later, he found Phebe able to talk and laugh and rid of the impediment in her speech and of her nervous symptoms, though still very weak. Only two weeks later, however, the spasms and lockjaw returned. At this point the doctors prescribed astringent douches and a pessary because her uterus was determined to be three-fourths of an inch below its proper position. In late June her father wrote to Ruffin much encouraged that Phebe's menstrual period had come on naturally without the help of medicines. Again there was improvement. In September her father reported that "Phebe at present comes on finely, eats with the family every Meal, went to church on last Sunday, & one day this week to Miss Burke's examination. She takes I am affraid too much exercise but it cannot be prevented."[8]

Her brother Alexander, in one of his confiding letters to Catherine Ruffin, told her, "My dear Phebe was quite unwell yesterday but says she is quite well again. I was reading to her at the time. I was much alarmed at her very sudden change of countenance."[9] In 1835 other attacks occurred as severe as those of 1830, in which she would lose consciousness during the spasms. A friend wrote to Miss Burke, "Phebe is better. I have not seen her. The girls and all that have seen her say there is a great change in her; at times she is quite silly, and [a] great expression of wildness out of her eyes; her sufferings have been greater this attack than any of her former ones."[10] Later letters spoke of no similar attacks, but a neighbor wrote to Eliza Bond in 1837, "Phebe has been a good deal troubled at the letters she wrote to your Aunt; poor girl, she is not herself."[11]

Long experience with his wife's and her sisters' attacks gave Thomas Ruffin some insight into their problems. Although he recognized that bodily weakness contributed to their mental ill health, he did not see the part that he and other men played in adding to their stress by expecting of women almost impossibly high standards of conduct, virtue, and moral perception. In writing to his wife about her situation he disclosed both the insight and the blindness. "Women, it is true, owe much of their superior influence & many of their virtues to the frailness of their bodily constitutions, as well as to the delicacy of their sentiments & moral perceptions, and, therefore, one cannot wish them much changed; yet one must acknowledge that *they* would have more comfort in frames somewhat more robust & with a little less nervous susceptibility."[12]

In those days medical aid was palliative at best; whatever healing occurred, nature effected. As a last resort, mineral springs were usually tried and, depending on the illness, could prove efficacious. Those whose illnesses benefited from relaxation, rest, and nourishing and tempting food could be restored to health or something approximating it. Even those in the early stages of consumption found a visit to the springs restorative. All through the century springs were popular as vacation spots for the healthy as well as the sick. Starting from rather primitive structures adjoining natural springs, at first usually near or in the mountains, and progressing over the decades to the most luxurious accommodations and entertainment and to locations in the piedmont, springs attracted the southern gentry for vacations at least once a year. The Virginia spas, such as White Sulphur Springs, Warm Springs, Red Sulphur Springs, and Sweet Springs, were older and more elite, but the Kirklands and their relations more frequently chose resorts closer to home: Lenox Castle in Rockingham County and Shocco Springs in Warren.

Richard Bennehan visited Shocco in 1825, expecting to meet Kirkland there. Joseph Caldwell, the president of the university and friend of both men, had told him that Kirkland recommended going after the middle of July when there would be more company. Bennehan was therefore disappointed not to find Kirkland there when he arrived as directed in July. As weeks passed without his making an appearance, Bennehan's son tried to mend matters: "I requested Dr. Umstead to state to Mr. Kirkland how solisitous his friends in Warren were to see him, and what good fare and good society you had at Shocco."[13]

In an earlier letter to his son, Richard Bennehan had described the resort:

> I arrived here on Monday the 25th where I found upwards of thirty Ladies & Gentlemen, the number daily increasing, Visitors to this most agreeable & highly improved watering place far exceeding any thing of the kind I have ever found beyond the mountains (that is) as respects good living, fine airy rooms, well furnished with every article necessary for the comfort and convenience of its inmates. The Springs in fine neat order, the one at this place surmounted with a huge building and good seats for at least one hundred Visitors, but I most sincerely regret the want of Baths both hot & cold which the proprietor says was almost impossible to have in readiness this season.[14]

Although Richard Bennehan always enjoyed Kirkland's company, Thomas Bennehan was Kirkland's friend and more nearly contemporary. In his usual way when sending Thomas Bennehan a bill, Kirkland added a personal note. "W. Kirkland will be extremely glad to see you & our mutual friend Mr. [Peter] Brown at his house & is in hopes when you do come that you will make it a visit worth while by giving him the pleasure of your company for some time."[15] Bennehan reciprocated the warm feeling. He wrote to his nephew Paul Cameron: "Please say to Mr. Kirkland that on examination I shall not have a Bushel of Cotton seed to spare unless he himself should want a few Bushels to plant; with him I would divide my last seed." Bennehan regretted not having had the pleasure of dining at Paul's while the Ruffins and Kirkland were there, instead of "eating my solitary crust, rat-like by myself."[16]

William Kirkland usually visited the springs once each summer and probably did not disappoint Richard Bennehan in 1825. Until a week before his death in June 1836, Kirkland was still planning to go to the springs, certain that they would again relieve him. Spas proliferated as the century proceeded, and the sick became a less noticeable component of the company as recreation became more important, entertainment more lavish, and competition among the resorts ever keener. Each resort retained a resident doctor, however, for those in the company needing his attention. Just before the Civil War a visitor described the daily routine at Kittrell Springs, Franklin County, which was probably representative of the other North Carolina resorts. "There are a great many fine folks here for pleasure who spend their time in dressing, dancing, and keeping company in the large ballroom, some times 50 persons on the floor dancing at once. They dance between breakfast and dinner, between dinner and supper, and from supper till 11 o'clock; breakfast at 8 dinner at 2½ o'clock, supper at 7. The table is pretty fair much better than last season. . . . The fare is very good and Dr. Blacknall very kind & attentive."[17]

Dancing increased in popularity as health-conducive exercise, and spas were not the only places in which it was enjoyed. When Anne Ruffin visited the Stranges with her Aunt Phebe in 1830, they attended a party at which the company began to dance about noon and kept it up until eight that night, and "they have been both much better ever since," William Kirkland told Ruffin. Undoubtedly dancing provided another acceptable outlet for high spirits; it temporarily relaxed taut nerves in happy abandon and helped restore health to body and mind. As frivolous as the springs may now seem as medical resources for serious disease, they were, beyond a doubt, a better alternative than the bleeding and blistering, purging and puking, sweating and "salivating" the patient invariably suffered at the hands of a doctor.[18] For tuberculosis and hysteria they were certainly the best resort.

❦ *Illustrations* ❦

The town of Ayr about 1800 (*Scotia Depicta*, London, 1804, plate 25). Courtesy Rare Book Room, University of North Carolina Library, Chapel Hill.

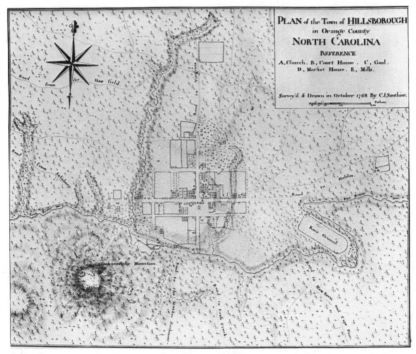

Claude J. Sauthier's *Plan of the Town of Hillsborough* (1768). The buildings to the east on the road to Halifax almost certainly represent William Few's home plantation and tavern. Courtesy North Carolina Division of Archives and History.

Archibald DeBow Murphey (1777–1832). Engraving by John Sartain.
Courtesy John L. Sanders.

Anne Kirkland Ruffin (1794–1879). Courtesy Southern Historical Collection,
Ruffin-Roulhac-Hamilton Papers, University of North Carolina Library,
Chapel Hill.

Thomas Ruffin (1787–1870). Portrait by James Hart in possession of the Dialectic and Philanthropic Societies Foundation, Chapel Hill. Courtesy National Portrait Gallery, Smithsonian Institution, Washington, D.C.

The Hillsborough home of Thomas and Anne Kirkland Ruffin from 1809 to 1829. In this house, built in the 1770s by James Hogg on property now known as Burnside, was organized an Orange County Chapter of the Society of the Cincinnati. Courtesy Southern Historical Collection, Ruffin-Roulhac-Hamilton Papers, University of North Carolina Library, Chapel Hill.

Sir Alexander Mackenzie (ca. 1764–1820). Portrait by Sir Thomas Lawrence.
Courtesy National Gallery of Canada, Ottowa,
Canadian War Memorials Collection.

Ayr Mount. Front (north) view. Unless otherwise credited, this and the following photographs of Ayr Mount and its furnishings are by Frederick Stipe Photography, courtesy Richard H. Jenrette.

Ayr Mount. River (south) view.

Lateral entrance passage: view toward parlor in east wing. Front door to the left and dining room door to the right.

Detail of hall and stairs. Photograph by Kenneth McFarland.

One of a pair of Sheraton-style card tables, mahogany and mahogany veneer on pine, original to Ayr Mount.

Parlor in west wing. The piano was acquired by William Kirkland in 1806.

The Broadwood fortepiano (1797) was restored to playing condition by John Watson, now of Colonial Williamsburg.

Dining room at Ayr Mount. The table and portrait were acquired with the house by Richard H. Jenrette in 1985.

Detail of dining room mantel and built-in walnut cupboard. Photograph by
Kenneth McFarland.

The Sheraton-style mahogany table, possibly original to the house.

Sheffield plate tea set and American coin silver cups (ca. 1840) were Kirkland family pieces.

Anglo-Irish cut glass, covered bowls, part of a large set owned by William Kirkland. The largest of the three bowls measures 11½ inches. The Museum of History, North Carolina Division of Archives and History, owns two of the three bowls at Ayr Mount.

Second floor lateral passage and stairs to third floor.

Detail of the larger of two third-floor bedrooms showing original paint finishes.

Locally made walnut tilt-top table (ca. 1840) belonging to the Kirkland family.

Map of the Town of Fayetteville (1825), published by John MacRae. The original settlement, Campbelltown, on the Cape Fear River, was slightly to the east of Cross Creek, a later and competing village. The two were incorporated as Fayetteville in 1783, the first of many towns named in honor of the Marquis de Lafayette. The Lafayette Hotel (shown at the right) was built by Robert Donaldson for Lafayette's visit to the town during his tour of the United States in 1825. Courtesy North Carolina Collection, University of North Carolina Library, Chapel Hill.

Robert Strange (1796–1854). Portrait by William Garl Browne. Courtesy North Carolina Collection, University of North Carolina Library, Chapel Hill.

Myrtle Hill (ca. 1817), the plantation house of Robert Strange, Fayetteville. The porches are later additions. Photograph by Nancy Mason. Courtesy North Carolina Division of Archives and History.

The Robert Strange town house (ca. 1817), Fayetteville. Now considerably altered, the house is locally said to have been the gift of William Kirkland to his daughter Jane Strange. Courtesy *Fayetteville Times*.

John Umstead Kirkland (1802–79).
Courtesy Richard H. Jenrette.

Schomberg House (1956 restoration), 80–82 Pall Mall, London. The left side of
the tripart house contained the office and apartments of Sir John Kirkland. Photograph by Sydney W. Newbery. Courtesy J. C. Kirk, Commercial Union
Properties Limited.

General William Whedbee Kirkland (1833–1915). Courtesy Duke University
Manuscript Department, C. C. Jones Papers.

Admiral William Alexander Kirkland (1836–98). Courtesy East Carolina
University Manuscript Collection, Kirkland Papers.

John U. Kirkland, Jr. (1838–1914) and his wife, Fanny Harriet McLaren
Kirkland (1844–1908), 1875. Courtesy Richard H. Jenrette.

Susan Mary Kirkland (1843–1914). Courtesy Southern Historical Collection, Frank Nash Papers, University of North Carolina Library, Chapel Hill.

Ayr Mount viewed from the northeast. Photograph by Tim Buchman.

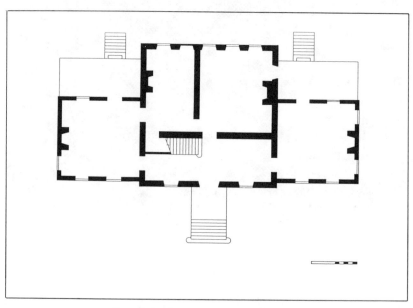

Plan of the first floor of Ayr Mount.

Family cemetery at Ayr Mount. The graves of Margaret and William Kirkland are in the left foreground. Photograph by Frederick Stipe Photography. Courtesy Richard H. Jenrette.

❦ 9 ❦

Fortune's Reverses

T HE LIFE William Kirkland had constructed for himself and his
family was threatened by financial indebtedness, incurred not so
much for himself as by his guarantees of debts incurred by friends
and relations. Nor was Kirkland the only family member afflicted;
George McNeill and Thomas Ruffin suffered with him. To be sure, living
on credit was a way of life for planters and farmers alike, and to lend
one's name as guarantor on notes of friends and relations was a function
of friendship and kinship. In the normal give and take of life things
balanced out, and no particular notice was taken of debts or loan endorsements until they became critical. Usually only the settlement of an
estate forced their repayment; otherwise they accumulated or were renewed and thereby became for the lender a form of investment.

Bank loans, however, were not gentlemen's agreements but formal and
serious business; the bank could decide not to renew a loan when the
principal was due or to sell property covered by deeds of trust when
notes expired, rending the web of interdependent debt and credit. Kirkland decried the banks' intransigence as counterproductive: "by harass-
ing & suing their Debtors [they] make them [the debts] ultimately bad."[1]
If Kirkland's financial ills were in part his fault, that fault was a com-
pound of generosity, loyalty, and a blind disregard of self-interest. He
was not naive, but he always expected people to be more fiscally responsible than they were.

William Kirkland's financial ills did not strike suddenly in a feverish
crisis but approached as a slow, steady weakening like an anemia, insid-
ious and irreversible. The first symptom of the malady appeared in 1815,
when Archibald Murphey made a deed of trust of some of his property
to Ruffin and Kirkland to secure his current debts. The property he
conveyed consisted of 1,300 acres of his home plantation, the Hermitage, on Great Alamance Creek and his distillery and mills on Haw River;
an additional 2,500 acres in the Hawfields, on the west side of Haw

River, with another mill; about 1,550 acres in Rockingham County on which the spa Lenox Castle and its springs were located; more than 31 acres in Pittsylvania County, Virginia, containing mills, distillery, cotton machine, and an adjoining plantation house and outbuildings; forty-two slaves; a thousand-volume library; furnishings, livestock, interest in the public house and store at Lenox Castle; and interest in the firm of John B. Troy in Randolph County and in that of Thomas Scott and Company on Haw River. Murphey knew the men he was dealing with and could count on their scruples. In 1820 he wrote to Ruffin, "I thank you and Mr. Kirkland for the Delicacy and Tenderness with which you have always treated me."[2]

When he was still unable to repay his debts by 1821, Murphey authorized James Webb and David Yarbrough as trustees to sell some of his property. Because of Ruffin's and Kirkland's admiration, affection, and familial responsibility for Murphey, a sale was no solution for them. John Scott's widow, who lived on Murphey's land, and Jane Scott Murphey would lose their homes, and with his lands Murphey would lose his investments, for land sold by the sheriff never brought more than a fraction of its true value. Kirkland and Ruffin could not allow this to happen, for their own money was also at stake. If time could help Murphey untangle his affairs, they were willing to buy it for him. At the sale, therefore, Ruffin bought 1,673 acres of the home tract, including the mills and distillery and the miller Jerry, portions of the Hawfields land, and 1,700 acres of Lenox Castle land. He also bought two tracts of land near Haywood and two Haywood town lots, fifteen slaves, and the thousand-volume library.[3]

The full amount of Murphey's indebtedness became known when Kirkland and Ruffin made out for Yarbrough and Webb a total list of his debts. They added up to some $70,000, a staggering sum for the time. The amount or character of Murphey's debt to Kirkland is not revealed in surviving documents, but it was undoubtedly as a signer of Murphey's many notes that Kirkland became responsible for some of Murphey's unpaid debts. The transfer to Kirkland of 5,000 acres of land in Tipton County, Tennessee, was to cover Murphey's debt to Kirkland. After the 1821 sale, McNeill wrote to Ruffin to commiserate with him and inquired how Kirkland had weathered his losses, a question that suggests that Kirkland's financial liability was not inconsiderable.[4]

To weather his own losses, besides establishing his partnership with

76

Chambers in the slave trade, Ruffin immediately tried to collect debts owed to Murphey that had been assigned to him. One was for $10,000 from Dr. Solomon DeBow, a Murphey relation, to whom Ruffin reported "the total ruin of our worthy friend" and "the very large sums of money which I have paid and shall have to pay as his surity. They are of such magnitude as to induce in me serious apprehensions of meeting with the same fate which has befallen him." He was facing the necessity of paying out $40,000 within a few months. Ruffin struggled along for several years, meeting the interest payments on his debts, but in 1824 he was compelled to convey in trust to Webb and Kirkland much of the land he had taken over from Murphey, directing them to sell it so that he might pay off some of his debts.[5]

That Kirkland still did not feel seriously strapped for money at this time is evident by his continued investment in land. In 1821 he bought sixty-five acres that lay between Ayr Mount and Ruffin's home tract for $1,000. In 1822 he bought two hundred acres of farmland. In 1825 he bought for $2,000 a portion of lot 25 in Hillsborough at the northwest corner of King and Churton streets, which would be identified for the next fifty years as Kirkland's corner. His experience with Murphey did not prevent his signing a note for the firm of Houze and Yarbrough in 1824. His directorship on the board of the Hillsborough branch of the Bank of Cape Fear, of which he owned forty-three shares of stock, appeared as public testimony to his solvency.[6] He still seemed to be very much on top of his affairs.

Kirkland's eventual financial crippling came as a result of cumulative drains on his resources and especially from the progressive indebtedness of the firm of McNeill and Kirkland, the business in Fayetteville. Without Kirkland's knowledge, McNeill wrote in 1825 to Ruffin, by then his brother-in-law through his marriage to Ruffin's sister Minerva in 1823, asking him whether he would be willing to endorse a note of from $10,000 to $20,000 for the firm, which, he explained, was laboring under credit difficulties. He did not consult with Kirkland before asking Ruffin because, as he explained to Ruffin, he did not want to cause awkwardness between Ruffin and Kirkland if Ruffin chose to refuse the request. McNeill, always optimistic, spoke of their offer to join another established business. He attributed some of the indebtedness to uncollected loans they had made to others, for example, to John Dobbin and Robert Strange, for the latter of whom Kirkland's endorsements "increased beyond his expectations."[7] But most of their indebtedness he blamed on the large orders of goods from abroad that the firm had made in 1816 and 1819. The nature of those purchases may be gleaned from an advertisement for McNeill and Kirkland's store in the Fayetteville newspaper, which announced the arrival of the British ship *Esther* in August 1816 and described some of their new wares among its cargo: 215 packages of dry goods, 12 boxes of plates, 140 crates of earthenware, 10 sets of elegant Liverpool china, 12 dozen Durham mustard jars, 90 dozen bottles of the best London porter, 50 pieces of Dundee bagging, 3 tons of copperas, and 7,500 bushels of Liverpool salt. The debts incurred with these shipments had mounted over the years despite McNeill's efforts to pay them off. Ruffin apparently agreed to McNeill's request. In addition, to ease Kirkland's situation, the next year Ruffin bought three-fifths of the five-thousand-acre tract of land in Tipton County.[8] How he was able to pay the $7,500 selling price is a mystery. Perhaps it was merely a paper transaction canceling a Kirkland debt to Ruffin.

The situation of the firm of McNeill and Kirkland became desperate in 1827 when McNeill's brother William L. McNeill went bankrupt. He owed the banks of Fayetteville $14,393, of which the McNeill and Kirkland firm had signed notes amounting to $11,393. When McNeill broke this bad news to Ruffin, he noted that the firm's own debt to the Fayetteville branch of the state bank was then over $20,000. They hoped to recoup something on the sale of William McNeill's property. Kirkland hurried down to Fayetteville and from there wrote Ruffin more details of the situation. William McNeill and his wife had assigned to the firm various debts owed them and additional property. As usual, George McNeill's hopes were unrealistic and bids were so low at the auction that McNeill and Kirkland felt compelled to bid in the property themselves, thus incurring even greater indebtedness. Ruffin offered to endorse any notes Kirkland wrote for loans. In accepting the offer, Kirkland replied, "I shall make it my business as well from inclination as duty to see that you never lose a cent by becoming responsible for any debt of mine; indeed, had I the most distant idea that such should ever turn out to be the case I would not permit you to do so." Having lost everything they owned, the William McNeills emigrated to Tennessee to make a clean start.[9]

Because of his Fayetteville troubles and various other debts, including notes he had signed for James Yarbrough in Franklin County, Kirkland dissolved his partnership with Henry Houze in 1828, taking three town lots in Louisburg, numbers 29, 40, and 41, as his share of the assets. Kirkland and Houze had already sold the two-hundred-plus acres of land they jointly owned.[10]

In 1828, William Kirkland deeded one-half of his store lot in Hillsborough to his son John. In place of the selling price of $1,025, William Kirkland received credit for that amount on the books of the firm William Kirkland and Son, and John Kirkland was to be charged with keeping the accounts. The firm's name had been changed at the time of John's return to Hillsborough in 1824. It was to house the new firm that Kirkland had purchased the corner store on lot 25.[11]

The debacle of the firm of McNeill and Kirkland came in 1829. In March, McNeill told Ruffin that the Fayetteville business was faltering and that they were moving to a store with lower rent, but by May his hopes for recovery were dashed. "Mr. Kirkland," he wrote, "will inform you of the ruinous result of our business."[12] He arranged to assign to Kirkland all his interest (in right of his wife) in Ruffin's father's estate. He also offered to sell Ruffin his gold watch, ordered from London when he thought he could afford it. "I think it rather a reproach for a *broken* merchant to wear such an article."[13] If Ruffin wished to buy it, McNeill asked that the first $50 of its price be sent to him to pay the store rent and the remainder credited to Kirkland.

At the end of the month the firm of McNeill and Kirkland was dissolved by mutual consent. A creditor of the firm, Thomas Irvin and Company of New York, to which McNeill and Kirkland owed $4,000, sent a personal letter to Ruffin: "We are truly sorry for the misfortune of Messrs McNeill and Kirkland that led to it [the dissolution]. We most sincerely hope it will not turn out so bad as to take all Mr. Kirkland's substance. It is a very distressing case for him at his time of life. We have not the pleasure of being acquainted with him personally, but we have always found him very punctual in transactions we have had with him. We hope he will still be able to go on with his business."[14]

Although Kirkland did not try to continue business in Fayetteville, McNeill started over again with a loan from John B. Troy of Randolph County. In 1831 he suffered further losses in the fire that caused enormous and widespread damage in Fayetteville, but McNeill was indestructible. He doggedly began again, and during the next thirty years, he was able to build up a large business and, as a pillar of the Presbyterian church and a leader in the community, won a respected place in Fayetteville's history.[15]

In June 1829, Kirkland learned that the Fayetteville firm's debt was $15,800, and he was driven to ask Charles F. Bagge of Salem for a loan of $5,000, which Ruffin and John Kirkland endorsed for him. "I am afraid," he wrote to Ruffin, "it will run me hard to pay the discount that will be due . . . without any of the principal, but I will scuffle along & do the best I can."[16] In the spring he had resorted to another tactic, an attempt to sell the western lands. Daniel Anderson's son George, who had moved to Tennessee and gone into the mercantile business, was to come through Hillsborough on his way home after a buying trip, and Kirkland suggested to Ruffin that they make him their agent to lay off and sell the land in lots. This plan was not acted upon. In August, David Yarbrough returned from a trip to Tennessee and reported that he thought Kirkland and Ruffin's land could be sold immediately if it were known to be on the market. By November Ruffin had drawn up a power of attorney for its sale through an agent in Tennessee.[17]

Kirkland must have felt, with Hamlet, that troubles came not singly like spies but in battalions. On top of these disasters came a distressing letter from a friend of Dr. de Graffenriedt in Columbus, Georgia, which

> brought a painful and disagreeable account of his present circumstances in life; he is very poor, & very needy, & it appears his brother intends selling his present residence unless he can pay the Debt he owes him. I think with Mr. Gordon [the friend] that the Dr. has a considerable degree of knowledge of his profession, but he lacks all other kind of sense, particularly common sense & has neither prudence nor discretion. Mr. Gordon it appears is unacquainted with my situation, but I should certainly, were it in my power, advance the money that my Dear Patsey & her children should certainly have a house over their heads, when it is probable the Dr. might be able to earn a scanty livelihood for them, which is all I expect he would do.[18]

Because of this final blow, Kirkland took what must have been the most difficult step of his life. Proud, self-reliant, honest to the core, and hardworking, he resolved to sell Ayr Mount.

I went down to Mr. [Duncan] Cameron's on last Friday week to endeavour to sell him the place whereon I live, but he has no notion of purchasing; he said the property was entirely too valuable, that all he wanted was about ten Acres of land nigh Hillsborough to build on for his family to reside at for about three months in the year. ... I shall therefore now do my best to sell the plantation, besides all my other real Estate, excepting for the present the place whereon I now reside. ...

I have written to Mr. Gordon that I will remit to him the $500 by the 1st of January, provided Dr. DeGraffenreid will consent to have the property conveyed to me, & by me to be conveyed in trust to you & John for the sole benefit of my dear daughter Patsey forever.[19]

Realizing that his affairs were hopelessly encumbered, Kirkland must have pondered long on ways to safeguard those closest to him and provide for the most helpless in the event of his death. Finally, he made his decisions, wrote them in his will, and hid it in his desk in the store. With characteristic courage, he went on with his daily life, his head unbowed. But ill fortune had not finished with William Kirkland. The death of a Fayetteville merchant resulted in a demand for repayment of a $1,600 loan made to the partnership of Webb and Kirkland. Again Kirkland appealed to Duncan Cameron and received the $5,000 that he requested. Kirkland assured him, probably with the will's provisions in mind, that "you will run no risque in loaning me this money, as its return shall be provided for in such a way as to prevent any possibility of the kind; at the same time I well know, that I have enough to pay all the debts I owe, & it shall be my endeavour (as it is my interest) to discharge them all as fast as I possibly can."[20]

Murphey's dreary business affairs dragged on. He owed Ruffin some $27,000 by 1829 so that land that had been conveyed only in trust and remained unsold was now conveyed in fee simple to Ruffin. Jane Scott Murphey, whose health had always been precarious, died in April 1829. Because Murphey's home plantation (now Ruffin's), with its elegant two-story house of ten rooms and eight fireplaces, was unoccupied and unsupervised, and because the Ruffins now had eleven children and must have felt unbearably crowded in their three-room Hillsborough quarters, they moved in 1829 to the Hermitage and attempted to make the plantation a paying proposition. In the midst of the gloom of that year, Ruffin was elected president of the State Bank of North Carolina, and that good fortune was exceeded by the honor of his election to the state supreme court at the end of the same year. A justice's salary was low, but it was certain.[21]

Still undaunted by the chaos of his affairs and the cost to others of his recklessness, Murphey continued to look for investments that might miraculously extricate him from his disastrous situation. Like many another deluded dreamer, he was dazzled by gold and invested in a North Carolina mine and the machinery to extract and refine the precious metal. In 1829 Kirkland noted in a letter to Ruffin that while he was in Fayetteville, winding up his affairs there, Murphey sent an order to the Hillsborough store for iron, promising to pay for it with the first gold he sent down to be fluxed; "but I expect he will never think of it again," Kirkland added realistically.[22]

Fortunately for all his friends and family, Murphey's health, which had steadily declined, finally failed entirely, and, on the first of February 1832, he died in Hillsborough, where he had lived during his last year. Dr. James Strudwick Smith believed he had died of an overdose of laudanum. Historians have been kinder to him than his contemporaries. Decorum required public lamentation, but privately there was only relief. Although he had asked to be buried beside his wife at the Hermitage, the Ruffins thought the shock would be too much for "poor old Grandmammy," as Mrs. Scott's great-granddaughter Anne Ruffin told her sister Catherine, and the roads were so bad that he was buried instead in the Hillsborough town graveyard.[23] Ruffin confided his feelings to his wife:

> For the sake of his Family & those other survivors who would *then* have been his surviving *friends* and have felt a deep interest in his name & character, it is a thousand pities that he had not gone down to his grave fifteen years ago. He would then have been "cut off from much of the evil to come" which he has since experienced & escaped many of those acts of positive crime, which repelled from him those friends, injured many persons, tarnished his character, & embittered his days with racking pains of body & pangs of remorse—But the ways of Providence are full of wisdom and mercy! He was suffered to continue so long as a standing impressive beacon

of warning to those who knew him & especially the young whom he had a faculty of fascinating & beguiling. I should think that not one of them can ever forget him or fail to think often of him as a distinguished mark & warning against disbelief & depravity; but he is gone, and Peace be with him! *My* wrongs & the remembrance of *them* be burried with him![24]

That Murphey was largely responsible for his plight cannot be denied; but that so many responsible persons also went bankrupt or sank so deeply into debt that they never got out from under it was symptomatic of the widespread and far-reaching problems peculiar to North Carolina. Its "poor, backward, and divided" condition, in the words of one historian, was directly related to geographical, economic, and political handicaps.[25] The lack of good ports for transatlantic commerce, of systems of road, canal, or river transportation for carrying goods to market, and of manufacture on any sizable scale resulted in a continual drain of money to neighboring states. Participants in the market economy, therefore, took their produce either to Virginia or South Carolina and there, or in northern cities, spent their profits on supplies for the following year and goods for house and family. This continual transfer of income out of state year after year made it impossible for North Carolina to thrive. Capital was hard to come by. Cash was scarce and banking was in its infancy. Primarily dependent on an agricultural economy, the state was handicapped by antiquated agricultural practices that exhausted the soil and returned poorer and poorer crops. Without proper roads or navigable rivers in the piedmont, distribution of goods and transportation of produce to local markets were difficult, restricting even internal commerce. Geography and commercial and agricultural practices conspired to impoverish the state.

The political disabilities were equally debilitating. Under its original constitution, North Carolina was run by an oligarchy of eastern planters, who ignored the large and growing population of the backcountry with its different needs and, following Jeffersonian philosophy that the least government was the best government, allowed the state to stagnate, refusing to vote appropriations for internal improvements and education which the state desperately needed. Nathaniel Macon represented the state's retrograde philosophy in Congress for thirty-seven years, conscientiously defending the status quo and voting against internal improvements, protective tariffs, and other legislation that would have helped North Carolina.

The economic, agricultural, political, and cultural stagnation that characterized the long period of North Carolina history termed the Rip Van Winkle era was responsible for another drain on the state's resources. An alarming proportion of its population packed up and moved out, seeking elsewhere the opportunity and scope for energy and ambition North Carolina could no longer provide. In this general quagmire individuals floundered or quit. Kirkland was a victim of circumstance and his friends. They were all victims of North Carolina's Rip Van Winkle era.

❧ 10 ❧

Aftereffects

THE DRAMATIC CHANGE in William Kirkland's fortunes inevitably affected his children. His three younger daughters, though undoubtedly as attractive as their older sisters, found no suitors clamoring to ally themselves with daughters of an aging and financially embarrassed merchant. In affairs of the heart prudence was frequently thrown to the winds, but marriage was a serious business and reinforced society's economic basis. As a result, Mary and Susan took on the roles assigned to spinsters and selflessly served their parents, married sisters and brothers, and even nieces and nephews as nurses and household managers wherever and whenever they were needed. Illness was so constant a component of nineteenth-century life that the mother of a large family needed all the help she could get, or, if she herself were indisposed, her household acutely required someone in her place to keep it going. Mary and Susan gracefully stepped into these roles.

For Phebe Kirkland, the result was different, probably because of her illness. When her father's affairs fell apart in 1829, she was going on eighteen years old, and from then until her mother's death in 1839, she suffered repeated periods of hysteria in the years when she would ordinarily have been preparing for and experiencing marriage and motherhood. When her mother died, her anomalous position in the family changed, and her hysteria did not return. In the conclaves following the funeral, the family apparently agreed that the house would be bid in at the auction stipulated in William Kirkland's will by Mary and Susan, but Phebe was not included in the arrangement. She may have made it clear that she would not stay in Hillsborough. Instead, right after the sale of the property in November 1839, Phebe went to Columbus, Georgia, on a visit, traveling with her niece Jane de Graffenried, who had come up for Margaret Kirkland's funeral.[1] Patsy de Graffenriedt, with a large family of children and in precarious health, may have been glad of an extra pair of hands and an extended visit from her younger sister.

85

Phebe was theoretically not without means, for her father's will had allotted her a share of his estate. Although no funds were ever legally transferred to her, she was apparently informally allotted one slave from her father's estate as her portion. On her arrival in Georgia, Phebe learned that slaves were hired out there for much better rates than in North Carolina. She immediately wrote home to John Kirkland, asking him to send her the slave Jenny, her inheritance. She asked that Jenny be provided with good warm clothing and new shoes and arrive in Georgia by the first of January, in time to be hired out for the coming year. Phebe appended the request that postage on letters to her be prepaid out of the funds held for her in Hillsborough.[2] In those days, the recipient of letters customarily paid the postage.

Another letter from Phebe two months later reported that she was delighted with Columbus, that she weighed more than she ever had in her life, and that she liked the Episcopal minister. She intimated that she would stay permanently. At the end of that year she was still singing the praises of Columbus: she had been well the entire year except for a day or two and had formed some strong attachments, was treated with kindness and affection by everyone, and would rather live anywhere in the world than Hillsborough. She also raised some anxiety at home about Patsy's situation. Dr. de Graffenriedt was in no way reformed despite rumors to the contrary, and the family feared that Patsy led a miserable life. Phebe wrote that Patsy had but one fault: she was too good-natured.[3]

In spite of the hints in her letter about strong attachments, Phebe's family must have been amazed to learn in 1841 that she had married one Nelson McLester of Columbus. The newlyweds appeared in Hillsborough on the heels of this announcement. Mary Kirkland, who was visiting at the Hermitage at the time, had to hurry home to Ayr Mount to entertain them. The governess in the Ruffin household, Mary McLean Bryant, formerly the governess of Duncan Cameron's six daughters, wrote to one of her former charges that Mary Kirkland would remain "till her sister McLester's departure—about a week 'tis said; I hardly think she will be persuaded to accompany the newly married pair on their return to Georgia—at least I hope not—Mr. Sterling [Ruffin] is expected to day from Hillsboro'—he having accompanied Miss Mary down—and then we shall hear somewhat of the new relation."[4]

A year later Phebe gave birth to a little girl about whom she wrote proudly to her beloved Miss Burke.

> I am the mother of a lovely and interesting daughter named Margaret after my dear departed Parent. She is just a month old tonight. . . . She promises to have a fair skin, dark blue eyes, a thick head of black hair about an inch and a half long, nose rather inclined to be pug, a most beautiful mouth. She is thought to be one of the prettiest new-born infants. The most prominent feature I forgot to mention—her forehead, which is much admired, thought to be very remarkable for so young an infant. Her father prides himself upon that one feature it being an indication of intelligence. She was one of the best babes I ever saw for the first week or so after her birth, but her Father who idolizes her has completely spoiled her: the first thing after coming into the house is 'My dear, let me have the baby.' I object to his awaking her but it appears he is obliged to kiss her; in that way he arouses her. She is very much spoiled.

Phebe was obviously very happy with motherhood, but she was traumatized by childbirth. She informed Miss Burke that "marriage is not what it is cracked up to be; I did not know we had to suffer half what we do. I have often heard it said that labour was the worst suffering that poor females are subject to, but I know it now from bitter experience, and had I known as much as I do now I would have staid single all my life." She was devoted to her husband.

> I have one of the best husbands that this world can afford, but it does not compensate for the bearing of children. I do wish you knew my old man. I know you would love him for his kindness to me, the most indulgent husband that ever lived; I have everything around me to make me happy and contented—the best of husbands, a comfortable home with every other comfort around me. My only troubles now are that he should die and leave me; what would become of me. I know I should go deranged. I could not bear up under that affliction. When we are happily married I think there is more pain than pleasure accompanying it. We shall have to give them up or we die and leave them.[5]

In the same letter she described the sickness in Columbus at that time and the consequent poverty. She recounted how needy people came to her door and how solicitous McLester was in seeing that their wants were met. They had a servant, Phebe explained, whom she used to send around the city to work for the poor. "Mr. McLester is not a religious man but he will I hope be rewarded in another world for his kindess to those who are in distress." Phebe admitted that he was "the pride of my heart."

Phebe's apprehensions were fulfilled and her happiness was short-lived: she died in 1844 at the age of thirty-three.[6] No surviving letter explains the circumstances or the cause of her death. She had apparently requested that her sister Mary raise her little daughter. As a result, Margaret (Maggie) McLester became another inmate of Ayr Mount. Maggie was a healthy child, grew very fast, and much resembled her mother. Her father made the long journey to Hillsborough once or twice a year to visit her. Those occasions gave rise to rumors that he and Mary were to be wed, though one sensible friend said she did not believe a word of it. The possibility of such an arrangement faded when McLester remarried and in 1850 died in Savannah on his way once more to visit his daughter. As his second wife, too, predeceased him, Maggie was his only heir. She was very well provided for. McLester left well over $12,000 lent out at interest, nineteen slaves, two gold watches, a gold locket, a ring, breast pin, lots of furniture, and, undoubtedly, real estate. Ruffin, who was informed of the details, told his wife, "Maggie is in a situation to be beholden to no one as her property is ample to educate her well, & give her the breeding & the enjoyments of a gentlewoman." On his deathbed McLester wrote to John U. Kirkland asking him to stand in the place of a father to Maggie.[7]

John Kirkland did not incur any additional expense from the arrangement, for he was able to charge her estate for her board and keep. Maggie became very much a part of John Kirkland's family and called him "father" and his wife, "mother." Ruffin, who was appointed her legal guardian, managed her money for her and gladly expended funds for her continued education at the Burwell School, where McLester had earlier placed her, both in Hillsborough and later in Charlotte, after the Burwells' move there in 1857. Ruffin proved exceedingly niggardly, however, about pin money, and Maggie was required to write to him to request money for any little necessities, even for clothing.[8]

William Kirkland's losses had equally affected his sons' lives, for their expectations of following in his footsteps as merchant-planters were seriously hampered. They had been well brought up and well educated, but their scope for action was drastically curtailed by their father's failure. Success in business could, of course, remove the handicaps; their father had started with nothing too; but Hillsborough was no longer the frontier town in the backcountry that William Kirkland had first known. Perseverance and prudence had been sufficient assets then; now the economy was depressed everywhere and Hillsborough had become a backwater. John Kirkland was sensitive about his financial position. Catherine Ruffin encouraged his interest in a Raleigh acquaintance of hers after his courtship of Mary Ashe had foundered. She wrote to him of a friend who had also been disappointed in love, hoping to elicit his interest and arouse his sympathy. He replied, "I feel for all unrequited lovers, tho I must confess I am glad that Miss H is determined not to be in too great a hurry to marry. I should like exceedingly to link my Fortune with that of so amiable a Young Lady, but Catherine—What a disparity there is, I mean in point of Wealth."[9]

Catherine's relationship with her two uncles reveals the differences between Kirkland's sons. Though both obviously enjoyed having Catherine as a confidante and wrote her long letters somewhat flirtatious in tone, John Kirkland, seven years her senior, was always more avuncular and interspersed his confidences with admonitions and advice. Alexander's letters were full of fun, gossip, and thoughts for her eyes alone. John addressed her as "My dear Niece," while Alexander wrote, "My dearest Kate." Alexander was obviously at ease with the written word and very comfortable with his niece, only three years his junior. Both, however, shared with her the ups and downs of their romances and sought her help and connivance.

Undismayed by his loss in Mary Ashe's coquettish game, John Kirkland before long found another girl to interest him, and by 1828 he was engaged to be married. He wrote to Catherine from the American Hotel in New York, where he was doing the semiannual purchasing for William Kirkland and Son, that he had dined with the Robert Donaldsons and been teased about his secret engagement.[10]

Robert Donaldson, a New York merchant and later patron of the arts, then lived on State Street in the former house of Archibald Gracie. Donaldson had probably become acquainted with John Kirkland a decade before in his native Fayetteville. Donaldson had grown up both in North Carolina and New York, the son of an import-export merchant with ties to London, where Robert's uncle Samuel Donaldson headed the family firm. Robert Donaldson had graduated from the university at Chapel Hill in 1818 and at his maturity had come into possession, with his brother James, of their father's far-flung business interests, which they had inherited at his death in 1808. Besides cash, the large estate consisted of real estate, furniture, personal property, and slaves, a number of partnerships with stores in Norfolk, Suffolk, Petersburg, Wilmington, and Fayetteville, and ships to carry their merchandise. In the early 1820s Robert had moved to New York, but he retained property and business interests in Fayetteville. Just nine months before John Kirkland's visit, Donaldson had married Susan Jane Gaston, the eldest daughter of William Gaston, a New Bern lawyer and later much esteemed state supreme court justice on the bench with Thomas Ruffin.[11]

At the Donaldsons', John Kirkland had found the Misses Burgwin and Gaston, a younger sister of Susan Jane, and had endured their teasing about Miss S., "with whom I believe you are acquainted. They say I am engaged to be married and so forth. How knowing they are, Catherine." Miss S. was Elizabeth Adam Simpson (called Betsy), a daughter of Samuel Simpson, also of New Bern, who had a house in Hillsborough to which the family retreated from the annual summer agues and the presumed dangerous miasmas of the coastal regions. In Hillsborough Betsy Simpson and her sister Maria had become acquainted with Catherine, her young aunts, and their friends. At the time of the Simpsons' earliest appearance in Hillsborough in 1824, Sally Nash had written Catherine, then at Rock Rest, "My troubles are not over; tomorrow I have to march off to see Maria Simpson and Mary Birch, the latter an ugly *little* thing not much larger than Louisa Clark although her mother says she is 14. I had much rather be shut up in the house for a month than to go see either but it cannot be avoided. . . . Mr. Bryans flame Miss Betsy Simpson has arrived. I suppose you have heard that she is very beautiful. I know that she dresses very much."[12]

In late 1828 Betsy Simpson wrote coyly to Catherine about John Kirkland, "Every one in New Bern has almost looked their eyes out looking for him. We are all the talk at present."[13] And Matthias Manly of New Bern wrote to his friend William Alexander Graham, a new young lawyer in Hillsborough, "Kirkland of your Borough has been here. He took I understand many long and solitary rambles with Miss Betsy S. Report says they are engaged to be married—the symtoms squint that way. The lady looks sober and matronlike—never goes out—has the headache—a bad cold—a sore throat—is pleased only when there is something pleasant and never laughs but when she is diverted."[14]

At first Ruffin refused to allow Catherine to go to John's wedding, which was to take place in New Bern, because he felt he could not spare the money to outfit her, but John Kirkland was so disappointed by her refusal that he wrote Ruffin himself to plead the case, and Ruffin relented. He told Catherine to get what she needed to be well dressed and not to skimp. She ordered two new dresses, a white one to use in her role as a bridesmaid and a colored silk for other festive occasions. Mary and Susan Kirkland received new silk dresses as well, given them by their brother John, whom they were to accompany to New Bern, but their father was not to know of this because he would not have allowed John to bear that expense.[15]

The wedding took place in February 1829, and the marriage was in all respects excellent for John Kirkland, for the young people proved to be permanently happy with each other, and Samuel Simpson was a prosperous man—not just a successful merchant but president of the Merchants' Bank in New Bern. John and Betsy returned from their honeymoon to Ayr Mount, but before the end of the year, they moved into a house in the village.[16]

Early in the year Samuel Simpson had put his house at the corner of Churton and Tryon streets up for sale or rent and bought three adjoining lots, 56, 57, 58, on Queen Street and an adjacent lot back of them, 154, on Union Street. On lot 58 stood a house that had been built by Eliza Hasell, and next door on lot 59 stood the Archibald Haralson house, then occupied by Dr. Edmund Strudwick and his wife, the former Ann Nash. No evidence definitely identifies the house into which the John Kirklands moved, but it is certain that it was one of Samuel Simpson's properties. The only clues to its identity are found in letters of 1837 and 1838. A friend wrote to Eliza Johnston, then in Alabama, the news of Hillsborough: "Ann Strudwick is housekeeping, and everything nice and good and greater style than any body about here except John Kirkland."[17] The house on lot 58, now called the Hasell-Nash house, is still probably the most stylish of Hillsborough's older dwellings. It is a tripart house like Ayr Mount, though built of wood instead of brick, its front door placed off center, and its three pediments turned to the front; it has unusually high-style decorative features. It could well answer Eliza Johnston's description and was probably the John Kirklands' dwelling place. They lived in Samuel Simpson's house only eight years.

In 1838 they bought the house and grounds of William Mercer Green, land that William Kirkland had sold Green and which adjoined Ruffin's Hillsborough property, Saint Matthew's Church, and Ayr Mount. Betsy was sorry to move, for she much preferred her former home. As a result of the Kirklands' move, Alice Ruffin reported to Catherine, Mr. Simpson had got John's old place for himself and Mr. Hill (another son-in-law).[18]

John Kirkland's financial position can never have been far from precarious, but besides a wealthy father-in-law to whom he could always appeal for help, he had the luck to inherit in 1830 from Dr. John Umstead, for whom he had been named, a tract of land in Tennessee, which may have helped later to pay off some of the debts he inherited from his father. He also was lucky in love. In December 1829 he wrote Catherine, telling her that he and Betsy had been keeping house almost a month and that "every hour of my life brings with it some endearing token of my Betsy's affection & promising anticipation of a life of comparative happiness."[19] Her affection for him was dramatically painted in a letter from her sister Maria, visiting her at Ayr Mount, before the John Kirklands' move to their own quarters in late 1829, while John was again in New York. Maria described how she and Betsy were in their bedroom, doing Saturday night chores, combing, brushing, and washing, when John unexpectedly returned. When she heard his voice downstairs, Betsy, despite her deshabille, threw her cloak about her and "*ran*" down to greet him. Presumably Maria's underlining of "ran" was a pointed reference to Betsy's advanced pregnancy. She gave birth to her first child not long afterward.[20]

Opinion about the John Kirklands' felicity seemed unanimous. An Asheboro lawyer wrote to George Johnston, a former clerk of William Kirkland's, that John Kirkland "must be the happiest man in all Hillsboro'. Who would not rather be a 'dog & bay the moon' than lead a single life when he can get a pretty wife."[21] And in 1835, after the birth of his first daughter, John Kirkland was described by a Murphey cousin as "fat & as happy as heart could wish."[22] In the choice of a wife and the conduct of his life John Kirkland proceeded to reveal himself the judicious and steady man he was expected to be.

❦ 11 ❦

Alexander and Anna

HIS SISTERS respected John Kirkland, admired him, and doted on him. Fifteen-year-old Mary A. Kirkland told Catherine that John was "as sweet as ches cake." Their feelings about Alexander, however, were more complex and more intense, including elements of anxiety and frustration as well as hero-worship and love. When he was sent to Partridge's Academy in January 1825, Mary wrote to Catherine, "Your Uncle A left us with a heavy heart on sunday morning. I never in all my life missed any one more than him. He left you a present."[1] Alexander was not the big brother and heir that John was marked out to be. He had not been schooled in Scotland to inherit the responsibility of his father's business. Neither had he been separated from his younger sisters for six years of their childhood when their bonds with each other were being formed. From August 1811 until December 1817, he had been the only son at home and had received the concentrated attention of the whole family. He was not a staunchly pious Presbyterian or a strict observer of an inherited social code. John went by the books; Alexander was unpredictable. There were in his makeup a Byronic streak, untamed physical vitality, and undeveloped intellectual potential. He was a giant of a man, six feet eight inches tall and proportionately heavy. In the family he is said to have been very handsome and able to carry his size with grace.[2] Although the years at military school had disciplined his body and mind, they had not sparked in him any discernible ambition. Thomas Ruffin expected him to pursue professional studies, for there was talk of Alexander's becoming a doctor. He might have studied law with his brothers-in-law Strange or Ruffin if he had so desired. He seems to have attempted neither course. The indecision about Alexander's plans can be seen in Richard S. Clinton's message to him through George Johnston. "Tell Alex Kirkland if he wishes to do well in life to come to Alabama."[3]

The path he chose or perhaps had chosen for him—to go into business

in Hillsborough—was a fatal one. There were already too many impecu-
nious shopkeepers in that small village, and the decade of the 1830s was
particularly depressed for trade in North Carolina and the nation. There
was also little to stimulate an active mind outside the professions or to
engage the talents of a man such as Alexander. There was ample bore-
dom and leisure to try the strongest will. In 1830 he lived "up stairs in
the store," where he spent one late evening writing to Catherine a letter
full of nonsense, snatches of poetry, and plans for a hunting trip at the
Hermitage. "Ask your mama," he wrote, "if for some fresh meat she
would be willing to accomodate three gentlemen and a couple of dogs
for a few days." He then speculated about whom her brother William
was in love with, what a letter to her from Maria Simpson might contain, and the comment that "love seems to occupy many if not most of
our young thoughts." He mocked himself when he described his "poor,
buffeted, love stricken heart," a matter he would discuss with her when
he saw her. His letter ended with the promise that though he had not yet
"performed one of your requests—kissed poor Grand Papa—if he comes
up clean shaved in the morning it shall be attended to." He closed by
asking her to give everyone at her house a kiss, but two kisses for "my
dear old Grandmammy," Mrs. Scott.[4]

In 1831 the firm of Cain and Kirkland was formed, consisting of
William Cain, Jr., and Alexander Kirkland.[5] They conducted a general
merchandise store in which their clerk, Victor Moreau Murphey (commonly called Moreau), did most of the work. In 1834, when Paul Cameron tempted Moreau with a partnership in his mill store in Person
County, he refused, explaining that he was the "wheelhorse" for Cain
and Kirkland; Cain was too busy settling his father's estate to come near
the store, and Moreau felt that he could not leave them. Shortly afterward, Moreau was asked to escort a group of slaves to Alabama for their
owners, the Strudwicks, who had invested in a plantation there. Moreau planned to see his cousin Patsy de Graffenriedt when they passed
through Columbus, Georgia, and hoped to receive a letter from Catherine there. It is likely that he was taking advantage of the chance to scout
out a possible location for a mercantile business, for two years later he
and Alexander established a store in Macon, Mississippi, and Moreau
moved to Macon to manage it.[6] When he took a tearful departure from
Hillsborough in May 1836, many other townspeople had already left:
Roswell Huntingdon, the silversmith, and his family, George Johnston,

94

who had married Eliza Bond, Polly Burke, the William Adamses, James H. Ruffin, Thomas Ruffin's brother, Dr. Edmund Strudwick's brother William, Duncan Cameron's nephew William Cameron, and others. They realized that Hillsborough's day as a backcountry trade center was over and prosperity was not likely to be found there.

Prosperity was not always found in the deep South either. Though he never returned to Hillsborough and eventually pursued a career as a physician in Mississippi, Moreau was discouraged at first. He confided his disillusionment to Paul Cameron and added, "This however I mention in strict confidence for fear that my dissatisfaction might create some uneasiness on the part of Alexander & now nothing but his interest keeps me here. He was entirely disinterested in his efforts in my behalf & of course I will suffer no exertion on my part to be wanting in the fulfillment of his expectation. And were his interest not connected with my own you would see me again in Carolina before the middle of May."[7] A year later he wrote again to Cameron, "Say to Alexander that as he has resolved never to write me again that he would do me a great favor by riding out to see how we come on."[8] Alexander seems to have acted on this suggestion after his employment in the business of Cain and Kirkland was terminated by debt in 1837.[9]

After he had set up as a merchant in his own right in 1831, Alexander was able to think seriously of marriage. He had enjoyed a series of flirtations—revealed in his letters to Catherine Ruffin—infatuated with first one belle and then another. In 1832 the particular lady was Eleanor Boylan, the daughter of a wealthy Raleigh businessman. "I declare most solemnly Cate that it is a gone case with me—and should I be so fortunate to get back home safe [from a stock purchasing trip], I will make a desperate effort if it is not too late."[10] The next year it was another girl, an affair only hinted at by Moreau Murphey's veiled reference in a letter to Catherine. He asked her why she hadn't written to her uncle: "His state of suspense is a wretched one."[11] Obviously she had been consulted about his chances with the current charmer.

Finally, in January 1835, a rumor reached Paul Cameron, which he passed on to his mother, that Alice Ruffin and Mary Kirkland were to be sent for shortly as attendants for a bride, "Miss Cameron, who as I learn will wear that name but a very short time. I don't know but I should judge from some things that the wedding is to be a 'great to-do.' With those kin folks of mine I should say that Economy cannot commence too soon."[12] As Paul's unkind remark makes clear, the Miss Cameron referred to was not one of his six eligible sisters, putative heiresses, but a daughter of his deceased uncle William Cameron, who had never been able to make a living and whose family survived through the kindness of William's father-in-law, Daniel Call of Richmond. Call had given his daughter land and slaves protected from William Cameron's debts, and since William's death the family had struggled along in Hillsborough, where Call had also provided the family with a house. Nancy Call Cameron gave music lessons to Hillsborough girls and, after its establishment about 1837, to the students at the Burwell School.[13] It was like Alexander Kirkland to have let no such sordid consideration as money stain the purity of his heart's desire; he had chosen Nancy and William Cameron's daughter Anna McKenzie Cameron as his bride.

Phebe Kirkland wrote to her friend Eliza Johnston that Alexander "has selected a very amiable Lady and what is more than all besides a devotedly pious one; all parties are pleased with the match. I have very little acquaintance with her but expect I shall love her very much as a Sister."[14] Anna was six years younger than Phebe and ten years younger than Alexander, who, at twenty-eight years of age, presumably knew what he was doing. They were married in January 1835 at her mother's house. Besides her own brothers and sisters, Thomas Bennehan, Thomas Cameron, Paul Cameron and his wife, and four of his sisters were present from the bride's family; in 1832 Paul Cameron had married Anne Ruffin, William Kirkland's granddaughter, so it was not the first alliance between the two families.[15]

Duncan Cameron received a firsthand account of his niece's wedding from his daughter Anne. Her cousin Walker Anderson gave the bride away in lieu of Duncan Cameron, whose position as president of the state bank kept him in Raleigh. Anna was surprisingly composed, but her mother dared not witness the ceremony lest her emotions overwhelm her.

> The house [at the southwest corner of Wake and Queen streets] was completely turned inside out; there was a very handsome supper set *up stairs* and that night poor Aunt Nancy had not a bedstead to sleep on. The next night Mr. John Kirkland gave them a large party which went off very pleasantly; on Monday night there was a dancing party at Mr. William Kirkland's. We staid all night [at] Mr.

K's and gladly turned our faces homeward next morning. Sister Margaret, Rebecca, Jean, and myself made "Lochiel" our home; [Lochiel was Walker Anderson's home west of Hillsborough on the Eno River]. Aunt Anderson and Cousin Mary of course staid there. Aunt A was quite well and seemed to enjoy the company not a little; the night of the wedding she looked at least ten years younger than she is.[16]

Walker Anderson also gave a party for the new couple, an event that Phebe Kirkland found "very dull." Perhaps Phebe's proprietary feeling for Alexander made her a little jealous of Anna, whom she described as "a very clever wife." A month after the wedding Phebe wrote to Catherine Ruffin, "They both appear to be very happy. She is a fine girl and will I expect make a good wife."[17] Alexander's character is difficult to reconstruct from the scraps of information about him and his few surviving letters. That he liked hunting is certain, and, with his military training, he was probably a good marksman. A puzzling incident mentioned in one of Susan Kirkland's letters, but found nowhere else in the records, must have been a hunting accident. Susan explained to Eliza Johnston why she had failed to say good-bye to her and Polly Burke the day they left for Alabama; that morning, Susan was on her way to see them when she learned that Alexander had shot Mr. Evans; she was too shocked to go.[18] Evans is not identified.

Although his wife testified to his gentleness, Alexander could become very angry when provoked, and on at least one such occasion he resorted to his fists. In 1836 he and Anna were setting out with Catherine Ruffin on a journey to the North and were taking their seats in the stagecoach in Hillsborough when an "uncouth person," as Catherine related, contested Alexander's seat. The driver intervened, became insolent to Alexander, and "with shocking oaths" called him a liar, at which Alexander "gave him some pretty severe blows in his face. The foreman of the grand Jury was present & witnessed it all and he was no other than my Grandpapa himself. I declare I never laughed so much in my life as I did after it was over. . . . I do wish you could have seen Grandpapa. . . . I never saw Uncle Alexander so enraged; he says he has positively been sick ever since."[19]

The Kirkland party made other arrangements and departed the next day in a private borrowed carriage, stopping the first night at Fairntosh because of a late start. From there they set out the following morning in snow, hail, and rain on awful roads. "About six miles from Fairntosh we were *mired* completely—carriage and horses—the poor animals could not move till they were loosed from their gear and *helped* out of the mud; then the carriage had to be prized out with poles which occupied at least two hours."[20]

That was only the beginning of their troubles. After spending the second night in Oxford, they left "bright and early" in good health and high spirits but on still intolerable roads. They made progress until three o'clock in the afternoon, when Anna felt indisposed. She made light of it but got progressively worse so that they were compelled to spend the night at Dr. Hall's. He scared them very much by suggesting that Anna was threatened by "an accident," Catherine's euphemism for a miscarriage. Her pain and fever were relieved by niter (saltpeter used as a diuretic and anti-inflammatory agent) and laudanum. After two days, during which Anna could not travel, they proceeded to Bellfield, where Catherine wrote her mother the details of their journey. Having shared a room with Anna and Alexander in the public houses where they stayed, Catherine had formed a different opinion of her uncle. "Of all the cowardly husbands I ever saw in my life," she told her mother, "Uncle Alexander exceeds."[21] Although she did not explain her remark, she was presumably referring to Alexander's behavior during Anna's illness.

The doctor's warning may not have been far off the mark. In July, Anna gave birth to a boy, whom they named William Alexander. A second son, Robert Strange, completed the family two years later. It is not clear from family letters where the young family lived, but probably they rented a house in town or lived over the store at Kirkland's corner. It is certain that Alexander did not prosper. In the summer of 1839, to cover his debts, Alexander made a deed of trust to Andrew Mickle, conveying not only a slave Polly and her three children but also all his right and interest in his father's estate and in the property of Nancy Call Cameron, his mother-in-law. His debts included many small sums to William A. Graham, Charles W. Johnston, Andrew Borland, Rawley Galloway, and others. To his partner William Cain he owed $8,500. He also owed money to his brother as the surviving partner of William Kirkland and Son and to his own partners in the firms of Brown and Kirkland, possibly a shoe store in Hillsborough, and Murphey and Kirkland, the general store in Macon, Mississippi. Apparently demoralized and debilitated, only four years after his marriage he was living without any employment at Ayr Mount. On a visit to her aunts, Catherine wrote home: "It grieves my heart to find uncle Alexander so altered; he has the appearance to me of a very intemperate man. He is fat and unnaturally flushed and is really stupid. Alice thinks he is *rough* to Anna and I was glad to hear she bore it so meekly for she is a high-spirited woman and I was afraid would resent such treatment. He is living in perfect idleness and I do think idleness *is* the root of all evil. I had rather see my poor brother a 'hewer of wood and drawer of water' than to be so entirely dependent for his support on anyone."[22]

Catherine described a very serious situation and one that may have had an underlying physical cause but was perceived by Alexander's family to be the result of intemperance. Three years later, in 1842, Anna's sister Lizzie reported that Alexander and Anna were still living at Ayr Mount.[23] His deterioration had continued, and his family obviously still had no place of their own. His death the following year nevertheless took his doctors and family by surprise. John Kirkland felt obliged to give a detailed account to their sister Mary, who was visiting the Stranges.

You have no doubt been apprised ere this of the melancholy tidings of the death of our dear brother, an event which no doubt was as great a shock to you as it was unexpected and distressing to all his friends here. I wrote to Mr. Strange by last mail giving him some of the particulars of it and desired to write also to you but knew not how to express myself. My Dear Sister, I can hardly realize it now. And I cannot express to you my feelings of sorrow & desolation when the thought, as it presently does, occurs that our Brother is no more. There had been no marked difference in his general health from the time you left us—if any it was for the better for Susy had been to see him a few days after when he expressed himself as feeling better than he had done for several years & indulged the hope that he was about to get well. On Tuesday morning after you started he sent for Susy & myself to go up & see him. We did so & found him not so ill as I apprehended. After staying with him an hour or two I had some business that required me at the store and I left him with the intention of returning as soon as I accomplished it. Before I did return he sent for me. When I went back I found him as

I had left him. His mind appeared to be restless. He complained of no pain or suffering of body; he talked a great deal evidently greatly excited. He spoke frequently of dying, of repentence and hoped that God would forgive him & permit him to go to heaven. Occasionally his mind would waver & he would say that he did not know what he was saying. He prayed frequently that God would have mercy upon him. Called over all his sisters by name & their children & expressed the wish that he could see them. He told me that he was going to die: & that when dead he desired to be buried at Air Mount. These were pretty much the subjects of his conversation all that day. We did not encourage him to talk but desired that he should be composed & sleep. No one who saw him apprehended any immediate danger. Dr. Strudwick who attended him had no idea that the closing scene was so near at hand. I staid with him untill the evening. He did not object to my leaving him. The Dr. was present & stated there was no necessity for my staying as he hoped he would (as he very much desired) rest well, that he appeared better & disposed to sleep. I came away in company with the Dr. & asked him to tell me what he thought of his case. He assured me there was no necessity for immediate alarm & that he did not know what might be ultimately the result but that if he would conform to his prescriptions he might get well. He had put himself for eight days previous to this upon an entire abstemious habit: had even quit chewing tobacco at the request of the Dr. with a determined effort to try & get well. Poor fellow, I fear he tried too much at once. About 12 o'clock in the night a message came for me to go to Mr. C immediately. I did not think to enquire nor did I dream of what was the matter, hurried on my clothes & lost no time in getting there. Imagine if you can, My dear Mary, my feelings when I entered the house & found that he had been dead about two hours, that he was dead before I had been sent for. Susan and Jno Cameron were in the room with him when he died & they did not know it for five or ten minutes after.

After night set in he rested pretty well & would sleep at times for twenty or thirty minutes and fifteen minutes before he died he sat up in bed without assistance & asked for water. They gave it to him. When he had drank as much as he wanted he handed the glass to Mr. C., thanked him, & laid down & drew up the bed clothes upon him, talked for a few moments, then dropped to sleep. The only thing that excited their apprehensions that all might not be right with him after this was that he lay so still. His sleep had been frequently disturbed & restless. To satisfy themselves they got the candle & held it close to his face, when the dreadful reality was manifest.[24]

John Kirkland concluded his letter with pious reflections on the meaning of death and the need to apply its afflictions to their benefit. Conspicuously absent from his detailed description was Anna Cameron Kirkland. As John's letter to his sister makes clear, Alexander was living during his last illness at her brother John Cameron's house.

One other account of Alexander's death was given by Thomas Ruffin to Catherine.

Your poor Uncle Alexander breathed his last on Wednesday night, a little after midnight—suddenly & to the surprise of his family & the astonishment of his physicians. He had no fever, nor, indeed, any particular disease known to his medical advisers; but his health gradually declined, & he finally ended his earthly career simply by the failure of an enfeebled & shattered constitution. Poor Fellow! He knew trouble early in life, & has encountered so many anxieties & distresses of different kinds, that for some years past, he has had few enjoyments. . . . He cherished in his retirement lively religious impressions, and felt them strongly in his very last hours, thro' which he passed with but little bodily suffering & closed without a struggle: indeed, without its being perceived for some minutes by his attendants![25]

It is impossible to know to what early trouble in Alexander's life Ruffin referred, but it is possible to surmise that some of the many distresses and anxieties were related both to his business and to his marriage. With Ruffin's assurance that he had no perceptible disease, it seems reasonable to reject his descendants' assertion that Alexander died of a cancer contracted on a long ride to his store in Mississippi. His doctors would surely have recognized that disease. It is probably safe to conclude that the intemperance detected by Catherine was the real cause and that over the years it took its toll of his constitution, as Ruffin said.[26]

The tragedy did not end there for Anna. Alexander's death may not have been the cause of Anna's malady, but it was certainly, as she herself testified, the precipitating factor. From the day of his death Anna became deranged, blaming herself for not having been present and feeling abjectly unworthy of God's love and redemption. She hid her grief and her overwhelming sense of guilt. A few weeks after Alexander's death, to be kind to Anna and her little boys, the Ruffins had them for a visit. If they detected trouble, it was not mentioned in family letters. Only in December 1845 or January 1846 did a crisis occur that could not be kept from her relations. Anna's behavior became alarming. Ruffin told his wife that she should be put in an asylum. Margaret Anna Burwell, the Presbyterian minister's wife and an illustrious teacher, wrote to Mary Kirkland, again in Fayetteville, about the situation at Nancy Cameron's house. When Anna Kirkland's crisis occurred, her mother had sent for Mr. Burwell. After several visits with her he concluded that the subject of religion ought not to be mentioned to her. It was on that one subject alone, which had become an obsession, that she was insane. She would not eat or sleep. She would not lie down on her bed but would crouch on the floor on her hands and knees, saying she was unworthy of a comfortable bed. She was convinced that God had utterly cast her out and that only by self-torture could she perhaps escape eternal damnation. She refused to eat, she dug her fingernails into her thumbs, she prayed incessantly, and she claimed that heavenly harbingers had predicted her death on May 25. Her nerves were wildly excited.[27]

When she did not improve, the family sent for Duncan Cameron to advise them what to do. He concluded that she was insane and should go into an institution. He probably offered to bear the expense. He had already paid for her brother William to attend medical lectures in Philadelphia, had sent her brother John to study law with Walker Anderson, and had earlier managed the property Nancy Call Cameron's father had settled on her. He discovered that insanity ran in the Call family; Anna's great-grandmother and a great-aunt had both been afflicted. In February 1846 Anna was taken to the Western Asylum at Staunton, Virginia. After only a week there, her condition improved. The doctor wrote encouragingly that she was sleeping in her bed and had begun to accept food. For breakfast she ate a buttered roll, a piece of cornbread, a small piece of beef, and a mug of coffee; for dinner she had wheat and cornbread, bacon or beef, and vegetables; for supper she had bread and butter with tea or coffee. She even agreed to do some knitting and would soon finish a pair of socks. Making clothes for the poor was part of the general therapy at the asylum. The doctor ventured to predict her complete recovery in time.[28]

Four months later, Anna wrote a long, perceptive letter to her uncle Duncan Cameron about her condition both before and after her arrival at the hospital. She was grateful to him for having sent her to the hospital and for his compassion. Her letter reveals her as well educated, articulate, refined, and intelligent. It also shows her to be completely obsessed with religion and the state of her soul. After having expressed her hope that she would again partake of divine redemption, she described her illness in detail:

> Uncle, I have been a deranged woman ever since the *fatal* night I was summoned to look upon the lifeless body of my *husband* whom I had left a few hours before apparently much better & in a fair way to recover. I would never have left his bedside but the physicians thought my presence excited him & prevented him from sleeping & after nursing him untiringly day & night unaided by a single person for years I was at last denied the priveledge of closing his eyes tho he *implored* me to let him breathe his last on my bosom. Oh! *God* my brain reels now when I think of that night. He was a man of modest merit; few knew his real worth & *none* save the wife of his bosom appreciated his gentle & endearing virtues, tho *my* family were tenderly attached to him. He was generous & forgiving almost to a fault & bore with the infirmities of my temper and disposition as no other man on earth would have done. I do not remember that he ever spoke harshly to me during the whole of our wedded life except once when I richly deserved it & then the words had scarcely passed his lips when he begged my pardon with tears in his eyes & Oh! how humbled I felt & how I worshipped him. He was my *life* my *all* and as I said before when I beheld him numbered with the dead reason deserted her throne. . . .
>
> From that moment, tho I complained but little & constantly attempted to assume a composure I did not feel, like the Spartan boy I concealed that which was preying upon my *life strings*, & known only to the *Searcher* of hearts is the torture I have endured. . . . I was all the time aware that something was amiss with my mind, but I

struggled against the conviction, little dreaming to what a fearful crisis 'twould come. I taught a school, sought out objects of charity, and busied myself with household cares hoping thus in time to be able to bow with submission to the blow which seemed to have blotted out creation, & left me a lone, & blighted thing. . . . Your judicious advice & kind assistance to my dear Mother have been the means, with the blessing of *God*, of saving not only my life but my *soul*, for if I had remained at home I am persuaded I should have committed suicide. . . . I am not gifted with excellency of speech, like some of my family, & am a person of few words in the way of thanks, being *painfully* aware of my *deficiency* in the upper story, but from my *inmost soul* I do feel your kindness. . . . I understand that patients sometimes blame their friends for bringing them here, but I have no feeling of the kind; on the contrary shall forever bless the day that brought me to this house of refuge. I know some regard it as disgraceful to have been an inmate of an asylum, but I cannot see that a mental malady is more disgraceful than a physical one; both come from *His* hand who doth all things well.[29]

She wrote pages more, relating her hopes that the knowledge of her infirmity would not injure her children and that her mother's tender care would not spoil them. Her brothers, she confessed to her uncle, furnished striking examples of the effects of her mother's indulgence. She spoke of her own reticence and inability to confide in anyone save her husband. She vowed to alter her habit and felt she could trust him as she had trusted her father. She blamed her mother for not keeping a tighter rein on her rebellious spirit. Her mother, she told Cameron, felt sorry for her because she lacked the personal attractions and mental gifts of her sisters.

This was only the first of many such lengthy letters from Anna, who never recovered sufficiently to live an independent life, although she had long intervals of sanity between her attacks. She seems to have tried several times without success to resume a normal existence. After Duncan Cameron's death, she was moved to the North Carolina asylum in Raleigh, and her sons paid for her care although she was admitted as a pauper. In 1857 she asked to join her son Robert in South Carolina, where he was working. Her sons appealed to Ruffin, probably unsuccessfully, to prevent her leaving Raleigh. A letter from Robert in 1859 informed Ruffin that she was with him again and talked of going back to Raleigh. She was then in a very excitable condition.[30]

During the Civil War, William Alexander Kirkland chose to remain in the United States Navy, but Robert Strange Kirkland volunteered in the Confederate forces in South Carolina and was serving in Virginia when the Confederacy passed a law exempting one son in a widow's family from military service. Because he was his mother's sole support and he could not manage on his $20 a month soldier's pay, he hoped to take advantage of the new ruling. Furthermore, he told Ruffin, despite his size and robust appearance (he was as large as his father), his health was "none of the best." Apparently his request for release was refused, for he was still in the army the following year and was shot in both legs at Gettysburg. He nevertheless survived.[31]

So did his mother. Anna Kirkland lived in the Raleigh asylum until her death in 1890. Her remains were interred at Ayr Mount "in the rain," Paul Cameron told his daughter.[32] Nothing about the tragic if ordinary lives of Anna and Alexander was transmitted by William Alexander and Robert Strange Kirkland to their descendants but their names, dates, and the barest of biographical information, stripped of the passion, the expectations of happiness, and the grim dénouement of their ill-fated lives.

❧ 12 ❧

An Interlude

COMIC RELIEF in this long saga of misfortune was not missing in the Kirklands' daily lives. It was supplied by young grandchildren and their schoolmates, some of whom lived at Ayr Mount, but particularly by the unfolding drama of William Kirkland's oldest grandchild. It might be called the courting of Catherine Ruffin, and it was played out over a dozen years before coming to a close with a happy ending, the qualification for comedy. The *dramatis personae* included, besides the heroine, the male leads, Thomas Ruffin, a baker's dozen of suitors, and the supporting cast of Catherine's closest friends and relations. Unfortunately, no picture of the young Catherine supplies evidence of her ravishing beauty; imagination will have to supply the deficit. Although Catherine's beauty was described as a poor imitation of her mother's, there can be no doubt that it was remarkable. As his oldest child, Catherine was clearly dear to Thomas Ruffin's heart; his letters to her show the confidence and respect almost of a close friend rather than of a father, particularly after her marriage. The long years during which one suitor after another placed her future in jeopardy were full of anxiety for him and her mother.

The finishing touches to Catherine's education were added during the years 1824 and 1825 at Mrs. Edward Jones's boarding school and on long visits to her aunts in Fayetteville. In his letters to her when she was fourteen years old, Ruffin reminded her of the advantages she was enjoying in the company of the Stranges and McNeills in the refined society of Fayetteville, acquiring the polish and social graces that would equip her to adorn any position in life in which she was placed. Although their correspondence never mentioned books, music, needlework, painting, and domestic skills, those were, presumably, the objects of her study. Her unmistakable resemblance to her mother as she approached the age at which Ruffin married Anne Kirkland must have made him acutely aware that her chances for future happiness could be determined by any young man, with or without the right credentials, who could insinuate himself into Catherine's good graces and who might, as likely as not, prove utterly unworthy of Ruffin's prize. In this gamble with fate, his own precarious financial situation must have been some consolation, for at least he could be sure that fortune hunters would not be among her suitors. Nevertheless, her future happiness was in peril, and waiting to see what Catherine would do must have kept all the family in suspense.

While Catherine was away at school, her absence from Hillsborough, as her uncle John Kirkland noted, removed much of the gaiety and sprightliness from the social scene. He and Alexander and her uncle James Ruffin, all only slightly her senior and clearly enchanted by her, missed her and wanted to write to her. Catherine recognized the hold she had on them and the nature of her attraction. Years later she confided with amusement to her husband the change in James Ruffin's attachment: "It makes me feel quite sad to see how much his affection has diminished for me from what it used to be before I was married."[1]

Even her father was not immune to her extraordinary charm and tried to please and entertain her with his letters, their tone at times reflecting more the gallant than the paterfamilias. He archly described, for example, his meeting on the road with George Burgwin and his daughters, her friends.

> Mag was seated on the Driver's box playing the [part] & the coachman to ease his jaded brutes was trudging on foot thro' a heavy sand. She knew me as soon as I came in sight & drew her veil aside & spread her *little* mouth something short of either ear. By the time I got up she had repursed it sufficiently to take a kiss which I very cordially imparted. The other young ladies fared better, that is, they escaped that salutation; for I understand that Miss Eliza's lips are forbidden fruit & Miss Julia is not enough a *daughter of Hillsborough* to appreciate so familiar a greeting from one so nearly a stranger.[2]

Catherine's mother, on the other hand, almost never wrote to her, to her other children, or even to her husband. She had a strong aversion to letter writing and whenever possible put the burden on others. Her unmarried sisters gladly accommodated her. In one letter to Catherine, Mary Kirkland described her sister Anne Kirkland Ruffin as "very busy at present preparing for a few gentlemen that dine with her tomorrow.

She is just as fat as Mama and as lazy as she can possibly be."[3] Thomas Ruffin put up graciously with her refusal to write to him. Once, however, in a letter to Ruffin for her mother, Catherine promised him that her mother would write soon. Consequently, he received the following rare lines from his wife:

> I perceive from your letter to me that she made a promise for me without my knowledge, that of writing very soon. I was in hopes I should have been spared that pain, for really, my husband, it is a pain to me to write. My letters cannot afford you any pleasure. I never could express myself or my feelings on paper and the older I get the more difficulty I find in doing so, and I do not think it a duty when I make the children write you. They have written every week since you left us; therefore let my love and prayers for your health and happiness be for my part and let our children do all the writing.[4]

Although she considered her obligation fulfilled if her daughters wrote for her, Anne Ruffin was something of a tyrant about her husband's writing. Their daughter Patty relayed to him a message from her mother: " 'Tell him . . . that this day two weeks ago, he left home & in that time he has written to me *once*!! Ask him if he is not *ashamed of himself* as a good Christian husband he ought to be, I am sure!' This is her message; I deliver it verbatim and without any comment, save to beg, that you will not think me a very saucy daughter, for repeating such a very saucy message to my Papa."[5]

At the beginning of Catherine's absence from Hillsborough, her brother William sent her a message from John Kirkland, who stood on ceremony; didn't she know that ladies were supposed to write to gentlemen first? Alexander felt no such compunctions. Catherine heard from him frequently. He stayed home from church one Sunday to answer a letter from her and to comment on disclosures she made to him that did not get into letters to her father. "Your description of the walk," he wrote, "I found very interesting, thou' I must confess, you were rather bold in hugging the little Dr., presuming at the same time that you were quite excusable, for such opportunities seldom occur."[6]

Alexander also informed her that her father had accepted as a law student Alexander's erstwhile colleague at the university William Alexander Graham, a recent graduate and a tall, good-looking youth. "I do not mean by any means to distress you by mentioning this," Alexander wrote, "but rather to put you in mind that the time is to come when Mr. G. will escort you to and from preaching when your uncle will be far off."[7] Things fell out as Alexander had predicted, and Graham became the first of Catherine's known admirers. Three years later Graham's sister Sophia Witherspoon wrote him, "Do write soon & let me hear all about Miss Ruffin, what you are about. I think setling in Hillsboro looks a little suspicious."[8]

Graham's brother James saw other attractions in the town. "I believe Hillsboro unites more advantages and inducements for a settled residence than other point in the state. It combines," he wrote his brother, "health, wealth, and intelligent and interesting society. These I conceive to be the '*Sine qua non*' to the enjoyment of life, to the fortune and fame of those whose aim and object is usefulness and happiness."[9]

Another of Graham's sisters, Mary Morrison, shared her sister's suspicions of his motive. "Fanny Webb has brought a report from your town, that you are going to marry Miss Ruffin; if it is the case I think it will do very well. I think that family makes fine wives."[10] That Graham would have been a proper *parti* in Ruffin's view is unquestionable. He was well-born, well educated, ambitious, hardworking, with a lively mind and engaging personality. He did not, however, engage Catherine. His illustrious future, if written in his palm, was not patent in his face. In any case, it would probably have made no difference to Catherine if she had known he was to be a United States senator, governor of North Carolina, and secretary of the navy.

While Catherine's friendship with Graham remained unresolved, she became linked in gossip's busy mill with Paul Carrington Cameron, another young man whom her parents could hardly have failed to approve. He was the heir to Duncan Cameron's fortune and a passionate, peppery, capable, and energetic youth. Catherine seems not to have disguised her interest in him, for his sister Mary Anne wrote to him at Trinity College in Hartford, Connecticut, "Catherine Ruffin often speaks of you to me & desired me to give her love to you."[11] In her own family her partiality was well known. The fourteen-year-old Anne Ruffin, in school in Hillsborough, wrote to her mother in Raleigh, "Tell Kate Friend Paul has been in town for the last week; he is quite a fine looking young man. He enquired very particularly after her & is to be in Raleigh next week. He says he intends staying half of his time at our house."[12] Obviously already an admirer of her future husband, Anne wrote soon again directly to Catherine, "I suppose you have seen Paul. Do you think he is as handsome as ever?"[13]

The reason for Mrs. Ruffin's and Catherine's presence in Raleigh was Ruffin's continuous work there after his appointment to the bank presidency in 1829, followed by the appointment to the state supreme court. He rented quarters where his wife and daughter joined him at the end of the year on a rare occasion when his wife was persuaded to leave her myriad burdens at the Hermitage. During their visit, Catherine, whose success and reputation as a belle were already well established, received some advice from her Uncle John. He feared that in Raleigh she ran the danger of having her head turned by admiration and unwarily losing her heart. He warned her, "Let me guard you, my dear Niece, in this season of gaiety & frolic in the metropolis to keep your affections fast from the efforts I have no doubt are daily made to wean them from your Friends & fix them supremely upon some one single object—I do not know that this is your case, but your many virtues & indearing qualities I presume are strong enducements to admiration."[14] She was too much the coquette to need the warning.

Her parents must have been disquieted by reports that reached them through friends when Catherine was at the Shocco Springs with the Boylans the following summer. Ruffin had heard that Catherine "was quite well & everybody says in high spirits enough to be called *wild*."[15] Her aunt Jane Strange, hoping to curb her headstrong niece, had seized the opportunity of John Kirkland's wedding to warn Catherine of marriage's drawbacks. "I hope he will make a good husband, for nothing can compensate a woman for giving up her freedom but a good husband."[16] The longer Catherine remained unmarried the more easily alarmed her father became when each new threat occurred. "What does Catherine mean about this Mr. Grist?" he asked his wife when yet another admirer appeared. "It was a comfort to me to think that she had kept unmarried until she had reached an age at which she would not throw herself away. I still hope so. But there is always danger in strangers."[17]

Catherine's friends could not help teasing her about her swains. Some time after she lost interest in Paul Cameron, who then switched his attentions to her sister Anne, his uncle Thomas Bennehan seems to have thought her fair game even though she was thirty years his junior. The perennial bachelor and owner of Stagville Plantation and old friend of the Kirklands could not be ignored, though obviously Catherine and her friends never took his interest in her seriously. Sarah Kollock Nash jested with Catherine about him and her other "beaux": "Tho' you have lost Uncle Tommy's fine estate (which by the by is your own fault; I *told* you to *keep the bracelets*: sending them back was as good as a refusal) and the tall, stately Mr. G[raham], whom Hillsboro' people were determined you *should* marry, yet the Quaker is still at your disposal. . . . Has Paul [Cameron] given Ann 'the bracelets?' Tell her to be wiser than you; a 'Stagville' does not offer itself every day."[18]

Obviously Anne did not send the bracelets back, and she became the mistress of Fairntosh and Stagville and much more, for Paul Cameron eventually inherited both plantations and was reputed to be the wealthiest man in North Carolina. Catherine's early flirtation with him turned into friendship when he became her brother-in-law in 1832, and the occasional letters they exchanged showed how much playfulness there was in their relationship. "I *love* to receive letters from you," she wrote. In 1833 she wrote him about the arrival of Mary McLean Bryant, former governess to the Cameron daughters, to assume the same role at the Hermitage. Miss Bryant had visited at Fairntosh on her way to the Hermitage. With Miss Bryant had come, Catherine told Paul, Anne Ruffin Cameron's white satin hat. She inquired whether it had come on a visit or to market. "It shall receive *great* attention and kind treatment," she assured him.[19]

He had great fun with his answer to this and also felt free to write her his personal views on topics and persons that he would not care to tell others. He and Anne invited Catherine to visit them, tactfully naming a time when Thomas Bennehan would be away from Stagville, which lay next to the Camerons' Fairntosh plantation. Paul explained that Bennehan "would escape the fatal influence of your beauty" for "he has taken himself off to Halifax on a visit to his dear cousin Jack Amis to talk about Rail Roads and the transportation of cotton and tobacco and flour to market. Upon these subjects our Cousin Jack talks long and loud, both learnedly and unlearnedly, but be that as it may I am ever amused with the bright and golden anticipations which are to him to be realized through no distant perspective. Mr. Bennehan will have his own sport out of Jack and his friend Willie Jones and for some reasons I should like to be with him."[20]

In another jesting letter to her, Paul made fun of more sacrosanct topics: "Conventions and Camp Meetings and all these sort of collections are getting to be notorious places for wiveing and I am 'anti' the entire concern upon principal! Now dear Kate is this not bold chat from one who was born in the church to a *high* church woman? I may talk thus to my sister Kate, but it would be worth the hair upon my head— red as it is—if I should speak or write this to my Aunt Susan [Kirkland] about a 'synod' or 'monthly' or 'protracted meeting.' "[21]

In early 1832 Catherine had the diversion of attending the bride in Hannah Gaston's wedding to Matthias Manly, a New Bern lawyer and former classmate of William A. Graham. John Kirkland's marriage to Betsy Simpson had strengthened the family's social ties with New Bern. Catherine stayed with the Simpsons during the festivities attendant on the wedding. She described William Gaston as "almost broken down I expect going to parties and seeing company."[22] Hannah kept up a correspondence with Catherine after her marriage and continued to visit Hillsborough in summer. When her younger sisters visited the Nashes there in 1837, Eliza Gaston was not so impressed with Hillsborough as James Graham had been. "Our time has been constantly occupied in receiving & returning visits, walking & riding about to admire the beauties of this far famed spot," she wrote her father. "I must confess the Town itself is the dirtiest place I have ever seen but some of the situations around are very pretty & the view from the third mountain is really very fine."[23] Gaston and his younger daughters visited the Ruffins at the Hermitage later the same year. Nine years after Hannah Gaston's early death in 1835, Manly married Sarah Simpson, Betsy's sister, forging another link between the Kirklands and New Bern.[24]

A common characteristic of Catherine's suitors was tenacity. Some of them proposed not once but again and again. Besides Graham, Cameron, Bennehan, and "the Quaker," who may or may not have gone so far as to make formal declarations of their affection, they included Major John Hinton, Mr. Winslow and Mr. Winston (neither otherwise identified), Rawley Galloway of Rockingham County, Moreau Murphey, Fred Hill, and Daniel Barringer. Alice Ruffin, always at home helping her mother at the Hermitage, was growing tired of playing confidante to Catherine's persistent suitors. Winston even went to the Hermitage, Alice wrote Catherine, to inquire of her how Barringer's suit was faring, having just been rejected for the second time himself. Barringer did no better. When Catherine was at home again she learned from James Ruffin, whose letter was hand delivered by Rawley Galloway, that Galloway had come to the Hermitage to propose again.[25]

And then there was William Mercer Green, the minister of Saint Matthew's Church. At the time of his courtship of Catherine, Green was a widower with five children. He had come as minister to Hillsborough in 1825 and started the Hillsborough Female Academy to supplement his meager salary. When Ruffin heard of his offer of marriage to Catherine and of her acceptance on condition of her parents' approval, he was disturbed. After a second proposal five months later, Ruffin reacted vigorously and told Green in no uncertain terms that his conduct was not only deceptive but unbecoming a clergyman. Still Green persisted. Catherine was partly to blame. Her conditional acceptance certainly suggested that she loved him and left him with the impression that if he persevered he might overcome the obstacles.[26]

Catherine's friends were fearful that Green's tenacity would prevail, and they bombarded her with advice. Sarah Nash disguised her serious concern in her usual teasing vein, saying she had heard that Catherine was engaged. Rumor had identified Moreau Murphey as the lucky man, but knowing Ruffin's opposition to the marriage of cousins, she could hardly credit that report. Could it be Major Hinton? She discounted Green, she wrote disingenuously; "I know you are too happily situated & have *too* much sense to marry a widower with 5 children."[27] Her aunt Mary Ruffin Cain also broached the subject. She advised her to marry "the next *clever fellow* that makes his bow *if he is not a widower; keep clear of them always, even to parsons.*"[28] From Maria Spear, an Englishwoman associated with Green as principal of the Hillsborough Female Academy, Catherine received different advice. Maria Spear told Catherine that there was nothing to the rumors that had circulated about herself and Green, that their association in the school had provoked such rumors before, and that Green was totally committed to Catherine. In a postscript came the real message. Catherine must make up her mind. The respect and esteem she had expressed for Green were not enough. She must "give all or nothing."[29]

They were right to be anxious. Catherine accepted Green a second time. Her father, though controlled, was almost beside himself because of the poverty of clergymen's families, Green's uncertain health, and the difficult role of stepmother that Catherine would have to assume. Catherine's close friend Eleanor Boylan wrote too. The advice may have had an effect; Catherine again backed out of her engagement, and all her friends and relations breathed a sigh of relief. The following year Green was successful in wooing Charlotte Fleming, and they were married before the year ended. In 1838 he removed himself from the painful scene and settled in Chapel Hill, where he taught at the university and filled the office of chaplain, preached to Episcopalians, and helped them organize a congregation. His talents were rewarded in 1849 when he became the bishop of Mississippi and in 1867 a founder and chancellor of the University of the South at Sewanee.[30]

In 1835 Catherine's brother Sterling was suddenly afflicted with inflammation in both eyes, which led to the blindness that blighted his long life. In an effort to save his sight, he was taken to Philadelphia to be examined and treated by Dr. Isaac Hays, an ophthalmologist and editor of the *American Journal of Medical Sciences*, who invented his own instrument for cataract surgery. While under Hays's supervision, both in the hospital and afterward in a boardinghouse, Sterling was cared for by friends and relations, including William Cameron and Moreau Murphey, who were in Philadelphia attending medical courses. When Sterling lacked a nurse in the spring of 1836, Ruffin delegated Catherine for the job and sent her to Philadelphia. She returned home in July, and a sudden resolution of her perplexing matrimonial options followed. She wrote to her father on her arrival, describing the health of the family, particularly that of her mother and Anna Kirkland, whose first son was born while Catherine was at Ayr Mount. Typically her postscript contained the most important item in the letter. "What has become," she asked, "of my *old friend* Mr. Roulhac?"[31]

Joseph Blount Gregoire Roulhac was the son of a French lieutenant who had come to America with Lafayette's forces to fight for American independence and had remained in America and married as his second wife Frances Gray of Bertie County. Joseph Roulhac had been born at the family plantation, Fairfields, in Martin County. He was sent to the university, from which he was graduated at the age of sixteen in 1811, and then studied law, but preferring a mercantile career, he had gone into business in Windsor, Bertie County. He had first proposed marriage to Catherine in 1833 and then again in 1835, the year he was elected to represent his county at the constitutional convention, and been refused both times. He was fifteen years her senior but at forty-one probably did not seem old to the twenty-six-year-old Catherine. The change of heart that Catherine apparently experienced had come about on her journey home from Philadelphia. Following her question to her father about Roulhac's whereabouts, she added, "I did not even thank him for his attentions as an escort from Philadelphia to Raleigh. I did not see him after I arrived."[32]

Catherine had reached an age of almost confirmed spinsterhood. William A. Graham was to marry that summer, William M. Green had married the previous winter, and the other less serious contenders had been dispatched. She must have realized on her long journey in his company that the mature Joseph Roulhac was, after all, the one for her. Roulhac had a passion for books, a talent for accounting and business, a strong attachment to the Episcopal church, and a sensitivity to people that probably appealed to the equally sensitive and now experienced Catherine. Her inquiries were doubtless relayed quickly to Roulhac by her father, and two months later they were engaged to be married.[33]

Roulhac could hardly believe his luck. He wrote her his feelings of joy and the trouble he had had to disguise them from friends who had yet to be let in on the secret.

I find myself at a great loss to say what I wish to you; my situation is so thoroughly novel, and a letter to one who engages so large a portion of my thoughts is so entirely out of my line of correspondence, that I assure you, the task though delightful is not without its difficulties. Catherine, I have been happy twenty-four hours of every day since I left you, and the sun of my joy has had no cloud to obscure its brightness, except that of *absence* from your presence.

I found it a very difficult experiment to keep my promise of secrecy as regards our engagement. I can inform you, it is not easy to compress the lips & knit the brow, when the heart is dancing to the measure of double quick time. But I flatter myself, I succeeded, all things considered, not badly; in Hillsborough your aunt Cain was so surprised by my gravity, as to forego her intention of asking me pointed questions; there were others than the family present, or I should not have begun my stage tricks at that house, because I number that household among my *good friends*. In Raleigh I left every person except two, perfectly in the dark; as a proof of good acting Miss E. Boylan told me that her father & mother pitied me very much, when attacked at dinner by our late Govr. Swain & the former said he would give you a good scolding for your conduct.

It was a great relief to me to get on the road, where I shout & laugh until the welkin ring and echo would occasionally give back the one loved name. . . .

You Catherine who have been loved & sought by many, on whom you had no claims by the ties of nature, who have listened to the outpourings of the admiration and homage of scores of captive suitors, can have but a faint conception, nay, can [not] by the utmost possibility, realize my feelings. I, who never before could so far interest any of the fair portion of creation, as to wring a confession of any feeling above a *high regard*, or some other like civil acknowledgement. I feel that the day is far, far distant when I can cease to be grateful, or forget that my first duty is now & will forever be to make you the happiest of the happy. Why Catherine, you have made me vain I fear, to a fault, (and as Shakspeare had made his Richd 3rd say) I have grown into favor with myself. I will entertain a tailor & purchase a looking glass to view myself, since you have discerned I am a *marvelous proper man*.

After telling her about the health of the village of Windsor, where he lived with his sister, he reverted to the all-engrossing subject.

I forgot to mention that I called on your grandmother, as you no doubt heard while on your visit, but I hardly saw your favorite Aunt Susan; she did not make her appearance untill a few moments before I left, tho: I prolonged the visit, waiting for her, & those few moments your uncle John employed in teasing her—I suppose she was unwilling to see the *cruel man* who was to carry away her favorite neice. I hope however, yet to obtain a fair standing in the lady's graces, & what I cannot accomplish, you as my *nearest & best friend* on earth, must do for me. Remember me kindly Catherine to your good mother (Heaven bless her, for her good opinion of me), your honored father, your mischevious & teasing sister Alice, your smiling and bright-eyed sister Betty & kiss all the little ones for me. Tell the boys not to forget me & to learn their books or I will recommend Miss Bryan[t] to try the virtue of some of those fine rods that grow on the Allamance. God bless you Catherine, and may you be as happy & have as many blessings showered on you, as is wished for you, by your betrothed, whose devotion is unutterable.[34]

Mary Cameron Anderson, feeling old and depressed, wrote Catherine her regrets that she would not be present at her wedding. She was on the way to Pensacola, Florida, to join her son Walker and his family. Preparations went on hurriedly at the Hermitage. Mary and Susan Kirkland were there "fixing and sewing." "The wedding cloths [sic] are the finest that ever was in these parts," Margaret Taylor informed Eliza Johnston.[35] The marriage bond was signed by Paul Cameron as bondsman early in November, and the wedding took place November 24, 1836, at the Hermitage. The officiating minister was not William Mercer Green.[36]

Catherine's life as Mrs. Roulhac was hardly idyllic, though she had chosen wisely, and the marriage apparently brought happiness to them both. Bertie County, however, did not meet with her approval as a place to live. Not only was it too far from home and out of the swim, but she was convinced that it was also unhealthy and a threat to their children. By 1846 her husband had acceded to her "long desire" and moved his business to Raleigh. Their home became a mecca for many relations. They were able to persuade Ruffin to occupy the office during the many months of the year when the court was sitting, an arrangement that greatly relieved his unhappiness in being away from his own home. George M. Ruffin, a son of James Ruffin, Samuel S. Kirkland, a son of John Kirkland, and Catherine's brother Peter Browne Ruffin at various times apprenticed for mercantile careers as clerks in Roulhac's store and lived with his family. When Judge Strange was in Raleigh, he too stayed with the Roulhacs. Besides running his business, in the 1850s Roulhac served as president of the North Carolina Mutual Insurance Company. A devoted husband and proud father of seven children, Roulhac was described by Ruffin as "one of the best of nurses as well as of men."[37] Ruffin respected and depended on him. When Duncan Cameron's life was ebbing in 1853, Ruffin told Roulhac his feeling of inadequacy to express his sympathy and grief to the afflicted family. He asked Roulhac to do it for him, "as you have a tact for doing such things in the right time & in the right way."[38] Catherine's aunt Jane called Roulhac "Catherine's gude man," an endearment that became the family's invariable name for him and caused Catherine delighted embarrassment.[39]

Quite suddenly, one evening after dinner, when he was alone in his store, Joseph Roulhac was stricken with apoplexy and died. He was sixty-one years old. Grief-stricken but resigned to widowhood, Catherine moved back to Hillsborough and took up quarters in her childhood home on the hill.[40]

❧ 13 ❧

William Kirkland's Last Years

D URING THE YEARS that witnessed John U. Kirkland's establishment as a businessman and family man, Alexander's entrance
into the partnership of Cain and Kirkland and his marriage to
Anna Cameron, and the diverting vagaries of Catherine Ruffin's courtship, William Kirkland was on hand—then in his sixties—to share the
suspense or enjoy the satisfaction that these events provided, for he had
approximately seven years to live after the nadir of his fortunes in 1829.
Patches of sunlight in an otherwise overcast sky were fortunately many,
and despite his continuously straitened circumstances, he apparently
never lost his equanimity or dignity. He grappled with debt, looking for
ways to manage it or pay it off, but mostly he learned to live with it as
best he could.

The peculiar difficulties of the southern economy were compounded
in the 1830s by those of the national and international scene. Unsteady
prices, credit expansion, and inflation accompanied by unprecedented
land speculation were followed by panic and depression, creating an
economic rollercoaster for those involved in commerce. President Andrew Jackson's war on the United States Bank and his other economic
policies have traditionally been blamed for these conditions, but more
recent studies question these influences and attribute the economic
swings to more far-flung and global conditions. Whatever the causes, the
result for small merchants was unsettled times, unpredictable and dangerous for those who operated on credit. After a low in 1830, a peaking
in 1833, and another low in 1834, prices rose by 50 percent in three
years, a period of unparalleled speculation. The value of public lands
sold by the federal government in the same years rose from $5 million in
1834 to $25 million in 1836, building up huge deposits in the banks. The
price of cotton, the foreign sales of which accounted for one-half the
nation's export income, doubled in the 1830s and caused an accompanying rise in the value of cotton-growing land and attracted much foreign

capital to the country. As a result, both bank deposits and the trade balance again rose. After the 1836 boom came the Panic of 1837 and the crash. Businesses failed and civil unrest erupted in riots in the large cities, and the tightening of credit, calling in of loans, and demand for specie made desperate times in financial circles.[1] Except for the crash, which he did not live to experience, this was the economic background against which William Kirkland's last years were played out.

He continued to look to the sale of his Tennessee lands as a way of raising funds without cutting into his plantation acreage or losing that source of income. The Tennessee property was vacant land, returning no profit. Because his earlier attempts to sell it through an agent had apparently come to nought, he resolved to go himself to inspect and assess it and try to make arrangements for its disposal. At first he planned to travel west in the fall of 1830, but Archibald Murphey, who had made the trip in 1822, advised him to wait until spring. He thought that the long drought they were experiencing would be followed by heavy autumn rains, making the watercourses too full for fording. Another consideration, Kirkland wrote to Ruffin, was that William McNeill expected "to make a great deal of money this winter by purchasing cotton in the seed," and "the chance therefore will be better then than now of getting money from him." William McNeill's debts to McNeill and Kirkland Company were still unpaid. Unfortunately, William McNeill, like Murphey, was a Mr. Micawber, foolishly optimistic. Kirkland's own mood was hopeful just then because he had sold his land "over the river" for $1,475 on credit of six, twelve, and eighteen months' interest.[2] This transaction, however, was never recorded in the Register of Deeds office, and possibly the deal fell through.

As usual in his communications, whether letters or bills, Kirkland concluded business matters with family news. Having related to Ruffin the land sale and travel plans, he wound up his letter with the information that all were well and that Alexander was at the horse races and Andrew was at Ayr Mount weighing seed cotton. Up to now only slight mention has been made of Andrew Mickle, but he was for many years a fixture in William Kirkland's store and family. He was born about 1812 in Edinburgh, Scotland, and emigrated as an infant with his parents early in the century. At the death of his father, another Andrew Mickle, which, according to family tradition, occurred in Hillsborough, the younger Andrew was still a child.[3] An orphan without means of support, he may either have been unofficially adopted by William Kirkland or bound out to him by the county court, a legal solution by which the appointed master relieved the county of the cost of an orphan's maintenance in exchange for the labor of the child until his majority. In addition, the master was required to instruct his apprentice in reading, writing, and a livelihood and at his majority to furnish him with a suit of clothes and a sum of money. If such an arrangement took place between Kirkland and Mickle, the court minutes failed to record it.

According to Mickle's own testimony in 1836, when he was twenty-four years old, he had gone to reside with the family of William Kirkland "at an early age."[4] He would not have been of much help in the store before he reached the age of ten in 1822 and in no position to become Kirkland's clerk until the late 1820s. He probably followed George M. Johnston in that post when Johnston went into business in a new mercantile venture with Walker Anderson in 1827. Mickle continued with Kirkland until February 1836, when he and Joseph Norwood established a business together, opening yet another store in Hillsborough. In 1837 Mickle rented the old Ruffin home place, where his sister kept house for him until 1838, when he married Helen Mary Norwood, Joseph's sister and a daughter of Judge William Norwood. Her old Hillsborough friend Margaret J. Taylor wrote to Eliza Johnston, "I should be afraid to venture my head under that old roof in a storm."[5]

With Andrew Mickle a trusty and experienced clerk by 1831, William Kirkland was able to leave the business to him and John, confident that it was in good hands, and at last set off in the spring for Tennessee. Letters to Hillsborough from a variety of correspondents kept the town informed of his progress. George Johnston's cousin J. S. Mulhollan (an emigrant from Orange County) wrote from his new home in Nashville: "Our worthy friend Mr. Kirkland arrived in this place on Tuesday last. I can say I have not been so much pleased to meet with any person since I left home. . . . I spend every leisure moment I have in his company which is very few as I am living at this time in the Post Office and have very little time to spare."[6]

Archibald Murphey heard from his brother-in-law and former Hillsborough resident Herndon Haralson in Brownsville that Kirkland had been there, inspecting his nearby tracts of land, and had since departed for Tipton to call on Dr. Holt.[7]

A week later, at the end of June, Ruffin received from Kirkland himself a report of his journey and the disposition he had made of their lands. He was staying with George Anderson's family near LaGrange when he wrote. He had seen the various tracts of land and found them all good except a tract near Brownsville. Two hundred acres of it were "broken" land, by which he probably meant irregular terrain, interrupted by rock or other natural impediments, poorly suited for agricultural use. An additional two hundred acres were flooded by the Big Natchez River, and two hundred more were very good land. Because Murphey's title to the tract was not considered good, Kirkland had decided to sell it to Herndon Haralson, who owned the adjoining land. Five hundred acres of another tract, which Kirkland and Ruffin owned jointly, had seemed to contain very good land but was so overgrown with cane and under-brush that he had been unable to get into it. Another seven hundred acres were flooded by the Natchez River, but the timber was said to be very valuable. He had arranged to rent the tract in half a dozen different parcels on six-year leases.[8]

By the beginning of August 1831, Kirkland was back home again, none the worse for his arduous journey and pleased with its results except for the complaint that he could not digest limestone water. His homecoming was undoubtedly sweetened by the news of Anne Ruffin's engagement to Paul Cameron. The Cameron connection promised more than future security for his granddaughter. It strengthened the present ties of both friendship and business between the families. Paul's uncle Thomas D. Bennehan yearly ran up the longest accounts with Kirkland and Son, and both Bennehan and Duncan Cameron were steady and good customers of the firm of Kirkland and Webb, purchasing large amounts of skins and hides to keep their huge slave forces shod. In the spring of 1831, for example, Bennehan ordered twenty hides and skins amounting to 326 pounds and Cameron bought twenty-eight hides weighing 401 pounds. When John U. Kirkland made his semiannual buying trips to the North, his customers gave him special orders for locally unobtainable goods. For Bennehan, for example, he bought a wig, and for Ruffin he ordered a carriage, an elegant conveyance that cost $550.[9]

Kirkland's friendship with Duncan Cameron made him privy to the alarming despondency that Cameron suffered in the summer of 1833 and gave him an intimate view of the havoc it created. Although a tall, well-built man, radiating power of mind and body, Cameron was susceptible to mental depression, a tendency intensified when he had no challenging intellectual work to distract him from his personal afflictions. He had given up both his judgeship and his legal practice and was then devoting himself to family and plantation matters. The poor health of his daughters and slaves became particularly trying to him in 1832 and 1833 and threw him into a decline bordering on melancholia. He could not focus his attention on anything and even refused to take his meals at the table. His family persuaded him to visit his friends in Hillsborough for a time, hoping that the society of "his old companions and associates," Frederick Nash, William Norwood, William Kirkland, and James Webb, might lift his spirits.[10] Still unrelieved after trying this scheme, in August Cameron was persuaded to go to the Virginia springs with his seriously ailing daughter Rebecca. The travelers stopped over at Ayr Mount on the way, and Kirkland described their visit to Ruffin:

> We had the pleasure of Mr. and Mrs. Cameron and their Daughter Miss Rebecca's company at our house last Tuesday. They arrived about one o'clock accompanied by Mr. Bennehan on their way to the White Sulphur Springs in Virginia. They tarried with us all night, & all excepting Mr. B. left us on Wednesday Morning accompanied by Mr. Green, & travelled that day as far as Milton & returned excepting Mr. G. to my house on the following day & remained with us all day on Friday & went home on Saturday. The cause of their return was that Mr. Cameron said he felt so bad on Thursday morning that he could not think of continuing the journey, not having slept a wink at Milton; he however the next day regretted very much that he had not gone on, & I did so too. He is in very bad health, very nervous, & starts at the least noise, eats scarcely any thing & sleeps very little, & looks badly & has fallen away very much.
>
> He told me on Saturday morning that he & the family would go up to your house that day—but he soon changed his mind. He has no decision about his movements & appears to be afraid of trifles. He told me he should certainly go up to your house before you left home for Raleigh & wished me to let you know if an opportunity offered, that such was his intention. He will no doubt be accompanied by some of the family. Several of his friends came down to my house to see him on Friday & advised him to go on to Philadelphia,

and to take the advice of Physicians there, which he said he would do, but before he left my house he told me he believed he should not do so as he could not go there by himself & he had no friend to go with him as Mr. B. & himself could not both be absent at the same time.

Mrs. Anderson staid with him all day on Friday, talked a great deal to him. He says but little himself unless spoken to, but sits moping & apparently in deep study. We were all very sorry to see him so poorly, but I hope he will get over it before long—His Daughter Rebecca was also very weak & feeble & look'd badly.[11]

Although Cameron's mental condition improved, it was his position as president of the state bank from 1834 to 1851 that rescued him permanently by removing him from the unhealthy atmosphere, isolation, and enforced idleness of life at Fairntosh and substituted the mental stimulation of daily work, unrelated to personal worries, and the sociability of urban living. His temperament was unsuited to plantation life.

Isolation was never a problem at Ayr Mount. Its location close to Hillsborough gave its inhabitants the best of both worlds. The family largely escaped the fevers associated with low-lying lands because of Hillsborough's elevation, yet they enjoyed the self-sufficiency of the plantation economy and the bonuses of the planter's life-style. They were also close to friends, church, and medical care—balm for minds, spirits, and bodies. After the Ruffins' move to the Hermitage in 1829, the older Ruffin boys, Sterling and Peter Browne, who continued their schooling in Hillsborough, lived with their grandparents at Ayr Mount. Miscellaneous cousins and friends were also in residence for the same reason, Duncan MacRae, for example, and James Boylan. In summer any of the McNeill or Strange children might arrive for a visit. In the spring of 1830, a day when the boys had a holiday, Kirkland wrote to Ruffin that they had "all gone a fishing." When "Uncle Strange" came to Hillsborough to court, he, too, stayed at Ayr Mount. And there were daily visits of Hillsborough friends and relations. Moreau Murphey described to "his dearest Kitty" Ruffin a dinner at Ayr Mount in December 1833. It was Susan Kirkland's birthday and Catherine's mother's wedding anniversary. They had enjoyed wild turkey and drunk a toast to her mother.[12] There was always plenty of company at Ayr Mount, where hospitality was virtually an article of faith and could not have helped depleted coffers.

Grandchildren at hand did not monopolize Kirkland's thoughts or affection; he remembered those absent as well. He wrote charming letters to the little ones at the Hermitage, always urging them to come visit him. When his carriage left Ayr Mount one morning taking Catherine's friend Eleanor Boylan up to the Ruffins at the Hermitage, he sent a letter with her to the small fry:

My Dear Tom & Betty,

When I wrote a letter to your Pa yesterday by Jesse [a Ruffin slave] I told him if I could get a little money in the course of the day that I would send you two, Susan Mary, & Jane Minerva some Goodies. Well as good luck would have it I got a little & have sent you by Miss Eleanor [Boylan] 5 Cakes made by a New Man but I have told Miss Eleanor that if she wanted she might eat one of them by the way but I do not think I told her she was to take any thing else as I expected you would maybe give her some when she delivered them to you. Also some Goodies that is what is called Confectionaries & Raisins & Almonds.

Now I think I can guess what you will do with them: that is in the first place you will very willingly like very good Children give your Pa & Ma some & also your big Sisters & maybe Mr. Galloway a taste but I do not think Brother Will ought to have any as he went away from my house on Sunday Morning without telling me he was going at all. But I think on second thoughts that you will do better with them still by giving them all to your Ma & let her divide them & keep them for you as there is too many to eat all at once. I want to see you all very much & so does Grandma & Aunts & I hope Pa & Ma will let you & Betty come down along with Aunt Susan & stay awhile with us.

I have not mentioned old Grandma's [Mrs. Scott] coming in for a share of the Goodies as I was sure within my own mind you wouldn't forget her. Give all our love to her, Pa & Ma & all your big Sisters & Brother Will, little Susan Mary & Jane Minerva & I am my dear Tom & Betty

Your very affecte Grandadie
Wil Kirkland

N.B. You see I do not say you ought not to give Brother Will some. I only say I don't think he ought to have any for serving me so shabbily. If you don't come down you must write me soon & give me all your news.[13]

Kirkland's mood and health fluctuated in these years. In 1832 he admitted that he was feeling better. He attributed his improvement to eating lots of ripe tomatoes and was able to indulge his taste for them by riding home to dinner every day. Receipt of a letter from Scotland dated 1832 but not received until 1835, however, plunged him into a very depressed mood at a time when his health was poor, and Paul Cameron reported that he looked very bad. According to Mary Anne Cameron, the letter reported the death of William Kirkland's brother John.[14]

Letters from the family in Scotland, though infrequent, kept the North Carolina Kirklands informed of changes there during these years, and there had been much to report when John Kirkland wrote to his nephew John Umstead Kirkland in late 1830, probably the last letter he wrote to his American relations. Although he had earlier informed them of the deaths of his wife, Sybilla, and of Nugent's wife, Phoebe Bingham, both in 1825, he had had no word in reply. The 1830 letter, unlike the earlier one, however, had only good news. His son John had finally got over his grief at his first wife's death and had remarried. His new wife was Louisa Bishop, whose father had been "comptroller General to George the 3rd, and left a great fortune, chiefly at the disposal of his wife," after making suitable provision for his children.

> [The comptroller] has been dead many years, but his widow is still in life, and with her eldest and youngest daughter, youngest son etc. live in a splendid mansion near Sunbury about 15 miles from Town [London]. The rest of the family with the exception of one in the [East India] Company's service are remarkably well married, and live mostly upon their Estates in the Country. Mrs. Kirkland the young and handsome (only 28) has as yet no family to my son, but she seems to discharge a great duty to his two children. The youngest, Sybilla, she educates herself being highly capable and the Boy has been at school at Sunbury for two years past, but always coming home at Holidays & as much made of in every respect as if they were her own, which to John must be very satisfactory indeed. . . . They live in a very pretty place called the Priory at Roehampton

about seven miles from town, where he goes & comes every day (Saturday & Sunday excepted).[15]

John Kirkland did not mention in this letter, probably having told it before, that his son John had stepped into his Uncle Nugent's job as general agent for the British army. Thus the transition to his next topic, his brother Nugent, was natural. "Your Uncle Nugent & his Daughter have been mostly living upon the continent since the death of his wife, and Ann & I, Kenneth etc, went & spent about two months with them at Boulogne & Paris rather more than three years ago."[16]

He next reported his son Alexander Mackenzie's marriage to Isabella Dowie (Alexander's first cousin) "about four years ago, who has since presented him with two as fine children as ever you saw. The eldest, a boy named John, and the other a Girl named Isabella." Alexander was then living in his father's former house on George Street in Glasgow, "carrying on the same business etc. to much greater extent & better purpose than formerly."[17]

John Kirkland explained that he had retired, leaving the business to Alexander, and had moved to the country, about four miles from Glasgow, and rode in to town a couple of times a week. His son Kenneth and daughter Ann lived with him. Kenneth had intended to be educated for the church, but he had had to leave his studies in England because of his health and had been living for the past two years with Alexander. "But in order to garner a more general knowledge of business, we intend shortly to send him to Liverpool for twelve months or so." Finally, John Kirkland reported that his son Nugent was in India at Kaire, "on the Bombay establishment," where he had a wife and son.[18]

Despite the rosy hues with which John Kirkland colored the description of his family, he was less than candid about the problems of his son Kenneth William. As later events would show, Kenneth's career bore striking similarities to that of William Kirkland's son Alexander.

Bad news from another relation and from an unexpected quarter disturbed William Kirkland's waning years. Paul Cameron informed him that the state bank had decided to bring suit against him as a guarantor of a loan of $3,000 to Robert Strange. Although John MacRae had also signed the note for Strange, the bank was suing Kirkland alone. Paul Cameron was distressed that the bank had sent him the case to prosecute. Kirkland wrote immediately to Strange and learned that Strange "had been renewing that Note for several years by paying Six Months discount in advance & installment of $150 each time & that was as much as he [could] possibly pay & meet his other engagements; that when it last became due about the first of January he sent up a Note for renewal with the installment and discount which they refused to receive."[19] Strange was informed that he had to pay the whole amount in four years by equal installments at three- or six-month intervals. Further letters do not reveal how this case was settled. Possibly Kirkland's relation of these facts to Ruffin elicited the usual response of monetary help, or possibly Robert Strange handled the repayment himself. Kirkland was able to conclude this letter on a happier note. William Gaston had sent him a small remittance from Archibald Murphey's estate against Murphey's debt to Kirkland.

Financial worries were not to harass Kirkland much longer, for in 1835 his health began to fail. Paul Cameron wrote to his father, "Our friends in Hillsboro are all well except good old Mr. Kirkland, who is complaining a good deal."[20] Kirkland was well aware of his condition, for he promised Bennehan in the fall of that year, "Should I be spared until the Spring I will then certainly do myself the pleasure of paying you a visit."[21] In February 1836 Paul reported that "Old Mr. Kirkland is indisposed, not able to get to town any."[22]

In May 1836 Paul gave his father a few details of his old friend's condition. "Old Mr. Kirkland is in very bad health, and I fear is not to be with us a great while; he has no appetite for any sort of food, nor can he take his grog! I have been urging him to set off and travel at his ease to the springs."[23] About the same time Phebe Kirkland, visiting at the Hermitage, received a letter from her sister Susan at home:

I write just a few lines by Uncle Tommy [Scott] to tell you how Pa is & I sincerely wish I could give you more favourable accounts. He continues about the same, rather weaker I think than when you left home. The Dr. has changed the medicine & is now giving him the blue pill & yesterday I thought he looked better & he said he felt better, but he is not so well this morning, still talks about going to the springs but has not fixed upon any definite time. As for myself I have but little idea that he will go at all, but I think if he intends to do so the sooner he does the better as he could stand the journey better now than a few weeks hence.[24]

William Kirkland was not to get to the springs. In mid-June, a letter from John Kirkland to Ruffin described his father's much deteriorated condition. He was confined to bed, weak, dropsical, and unable to turn over in bed.[25]

A few days later, William Ruffin sent his father an urgent message from Ayr Mount to come at once; his grandfather was declining and was "suffering beyond expression."[26] William Kirkland died the next day, June 21, a month past his sixty-eighth birthday. He was buried at Ayr Mount, where the bodies of his four infant sons were probably interred, though their graves are unmarked. Samuel Hancock, the brickmason in Hillsborough, walled the grave and laid the tombstone, a marble slab, ordered from Petersburg, on which was inscribed

William Kirkland
of Ayrshire, Scotland
died June 21, 1836
Aged 69 years[27]

Reactions to Kirkland's death came from many different sources, but the consensus was clear. He had been a man of great integrity, hard-working, fair to all, and much beloved. Duncan Cameron wrote to Paul in his characteristically bland and balanced prose:

> On our return here [Raleigh] we heard of the death of our es-teemed friend Mr. Kirkland—an event for which we were prepared by your last letter, as well as from Dr. Strudwick's letter to Mr. Ruffin on Saturday last.
>
> I have lost a highly esteemed friend of nearly forty years stand-ing—his family, a husband and father of inestimable value—& the community in which he lived, an honest man.[28]

The *Fayetteville Observer* said that he had emigrated to this country soon after obtaining his majority. "He was liberal, kind-hearted and hospitable, and noted for his sterling and unsuspected integrity," an odd use of the word but obviously equivalent in the writer's mind to *unques-tioned.*[29]

John Cameron, Anna Cameron Kirkland's brother, wrote to William A. Graham, "I have just heard of the death of old Mr. Kirkland, poor old gentleman; his loss will be severely felt by all who knew him, & his kindness and hospitality remembered long after many who made more fuss in the world shall have passed away."[30]

After the funeral, Anne Ruffin Cameron went back to the Hermitage to stay with her mother, who was pregnant with her fourteenth child. She confided to Paul, "As I expected, Mama has given way more to her feelings since she got home, than she did all the time she was in Hillsboro; the news of my poor aunts situation has greatly distressed and depressed her; she has come to the conclusion of going down the last of next week and taking up her quarters at Aunt Mary's, there to remain during her confinement."[31] It is not clear to which of her aunts Anne referred. It may have been Patsy de Graffenriedt, for civil disturbance in Columbus, Georgia, caused by refugees from Indian raids, made her family fearful for her, or it might have been Mary Ruffin Cain, who was dying of tuberculosis; it might have been the hysterical Phebe, who had taken her father's death very hard, or it might have been the unstable Anna, who was expecting her first child.[32]

Catherine Ruffin wrote to her father of the family's reaction and her own grief:

> I was truly glad to find them all so much calmer than I had expected; indeed I think they bear their late heavy bereavement with much more fortitude than I had imagined possible. Poor Phebe! looks thin & feeble but is improved greatly. She goes about now and evidently strives to submit as a Christian to the will of God.
>
> I find it so hard to realize this dispensation, my dear father; I cannot believe that I have seen the good old man for the last time in this world; he was always the first to welcome me when I returned to Hillsboro. I cannot describe my feelings when I passed his store and missed his much-loved form from its accustomed spot. I saw him everywhere; everything and every place is associated with my dear old Grandfather. Oh! how I missed him.[33]

Mary Anderson remembered the welcome he had given her on her return to Hillsborough. She had written to Catherine in January 1835, "Your dear old Grandfather, Cate, met me so like himself that but for shame I would have kissed his cheek."[34] William Kirkland had always been a favorite of Mary Anderson. When she had first moved to Hillsborough, she had written to Duncan Cameron of her gratitude to Kirkland for the interest he took in her sons. "I hope & believe he will at all times advise & correct the boys in any impropriety they may fall into—I cannot but be gratified that they are so near a man I have so high a respect & regard for as Mr. Kirkland."[35]

Kirkland's death stunned the family because he had been its keystone all their lives. And for the town, too, his death represented more than the regretted changes in the passage of time; he had been sincerely loved and was sorely missed. Anna Webb, the doctor's wife, wrote to Polly Burke, "Our town is full of strangers & we are all dull. Mr. K.'s death through [sic] a gloom over the town."[36]

Moreau Murphey's tribute gave the measure of the man himself; it was a mature judgment rendered thirty years after Moreau's departure from Hillsborough, and it objectively epitomized the uncle he had known in his youth: "In point of sterling integrity of character endowed with a degree of disinterested benevolence universally acknowledged where known, with a constant & unwavering desire to discharge promptly & faithfully every duty to God & man, I must confess that Uncle Kirkland had no superior, if an equal, in the catalogue of my acquaintance."[37]

If none of these eulogies caught the wonder in William Kirkland's life or its symbolic splendor, it is because none of these observers had the vantage of a full perspective from start to finish: they had not known him in his youth, and they could not see him in his historical niche against the backdrop of a vanished southern culture. They were too close both to the man and to the times. They saw only the magnified present. The distance from a butcher shop in Ayr to a distinguished plantation house in the heart of Carolina was far more than three thousand miles or sixty-eight years. It was a journey from one world to another. Only his son John of his crowded household and none of his numerous grandchildren had ever glimpsed its origins or could begin to understand what he had achieved. No obituary could encompass the courage, the determination, the hard work, the self-discipline, and the risk to dream that had gone into the journey from Ayr to Ayr Mount.

Days of Reckoning

EVEN WHILE THE family absorbed the initial shock of William Kirkland's death and dealt with his funeral and burial, one question must have been uppermost in their minds—had he made a will? William Kirkland had repeatedly assured John Kirkland and Thomas Ruffin that he would safeguard them from the effects of his indebtedness, and his known conscientiousness would have been additional reassurance that a will would be found.

After the funeral, Thomas Ruffin took his wife and daughter Anne Cameron, both pregnant, back home, leaving John Kirkland to initiate the search for a will. After a few days of apparently futile looking, John turned to Andrew Mickle for help in locating the elusive paper. Mickle found the will at the back of a locked desk in the store.[1] Mickle's deposition, in Ruffin's handwriting, given to the county court, described the event:

> The said William Kirkland departed this life at his own house in Orange County near Hillsborough on the 21st day of June last past and within three or four days thereafter he was requested by the family of the deceased to examine his papers & desks for the purpose of finding his will if he had left one; and this deponent [Mickle] in the presence of several persons (among whom were the said [Nathaniel D.] Bain & [Leo] Heartt) proceeded to make such examination in one of the stores in Hillsborough in which the said William deceased was concerned & which was conducted more immediately by himself & by the said Bain & Heartt as clerks therein. And he saith that in a desk in the said store in which for many years past the valuable papers of the said William & of the store, such as money, bonds, deeds for slaves & land were usually deposited, he & they found the said paper writing which is here shown to the deponent & offered as the last will & testament of said deceased & also found in

the said desk with the said testament money, bank notes, bonds for money payable to said William & to the said William Kirkland & Son & deeds for lands & slaves; & that he, the said Andrew, hath ever since kept the said will in his possession until the present day and the said Andrew doth further on his said oath depose that the name of the said William Kirkland (now deceased) inserted in the said paper writing & also subscribed thereto & also the said paper writing & every part there of is, as the said Andrew doth verily believe, in the handwriting of the said William deceased.[2]

The holographic will was unwitnessed and therefore a careful court proceeding was necessary in which Andrew Mickle, Bain, and Heartt proved its authenticity to the court's satisfaction. Paul Cameron wrote to his uncle the same day the will was found, "Mr. Kirklands will has been found—it is *just* the will we all wished he should make. The family are better."[3] Obviously the matter had been of grave concern. Behind the scenes, however, John Kirkland and Thomas Ruffin probably knew more than they were saying, as disclosed by a letter from John U. Kirkland to Ruffin on June 29: "I enclose you the original of a paper found among my fathers papers in his Lock desk found by Andrew Mickle & Wm. [K. Ruffin]. I was certain that such a paper had been prepared by him & could be found. It is exactly a Copy of the paper now sent you. I have no time to say more."[4]

The paper he enclosed without comment was in Ruffin's handwriting, obviously the original, as John called it, from which William Kirkland had copied his will. Its existence made plain that William Kirkland had consulted with Ruffin about the disposition of his worldly goods and had asked Ruffin to turn his expressed intentions into acceptable legal language. Some time later, William Kirkland made a copy of the model Ruffin had drawn up and signed it, an entirely legal procedure. Ruffin's copy was dated only June 1829; William Kirkland's will was dated October 16, 1829. Kirkland had waited four months before getting around to the task.

John Kirkland's certainty that his father had made a will and his absence of comment about Ruffin's original, except to say that the will matched it exactly, suggest that John Kirkland knew of Ruffin's assistance to his father but that he and Ruffin did not know until the will was found whether William Kirkland had followed his original intentions or changed any of the provisions. Ruffin had probably instructed William Kirkland where to keep his will and John Kirkland where the will was likely to be found—among William Kirkland's valuable papers—and how best to arrange for its discovery. Ruffin's immediate departure for home after the funeral, a few days of unproductive searching for a will by the family, its discovery by a disinterested party, Andrew Mickle, in the locked desk in the store among William Kirkland's other valuable papers—all were careful steps in a procedure that had probably been stage-managed by Ruffin to assure the will's acceptance as genuine and to allay any suspicion of impropriety on his own or John's part by discreetly concealing their prior knowledge of a will and its probable contents.

It is understandable that Ruffin wished to distance himself from the will's composition because he was not only one of Kirkland's largest creditors, protected from financial loss by the will's provisions, but also because he was designated a trustee and executor. He meant to avert any possible charges of undue influence in the formulation of the will, which read as follows:

> Whereas I am largely indebted to sundry persons & especially on Notes made by myself or by McNeill & Kirkland and indorsed by divers of my friends, particularly David Yarbrough, John U. Kirkland, and Thomas Ruffin . . . and it is my sincere desire effectually to indemnify my said indorsers and to secure the payment of the said debts & finally to pay them and all others which I may owe or be bound for Now to that end, and to dispose of my worldly substance, I do hereby give, devise & bequeath my whole Estate, both real and personal, wheresoever situate, & all debts due me and every interest & valuable thing to me belonging to my son John U. Kirkland and my son-in-law Thomas Ruffin Esquire (whom I hereby appoint my Trustees and the Executors of this Will) in absolute property. . . .
>
> In trust to collect all monies due to me, and also to make Sale of my Lands and real property and my personal Chattels & Slaves or such part or parts thereof as my Trustees and Executors or the Survivor of them shall in their or his discretion deem necessary or proper . . . at public or private sale, and out of the monies thus collected or arising from the sales of my said Estates, pay off my

funeral Expenses, and the other charges of managing and administering my Estate, and then pay off and satisfy all Debts by me owing in the order following—

any debt or debts for which the said David Yarbrough is my security, or any Note or Notes made by me which the said Yarbrough hath endorsed or shall have endorsed for my accomodation in the first place; And in the next place, such other debts or Notes of mine for which the said Thomas Ruffin and my son John are, or either is, or shall be sureties or security by endorsement or otherwise; And in the third place, any other debt or debts in any manner owing by me as the principal debtor or one of the principal debtors; And in the fourth place all and every other debt or debts which I may be legally bound and liable for. . . .

After the payment of the debts, the residue was to be

for the Use and benefit of my wife Margaret for & during the term of her natural life. . . . My said Trustees or the Survivor may in their or his discretion sell the whole of my said Estates or only so much thereof as shall be sufficient to pay the expenses, charges, and debts aforesaid; and that as to such parts as shall remain unsold after making the payments aforesaid, or as to the surplus of money if there be any after those payments be made, that my said Trustees or the survivor shall stand seised of the real Estate and possessed of the personalty to the use and benefit of my said Wife, & suffer her to receive the profits thereof, and put out the monies to interest, and pay over to her annually the accruing interest to her own use during her life. And upon the further Trust upon the death of my Wife, to make sale of all parts of my Estate of what kind soever it may be then remaining unsold, and the proceeds thereof as well as the Money then on hand or at interest and the whole residue of my property to divide into five equal parts or shares, of which I give & bequeath one to each of my four children Alexander, Mary, Susan, and Phebe absolutely; and the remaining fifth part or share, I order and direct to be put out by my Executors to interest to and for the separate use and benefit of my Daughter Martha during her present coverture and not subject to the debts, contracts, or disposition of her present husband. . . .

The situation of my affairs is such as to make it very uncertain what surplus of my Estate will remain after the payment of my debts; and feeling, as I do, the duty of providing with the greatest certainty in my power for the comfortable livelihood of my Wife in her old Age, I have considered it most proper and prudent to bestow upon her as I have herein done the profits of my whole Estate after the payment of my Debts to discharge which, I think is the first and highest duty. Hence, I have not made any provision for my younger Children during their Mothers life, as I doubt not that according to her ability she will with Maternal feelings afford them proper aid, and provide for them as members of her family—I mention this in explanation of my Motives and Hopes in framing this my Will, and not as creating thereby any legal obligation on my Wife to maintain the Children—which, I trust, is altogether unnecessary, seeing that they may be useful to each other, and their mutual Affection will form a sufficient bond between them.[5]

John Kirkland closed his June 29 letter to Ruffin: "I should like much if you can consistently with your own feelings act with me in the management of the estate."[6] Despite this personal request from John, Ruffin declined to serve. A number of reasons could explain his refusal after having allowed William Kirkland to write his appointment into the will. Probably the most cogent was the simple fact of Ruffin's removal from Hillsborough after drafting the will for Kirkland. Supervision of Kirkland's tangled affairs would have required his frequent presence in Hillsborough and access to Kirkland's documents and accounts. This he could not well manage when living in Raleigh, burdened with his responsibilities as chief justice of the state supreme court, or when home at the Hermitage, where the family moved in 1829. Another reason may have been an aversion to any further financial involvement or accountability in an affair that promised to be lengthy and vulnerable to legal actions.

Since Ruffin declined the appointment, John Kirkland was left to handle the difficult estate by himself. He had the benefit of Ruffin's advice when he wanted it, but he seems to have managed mostly alone, keeping meticulous accounts of the estate's receipts and disbursements until the early 1850s. As these accounts reveal, William Kirkland's largest debts were those to Duncan Cameron, $10,000, to C. F. Bagge, $7,000, and to Ruffin, over $9,700. There were, in addition, smaller loans from the Cape Fear and state banks to be repaid.[7] Whatever the amount of the debt William Kirkland owed David Yarbrough, whom he had specifically wished to indemnify by the provisions of his will, it had apparently been repaid or canceled before Kirkland's death.

John Kirkland first made an inventory of the estate in preparation for a public auction.[8] Not everything included in the estate was offered for sale. Obviously the family intended to hold on to Ayr Mount and most of its possessions, but there were items belonging to the plantation— tracts of land, livestock, produce, tools, and slaves—that were expend- able. While John Kirkland made his lists and arranged for the sale to take place in early November, after harvest, life's multiplicity of daily incidents ran on, accompanied by speculation and varying degrees of anxiety about the coming sale.

Anna Webb wrote to a sympathetic Polly Burke about the Kirklands and the auction, "I am afraid Mr. Kirklands property will sell very low; everything is to be sold & if there is anything left Mrs. K. is to have it her life time & then to be divided between Mary, Susan, Alexander, Phoebe, Patseys children. They are a very distressed family." Her sympathy for their plight, however, could not suppress the humor she found in an incident arising from their Episcopal leanings. She obviously did not look kindly on what she saw as the apostasy of some of the family members from Presbyterianism. "They had a grand farce there [at St. Matthew's] yesterday. Mrs. Ruffin had two children, & A. Kirkland one babtised [sic]. They found out in the evening Mr. Green had forgotten to conse- crate the water & they had the children babtised over. Dr. Webb says Roman catholick mum[m]ery." Mrs. Webb also spoke of her alarm at the number of girls attending the Episcopal Female Academy. (Mrs. Bur- well's Presbyterian school did not open until 1837.) "Our sons will get them as wives," she lamented.[9]

Margaret Taylor also testified to the family's distress. "The Kirkland family are much bowed down. Susan more than any of them. Mrs. Strange is here now; her health has improved since she came up."[10]

At the Hermitage, the health of old Mrs. Scott, "the mother of our family," as Thomas Ruffin called his wife's grandmother, began to fail. "Our beloved Grandmother continues in a very low state," he told Paul Cameron, "& cannot, we fear, last many more days, if hours."[11] Prep- arations had already begun for Catherine's wedding so that the family's emotions alternated between happiness for Catherine and sorrow for Mrs. Scott's impending demise. Again a letter from Margaret Taylor carried the news to Alabama. "Old Mrs. Scott died a few weeks ago; it was a great relief to them all; she was so deaf that you could not make her hear or understand anything."[12] Betty Machen Scott had endured hard times most of her life, beginning with the forced sale of her father's possessions for debt in Dumfries, Virginia, through the long, ignominious decline of her son-in-law Archibald Murphey's affairs, which in turn impoverished her son, on whom she depended for support.[13] When she lay dying, the prospect of yet another sale, the property of her last son-in-law, must have darkened her remaining weeks. None of her children had prospered long. Both Jane and Lettie had died young, and now Thomas and Margaret were living on debt's precarious edge.

Mrs. Scott's illness and death were kept from Anne Ruffin Cameron because she was pregnant again after several miscarriages and one still-birth of a premature infant. Her mother gave birth to her fourteenth child at the end of July, little more than a month after William Kirkland's funeral, but despite their caution, Anne Cameron was delivered of another stillborn child in December.[14]

The sale on November 1, 1836, which included only the personal property of William Kirkland, did not accomplish very much toward paying off his debts. The largest sum realized for that purpose was from the sale of ten slaves, which had taken place in September, when Dr. Edmund Strudwick made his purchase of what John Kirkland called the "blind, halt, and diseased" but whose sale brought to the estate over $8,000. At the November sale Alexander was delegated to buy in for his mother most of the house furnishings. As customary on such occasions, in a gentlemen's agreement, no one bid against the widow so that she might cheaply regain possession of things which, under more equitable laws, would already have been considered her own. When the sale was over, Margaret Kirkland owed a little over $2,000 for most of the contents of her house and outbuildings. A few household items and some plantation gear, stock, crops, and tools were sold to others, but these sales to outsiders amounted only to something over $600. The Kirklands' nine remaining slaves, much real estate, and William Kirkland's businesses had not been offered for sale.[15]

If John Kirkland thought that by waiting to sell land he might get better prices, he was badly mistaken. Instead of prices continuing to rise, 1837 brought financial panic and the collapse of the already much inflated prices and difficult times for those involved with financial markets. In March, John Kirkland appealed to Ruffin for help. Although he had sold a tract of his father's land near Louisburg for $600 and twenty-six shares of the Bank of Cape Fear stock ($650), he was facing imminent interest payments of $3,800 due on loans. He needed $1,870 immediately, and money was not to be had.[16]

Joseph Roulhac could testify to the serious financial panic and described the situation he found in New York in April 1837. "It is impossible for you or any other person not in the city," he wrote to Catherine, "to form any idea of the commercial distress now bearing on this city. It exceeds any thing of the kind ever before known. Failures to the number of 20 to 30 take place daily. I have heard of men with a large estate 6 months ago, who have been compelled to stop payment after having made great sacrifices."[17] Historians have calculated that $100 million worth of mercantile failures occurred in New York City within a single fortnight that April, a sum almost three times the annual expenditure of the entire United States government at that time.

During the years from June 1836 until July 1839, estate matters remained in a holding pattern for the Kirklands. John Kirkland periodically met interest payments on his father's debts, often with money raised through the sale of real estate. He sold three tracts of land in Orange County: the Cook, McKerall, and Cabe tracts, which encompassed together about 650 acres, for $1,400, just a little over $2 per acre. He sold a tract of land in Franklin County for $600. He had repaid Duncan Cameron's $6,000 loan and C. F. Bagge's $2,000 on a bond immediately after the sale of the slaves, and during the next years he paid off several other smaller loans. Not much changed in the family's manner of living. Alexander (with his family), Phebe, Susan, and Mary continued to live at Ayr Mount with their mother. In 1838 John vacated his father-in-law's house and bought and moved into the recently vacated property of William Mercer Green, lying between Ruffin's old place and Ayr Mount, a tract originally sold to Green by William Kirkland.[18]

Surprisingly, at this unpromising time, both Mary and Susan had offers of marriage. Was it because both had been named heirs of their father's estate? Mary's was from William Graham's older brother John, whose wife of many years had died just a month before William Kirkland. "Mr. John Graham has been down to see Mary Kirkland," Margaret Taylor told Eliza Johnston; "he is to be down again next week on his way to Fayette when Mary is to get his answer as I believe it has been a matter of consideration with her. She was very much opposed to going to Fayette. He has eight or ten children, one married, one or two of the others grown."[19] As nothing more is heard of this affair, they apparently could not agree and the matter dropped. Margaret Taylor's details of Susan's offer are even more enigmatic. Her suitor was a Mr. Bird. "She treated him very badly, would not come out of the room to see him the last time he was hear [sic]; he took it in good part, that she did not want to hurt his feelings."[20]

Some of William Kirkland's grandchildren were having their own problems. Betty Ruffin, always a favorite with her grandfather, developed a serious heart condition, possibly from rheumatic fever, and died in December 1838. In the same year both her brother William Kirkland Ruffin and her cousin Duncan Kirkland MacRae ran amok, causing anxiety and pain to the whole family. William's addiction to gambling, drink, and drugs brought him spiraling debts, which, in a vicious circle, led him to wilder excesses. He became so excitable early in 1838 that his father had to go to Salisbury to bring him home. In the fall of the year, while his parents were away in Philadelphia, he left the Hermitage, went to South Carolina, and, in a drunken fury, shot the landlord at the inn where he had holed up. He landed in jail.[21]

In the same year, Duncan MacRae, as hot-tempered as he was brilliant, was the principal in a duel while a college student at Chapel Hill. Distraught by his own behavior and fearful of his father's reaction to the news of his expulsion from the university, he attempted suicide by shooting himself through the lungs. His life was despaired of, but he recovered. Fortunately, Duncan's adversary was not fatally wounded in the duel, though Duncan went to jail until the matter could be investigated.[22]

More bad luck occurred in October 1838: the barkhouse at the tanyard caught on fire and occasioned excitement for the neighbors and a grand spectacle for those not dangerously close, like Robina Hogg Norwood, who described it to her daughter Jane:

> We had a fire on Friday night which at first caused great alarm but was soon found to be confined to Mr. Kirkland's Barkhouse full of bark, a large quantity. The wind had been quite calm and as it occurred a little after dark & plenty of help & water being at hand, not withstanding the other buildings belonging to the establishment

were within a few feet, the fire was happily prevented from spreading. It indeed appeared almost miraculous & must have been owing to very great exertions. It was a splendid sight. The town was illuminated the whole night & the fire continued burning until Sunday afternoon.[23]

During the fire, perhaps to prevent its spreading to adjacent structures, the town apparently blew up the barkhouse, for a sum of $118 was paid by the town commissioners to William Kirkland's estate as indemnity.[24]

Margaret Scott Kirkland died in 1839. Of all the members in the Kirkland portrait she is most in shadow; if she ever wrote any letters, they have not survived, and even letters that tell of other family members rarely mention her. On one occasion she visited her daughter Anne, when the Ruffins were living on the almost adjacent property, sufficiently rare an event to put in a letter. She seems to have stuck to her job of managing the house and servants, eschewing holidays at the springs, sojourns with her daughters in Fayetteville, or even with Anne at the Hermitage after the Ruffins' move, despite the presence there of both her mother and brother. Her daughter Phebe described her as fat, and it was undoubtedly from her that her daughters and granddaughters got their tendency to overweight. But from her, too, they seem to have inherited their love of flowers, particularly Anne Ruffin and Anne Ruffin Cameron. Like many another plantation dweller in the early nineteenth century, Margaret Kirkland pinned her hopes on silkworms. "Mama is very busy with her worms," Susan wrote. "They have nearly all commenced spinning & I wish they had all finished for they smell so offensive they keep me sick at the stomach all the time."[25] One lone mulberry tree survived until recently at Ayr Mount to testify to this effort.

Perhaps frugality was one of Margaret Kirkland's virtues. Mary wrote to Catherine that her mother had put such coarse sheets on the bed they were "enough to have rubbed my *behind* clean off and I would have had none in the morning to have sat down upon."[26] This was an example of the twenty-year-old Mary's sense of humor; she was said to have been full of fun and laughter and "in a gale of good humour always."[27] By contrast, Susan, the serious one, took life hard. She was the best of nurses, however, when someone was sick, but her pride was easily wounded. She closed a letter to Catherine, who had not written to her for some time, "Your affectionate but slighted Aunt Susan."[28] Neither

Phebe, Mary, nor Susan had much polish; the education they had been exposed to at Polly Burke's school had not done much for their intellectual cultivation and refinement, possibly a reflection of their mother's deficiencies. The tone of their letters—and the one just quoted is a good example—is strikingly childish and trivial in comparison, for example, with letters of Catherine Ruffin Roulhac, Susan Jane Gaston Donaldson, or Anna Cameron Kirkland. The younger Kirkland daughters exercised their minds on little else than family news and local gossip. Their father, unlike William Cain, seems not to have noticed their failings. They might well have profited from William Cain's advice to his motherless daughter Minerva: "When in company bring the conversation to some useful subject and avoid, oh do avoid *trifles*."[29]

Whatever her failings, Margaret Kirkland seems to have had generally good health. She apparently escaped the "vapors," the neurotic episodes that plagued her daughters, and only once does a letter mention her suffering from chills and fever. In 1839, however, Phebe said her mother was complaining of her breast; six months later Anne Ruffin reported that her mother was sinking fast and the doctor thought her disease had descended to the lungs, a description, which, taken with the earlier report, could suggest breast cancer. Margaret Kirkland died in July 1839 at about sixty-six years of age, with only a notice in the local paper to mark her death and not even that in the surviving family letters.[30] Unless a woman was a good correspondent or a diarist or had literary relations to chronicle her life, her chance of leaving any individual imprint in history's annals was minimal. It is not surprising, therefore, that so little is known of Margaret Scott Kirkland.

Her death cleared the way for further steps in settling William Kirkland's estate. John Kirkland once more prepared for an auction sale, at the same time, no doubt, wondering how the house might be saved for the family's use. This time, all the real estate and business partnerships would have to be included. Oddly enough, Thomas Ruffin was not part of any family councils that must have taken place, but he was present at the sale on November 6, which he described to Roulhac:

> We went to Hillsborough last week as the family there wished us to be at the sale of the estate. Mary & Susan purchased Air Mount & most of the negroes & furniture at moderate, though reasonable, prices upon the whole, considering the times. I was not consulted as

to any arrangements & do not with any certainty know what is intended finally. I suppose they desire their brother John to repurchase from them; and, if that can be effected, it will be well. But he tells me that it will depend altogether upon future matters, whether he can meet their views; such as meeting with a fair sale for his own place, the prices his sisters would ask, and the terms on which they would reside together. I hope all things will work propitiously; and, at all events, I trust that no disagreement will arise between the members of the family whose feelings hitherto have been so harmonious.[31]

Paul Cameron was also present at the auction and gave essentially the same information to his father: that Mary and Susan would take the homestead for $5,000. "I have no doubt Judge Ruffin would have purchased had the members of the family wished it."[32]

John Kirkland's sale accounts showed that Mary and Susan bid in the house and the 503 acres of Ayr Mount for $6,461. As their mother had done in the previous sale, they also bought back much of the furnishings and, in addition, seven slaves for $2,636.50, so that their total bids amounted to $10,386.46. John Berry, with his purchase of the 325-acre plantation tract of land for $2,800, was the second largest buyer at the sale. Two slaves were sold, Jenny and Charity, to William Cain and Harrison Parker respectively, for something over $1,000. Total bids for the day's sale amounted to $14,654.43.[33]

Possessions sold out of the family consisted of miscellaneous furnishings, produce, plantation stock, and tools. The Kirklands must have regretted losing a few items, for example, the mahogany sideboard bought by Catlett Campbell for $31.50. But old friend that he was, he may well have returned what he bought to the family. Isaiah Spencer, the proprietor of the Orange Hotel (now the Colonial Inn), built in 1838, bought six green Windsor chairs ($3.50), four walnut small tables ($6.20), and a high post bed ($2.00). Another purchaser was Jean Odend'hal, the French teacher at the Female Academy and also an experimenter with silkworms. His purchases included two bedsteads (one of cherry), old knives, forks, and a knife box, five old damask tablecloths, and two bureaus (one mahogany, one walnut). Thomas Ruffin bought eleven Windsor chairs, a bed chair (perhaps a chaise longue), steelyards, and a red and white heifer.[34]

Two days later additional real estate and business interests were sold. At his brother's and sisters' urging, John Kirkland purchased (for $1,200 and $7,500 respectively) the store belonging to William Kirkland & Son and the tanyard with all its stock of leather, bark, and hides, in both of which he already had one-half interest. After two independent assessors inventoried and evaluated it, John Kirkland also bought the stock on hand in the store for $6,000, a purchase he described as highly injurious to him because the goods were old and would not have brought as much money if sold in the usual way.[35]

Other real estate, sold at the same time or later, included town lots: number 2 (the storehouse William Kirkland had bought from Yarbrough), $705, and another portion of the same lot, $275; number 44 (the hatter and blacksmith shops), $200; part of number 6 (the shoemaker's shop in which the tanyard surplus leather was made into shoes and sold), $600; and number 179 (unimproved), $20. The storehouse in Louisburg was sold for $725.[36]

For all the outside world knew, the settlement of William Kirkland's estate was progressing smoothly and to the satisfaction of the court and the family. Appearances suggested that John and his sisters had been able to reach an agreement and that John had repurchased from them the Ayr Mount tract with its improvements, slaves, family house, and furnishings. A letter from Margaret Taylor to Eliza Johnston in 1840 described what might have been taken as persuasive evidence. "John Kirkland has moved to the old place; it has been painted, white washed with many of the trees cut down around the house; it looks like a new house. Mary and Susan live with them."[37] For those who may have wondered how he paid for it, the assistance of Samuel Simpson, his well-to-do father-in-law, was a logical and satisfactory answer. Having moved into his father's house, John could sell off his own adjoining property, which he had purchased from Green in 1838. This he did in 1842, conveying to William A. Graham the fifty-six acres adjoining Ayr Mount and fifty-nine additional acres of nearby land. (No recorded deeds show John Kirkland's purchase of either of these tracts.) By this sale, John Kirkland received $3,200 and three Hillsborough town lots (not specified by number), on which Graham then resided.[38]

Thomas Ruffin was right to foresee trouble. In 1842 a lawyer in Salem notified Ruffin that he had been asked to bring suit against John Kirkland for repayment of $3,000 owed by William Kirkland's estate to C. F.

Bagge on which no interest had been paid for three years. Alarmed, Kirkland wrote to Ruffin explaining that he did not have a cent and did not know where to borrow. His friends in Hillsborough were in a similar predicament. Would Ruffin lend him the $200 for part of an interest payment, which would satisfy the lawyer temporarily? Close reading of the letter discloses that the estate's debt to Ruffin, or the interest on that debt, was being partly paid with merchandise in the store. Kirkland suggested that the current charges against Ruffin be applied to this loan of $200, though he admitted that the amount ought to be applied another way. To be sure, in 1841 Kirkland had made a payment to Ruffin of $1,201.55 on his claim, an amount recorded in the estate accounts. Presumably Ruffin acceded to his wishes and the payment was made. The accounts show that John Kirkland continued to make payments of interest and capital on Bagge's bond and in 1851 paid off the remainder in full.[39]

In 1843 E. L. de Graffenriedt, his wife Martha (Patsy), Alexander Kirkland, Andrew Mickle, Mary and Susan Kirkland, and Phebe and Nelson McLester brought suit against John Kirkland for fraud and improper conduct in his office of executor.[40] The complaint has not survived so that the exact charges are not known. From John Kirkland's answer it is possible to guess that he was charged with withholding money due William Kirkland's heirs and being unwilling to transfer title to a lot in Columbus, Georgia, which William Kirkland had bought for the benefit of Patsy de Graffenriedt. John Kirkland's answer made no mention of Mickle or the nature of his demand, but it was probably Mickle's claim through a deed of trust from Alexander Kirkland in 1839 to all Alexander's right and title in his father's estate.

Dr. de Graffenriedt had written Ruffin in 1840, mistakenly assuming him to be one of William Kirkland's executors, complaining about the title to the Columbus lot. He had made improvements to it of stores and a dwelling for his family and resented paying taxes on a property that he did not own. He wondered what provision for transfer of the title from William Kirkland to Patsy or a trustee had been made since William Kirkland's death. Ruffin had written back to explain that William Kirkland had purchased the lot after he had written his will so that title to the lot became part of his estate, subject to division among the five named heirs. Undoubtedly the suit requested clarification of the lot's ownership and designation of a trustee for Patsy.[41]

William A. Graham, whom John Kirkland engaged to defend him, wrote out John's answers to the allegations, detailing John's actions up to that time in the settlement of the estate. They included the results of both auctions and the sales of the real estate and Negroes. One item in the list was "Ayr Mount Tract to Mary & Susan Kirkland Novr 1839 at 1, 2, & 3 years with Int[erest] not paid."[42] John disclosed that he had sold real estate amounting to $13,606. A list of estate property that remained unsold was also included. He explained that contested titles to lands in both Tennessee and Florida had delayed their sale pending decisions in those cases. (This is the only mention of William Kirkland's ownership of real estate in Florida, described as between five and ten thousand acres. Like the Tennessee tracts, it seems to have been assigned to him for a debt of Archibald Murphey's.) John Kirkland disclosed his purchase, at the insistence of the family, of the businesses in which he and his father were partners for the sum of $14,700 (only half of which was owed the estate) and confessed that he had not yet reckoned the accounts of these businesses to know what they showed. He explained that for several years before his death his father had customarily taken large sums from their receipts to reduce his heavy indebtedness. What these withdrawals totaled John did not know. John also mentioned the still unknown amounts that might be due him from the business accounts and as commission in his role as executor. He gave $16,724.93 as the sum of the disbursements he had made from the estate for one purpose or another, among them a large amount for the maintenance of his mother during her widowhood, the benefit of which most of the plaintiffs had shared as members of her household. John admitted that Alexander might claim payment of a debt of $650 to the firm of William Kirkland & Son against his legacy; and John finally itemized advances he had already made to each of the plaintiffs. These totaled $4,250. He appended a list of debts for which the estate was liable in whole or in part. These were the $5,000 bond to Bagge and $9,701.55 to Ruffin.[43]

How the case was settled is not known. Records of the court of equity, in which the case was presumably tried, since Graham's document was headed "Court of Equity, Fall Term 1843," do not mention the case. Possibly it was settled out of court with the conveyance of the title of the Columbus lot in trust for Patsy and with the heirs' agreement to await a final accounting of the estate. Possibly the deaths of Alexander and Phebe weakened the desire of the remaining plaintiffs to continue the action. In any event, John Kirkland's accounts of his father's estate, which continued up to 1852, itemized no payments to any of the heirs. The papers in the equity case, however, were made part of the court's record of William Kirkland's estate settlement.

As John Kirkland continued year by year to add to the accounts of receipts and disbursements of his father's estate, he noted receiving repaid debts of Henry Houze amounting to $1,600, Cape Fear Navigation Stock Company dividends ($896) and sale of 112 shares of its stock ($1,680), and payment on sales of Tennessee lands ($1,092), among other smaller sums. Receipts up to 1852 exceeded disbursements by $16,000, but there were never any payments recorded for John's purchase of the store, its goods, the tanyard, or Ayr Mount. And there the matter rested until 1883.[44]

One can only speculate about John Kirkland's actions. How did he square them with his Presbyterian conscience? Why did he make no attempt to legitimate his possession of Ayr Mount, if only on paper? Why did he make no payments to the estate for the shares of the businesses he bought and continued to operate profitably? Even if he had not paid for Ayr Mount with its furnishings and slaves or for the tanyard and store with its stock in trade, amounting in all to more than $24,000, surely he might have paid off the debts to Ruffin and Bagge and given small legacies to his sisters Mary and Susan. Perhaps his agreement to support them for the rest of their lives satisifed their claim. Perhaps Patsy's claim was satisfied by the transfer of the title to the lot in Columbus and the advance of $900 he had made to her. Perhaps the nurture and care of Maggie McLester, despite the payment John received for her board and keep, were due compensation for Phebe's share. But how did he account to Alexander's sons, who were raised in Hillsborough by their grandmother Cameron, a widow dependent on her father's generosity for her support? What claim of theirs did John Kirkland recognize? The answers to these questions lie in the grave.

Yet it is possible to imagine the thoughts that might have run through the mind of the still young man, only thirty-four years old when his father died. To sell the tanyard and store and start anew would not have furthered his father's intentions for him. Fairness surely did not lie in sacrificing himself, his wife, and children for his father's debts. Against such an eventuality William Kirkland had specifically tried to safeguard John. Nor would anyone have gained by John's impoverishment. With his dependent sisters to support, he may have realized that keeping the family together at Ayr Mount was the most efficient solution. John may also have totted up the business accounts and discovered that what his father owed the businesses when added to his own commission as executor totaled more than John's debt to the estate. There is not sufficient evidence on which to render a judgment. As for giving up Ayr Mount, John may have felt that more important than individual justice was collective family pride, symbolized by the house itself. Aware of what his father had surmounted in building Ayr Mount, he may have rationalized that to maintain the symbol of that achievement was his paramount duty.

❦ 15 ❦

Antebellum Years

JOHN KIRKLAND and his family moved to Ayr Mount in 1840. For almost forty years they reenacted, with some important differences, the life his father's family had lived there. The decades divide conveniently into two periods separated by the Civil War. During the first, John Kirkland went daily to town to tend his tanyard and mercantile businesses. Betsy, almost as prolific as her mother-in-law, soon filled the house with children. The slaves, under John Miller's direction, kept the plantation producing for home and market consumption. A new business partnership was established by Kirkland and John Berry called Berry and Kirkland.[1] Repeated purchases of bar iron for this business suggest that they ran a blacksmith shop; but the fact that a new courthouse, designed and being built by Berry, was taking shape in 1844 and 1845 may bear on the question. Perhaps they stocked and supplied building materials for the project.

Unlike his father, however, John Kirkland early involved himself in public service, beginning in 1831 as a town commissioner. By 1832 he was a member of the Wardens of the Poor, an oversight committee for the running of the poorhouse, and he became chairman of the wardens in 1846, a position he retained until 1868. In 1844 he served on the building committee of the new courthouse that gave the county a handsome Greek Revival structure and Hillsborough its most distinguished landmark. In 1851 he was appointed a councillor of state. By 1852 he was a justice of the peace, a position with administrative and judicial responsibilities.[2] Justices collectively ran the county: they made the laws, levied the taxes and appropriated the tax money, and presided at the county courts. They traditionally appended "esquire" to their names, a title connoting not only status and respect but also power.

John Kirkland interested himself in politics, too, with mixed success. In 1845 he ran for the office of clerk of the superior court, a coveted job, but he was defeated. In 1856 he may again have run for public office, for

Ruffin alludes to his electioneering. When the Civil War was over in 1865 and a new legislature was setting the wheels of state running again, Kirkland wished to be reappointed justice of the peace and clerk and master in equity (the latter a job similar to clerk of the court but confined to the court of equity), which he had held before the war for a short time. Samuel F. Phillips wrote to William A. Graham that he hoped Kirkland was reappointed a justice but not clerk and master in the court of equity. "Kirkland and Dr. Strudwick," he wrote, "have been sufficiently unpleasant in political matters, but their merits as gentlemen, and guardians of county interests and of peace (the latter qualities apply particularly to Mr. K. upon the bench) are so considerable that I am disposed to overlook the figure they have made in politics."[3] Phillips, a lawyer, recognized Kirkland's genuine capacity for fairness and correct judgment. John Kirkland was reappointed justice of the peace and continued until the new constitution in 1868 did away with the county court and substituted in its place five elected county commissioners and township officials to conduct local government. Kirkland was then elected county commissioner and served two terms, 1868–70 and 1874–76.[4]

During the 1840s, John Kirkland's family was not only growing but growing up. All but one of his eleven children had been born by 1850. Margaret Taylor told Polly Burke, "Betsy Kirkland has another daughter; they call it Margaret Jane. Sam is taller than his mother, very much like her family; William is like the Kirkland's. Mary and Susan [John's sisters] are very fleshy. Mary has an unbounded flow of spirits, Susan one of the warmest Presbyterians you ever knew. Mr. Kirkland looks well."[5] But Sam's maturing had begun to be a problem; she noted, "all friends fear [he] will be a great trial to his parents."[6] Fuel for this anxiety was an incident in 1844 when Samuel and William, then thirteen and eleven years old, were hunting; Samuel shot William above the hip. William was carried home in a sheet but was not seriously hurt. The gun had been loaded with an "oak-ball." The Kirklands took this incident in stride. A few months later all was as usual at Ayr Mount. "Mrs. K. looks as young & pretty as ever; she has a very sweet, pretty infant."[7]

In general, however, the 1840s were a difficult decade. The economy was unstable for merchants, the weather was bad for farmers, and the widespread prevalence of fevers was dangerous for everyone. The decade opened with Thomas Scott's stroke; it was not fatal, but it heralded a long, slow decline. In 1844 Ruffin described him after an attack of unspecified fever as having "but little disease at present & has had but little fever for a week past. But his system is much prostrated & his mind is in a feeble & wandering state. His complexion wan & his countenence haggard & eye vacant & his conversation not always connected or rational."[8] Scott lingered, however, until 1847. Two sons, John and Lewis Mitchell, survived him. A daughter, Nancy, had died early in life of tuberculosis.[9]

Jane Kirkland Strange finally succumbed to tuberculosis too. Susan and Mary were summoned to Fayetteville in late 1845 when her condition became critical.

> Susan and Mary Kirkland are at Mr. Strange's; no doubt you have heard she is dead; the girls were sent [for]. They left here on Saturday, reached there on Monday. They did [not] think she was so low, went to bed. She slept quietly the first part of the night; she waked and told Susan she felt as if she was dying. The family got up, sent for the Dr.; he came and said she was no worse. She insisted that she was dying, gave some directions about different things, and what a happy thing it was she should be taken as early in the winter, that she would be spared great suffering and friends, a great deal of anxiety; then she wished to spend the little time she had in prayer, died calmly early on Tuesday. Judge Strange was at Smithville at court.[10]

Strange's absence from home was not as callous as it might seem. He had become used to his wife's bouts of illness and close calls, and he fully expected her to rally as usual. He was shattered by her death. He answered Catherine Roulhac's condolence letter eight months later, still in unabated misery: "Everything that reminds me how lately I was a happy husband and how many friends I had for the sake of her who is no more renews the bitterness of my grief and my heart is melted within me. Men do not often die it is said of a broken heart, but God knows what is to become of me. I often feel as if I should die immediately. None but those who have felt it know the bitterness of a broken spirit."[11]

Besides her husband, Jane left five sons and a daughter. Strange managed to put his life back together, and the children, dutiful and responsible, were a comfort to him. The association with their mother, however, turned out fatally for two sons, John and Alexander, who died of tuberculosis in young manhood within a year or two of each other. Twenty-year-old Alexander had been sent to Scotland in the hope that a change of climate might restore him, but death overtook him in the house of his cousins and John Kirkland's friends the Strangs. Until the second son's death, there was a coolness, even animosity between Robert Strange and Thomas Ruffin that prevented the development of real friendship or even cordial relations. An encounter at court, the only place their paths crossed, would result in little more than a few verbal exchanges, not always friendly. Ruffin's detachment is reflected in a comment in a letter to his wife after such a meeting that Strange had become "fatter than I ever saw him; in a few years, he may be a match for Mr. Bennehan."[12] Ruffin was punctilious in observing social conventions, however, and he wrote to Strange when he heard of John Strange's death in 1852 and apparently hit a responsive nerve. Strange wrote back regretting the long rift, which he attributed to stinging remarks Ruffin had made to him, and acknowledging the gratitude he still felt for Ruffin's having introduced him to Jane Kirkland, from whom, he said, all his earthly happiness had flowed.[13]

Unfortunately, although his old spirit was broken and his life was drawing to a close, Strange remarried in late 1853, possibly to have someone to take care of him, and he died within three months after a stroke. Between the time of his stroke and his death he wrote a new will, which outraged his eldest son, James W. Strange, because it left his entire estate to his widow, to be divided among his children only after her death, and it made no provision whatever for his youngest son, French, still a minor. After considerable negotiation with the widow, George McNeill and Robert French, representing the children, persuaded her to take a child's part of the estate. Thus Robert Strange passed from the scene causing contention to the end.[14]

In the last year of the 1840s new graves were added to the cemetery at Ayr Mount. John U. Kirkland's daughter Betty Kirkland, four years old, fell ill in late 1848. In the new year her worried father wrote Ruffin that she had had fever for five weeks and was skin and bones. She continued to eat a little every day, particularly ice cream. He also reported that his cousin Kenneth was declining rapidly. "Gets out of bed with assistance only to have it made up."[15] Kenneth was Kenneth William Kirkland, the son of John Kirkland of Glasgow, whose ill health had precluded his studying for the ministry many years before and who had been trained for business instead. As the local newspaper explained, Kenneth Kirkland "had lately come from Scotland, commenced business in New York but was taken sick & came south to stay with his relatives."[16] The sick at Ayr Mount prevented the presence of any of the Kirklands at the marriage of Margaret Strange to the Reverend Joseph Caldwell Huske. James Strange wrote of John U. Kirkland's situation to his brother Robert: "He poor man has the hand of Providence pressing heavily upon him at present. His little daughter Betty has been quite ill for several weeks & from all accounts I fear will never recover. Our Scotch cousin too is in ill health there so that none of the family will be able to leave home."[17]

Both patients died within a day of each other, Kenneth of tuberculosis.[18] James Hogg's daughter Robina Norwood attended the funeral and dwelt on the event in a way typical of mid-Victorians, who had a lugubrious appetite for deathbed minutiae and the pathos of mortality.

> A short time ago I witnessed a most solemn melancholy funeral scene at Mr. John Kirklands—a cousin of his wife who was in bad health but not apparently ill came to pay a visit & spend some time for his health—was taken ill & died. On the following day a lovely little daughter of Mr. K.'s who had been long sick (but was then believed to be recovering) died—were both buried at once. The gentleman was in middle life—had a wife & four children in Scotland to whom he hoped to return; but how vain are human hopes & wishes—there lay side by side in their coffins, the man in life's prime & the blooming infant. I cannot paint the grief of the parents. This was the second lovely infant they had lost but tho' I sympathize with the Bereaved I cannot grieve for the death of an infant. . . . But the man at a distance, his fate unknown to his bereaved family, was an object of real & true commiseration—relieved however by the consideration that he was believed to be a consistent Christian.[19]

All John Kirkland's epistolary talents must have been called into play by the letters he next penned to Scotland. In reply he heard from Kenneth Kirkland's brother John. He thanked his cousin for the news of his "unfortunate brother" for whose death an earlier letter had prepared them.

> I have alluded to poor Kenneth as our unfortunate brother, but he cannot justly be now so considered when we know that a Merciful Providence consigned him to the affectionate care of yourself &

your most amiable family at a period when it was of such infinite Importance to his Eternal Welfare that he should have time & opportunity to reflect upon the necessity & best means of preparation for it.

Poor fellow. He had those qualities you so well describe—but his besetting sin—of recent years—had well nigh extinguished them. Deeply grateful to the Almighty & to you are we all on this side of the Atlantic for the Serenity of his latest days.[20]

John Kirkland of Ayr Mount must have been painfully reminded of his brother Alexander as history seemed to have repeated itself in Kenneth Kirkland's life: a younger son, very tall and robust in appearance, his hopes for a career blighted—in Kenneth's case by both tuberculosis and drink—and a premature and unexpected death at the nadir of his worldly fortunes.

The letter from 80 Pall Mall, London, also contained much family news, probably one of the last communications between the Old World and New World Kirklands. The man who wrote it stood close to the top of the heap in a nation that then preeminently ruled not only the waves and international finance but was also close to completing an empire that would include one-fourth of the world's peoples. In 1838 John Kirkland had been knighted by Queen Victoria at the Palace of St. James's. He did not mention this triumph in his letter—perhaps he had earlier communicated it to his American cousins—but he discreetly referred to his wife as Lady Kirkland. During twenty-one years of marriage she had not produced any children but continued to be an exemplary mother to his two children by his first wife. John A. Vesey Kirkland, then twenty-nine years old, had made a career in the army and was "military secretary to the Commander in Chief of our North American Provinces," in other words, Canada. "He married a Canadian lady when he first visited that country with his Regiment the Coldstream Guards ten years ago & altho' his marriage at the early age of 19 was a great mortification to me at the time, he has been happy & respected & Mrs. Kirkland is an excellent mother of their 3 little children."[21]

Sir John Kirkland's younger child, Sybilla Augusta, would soon be twenty-eight years old. Although she was very pretty, her father explained, she had not yet been tempted to leave the paternal roof.

For the American John Kirkland, 1849 ended not much better than it

had begun. Anna Kirkland's insanity recurred, and Susan Kirkland suffered a long period of ill health. John Kirkland wrote to Roulhac, to
whom he had just apprenticed his difficult son Samuel, "Susan is still
ill—she thinks she has consumption." He thought it was only her nerves,
a variety of the Kirkland female malady. She felt constriction across her
breast accompanied by great oppression and excited heart action. Her
appetite was poor.[22] Margaret Taylor described her case to Polly Burke:
"Dr. Strudwick thinks her lungs are affected; great depression of spirits
on the subject of religion; her family try to think there is not so much the
matter with her; I fear they have tampered with her case too long."
Mary, on the contrary was "the picture of health, grows more like her
mother every day." Susan improved temporarily, but in 1853 Margaret
Taylor again wrote, "Susan Kirkland is not in good health. I see very
little of her; she is not able to walk to town."[23]

The Kirklands did not lose touch with their Georgia kin, but there
were few opportunities for communication or meeting. Edwin Louis de
Graffenried, Jr., visited Hillsborough in these years and his relations
liked him very much for his piety and resemblance to his mother. Miscellaneous letters brought other scraps of news from Columbus. Polly
Burke heard from her niece Mary Ashe Moses, John Kirkland's old
flame: "I saw Mrs. De Graffenreidt in Columbus; she is very fat & looks
remarkably well, very much like poor Phebe. Her eldest daughter Jane I
did not see as she was quite sick. Victoria is a beautiful girl not like her
mother's family. She says she is color'd like her father, who I do not
recollect."[24] Later, a Georgian acquaintance informed Ruffin that Jane
de Graffenried was to marry Judge Thompson of the Florida Supreme
Court, "certainly the very ablest lawyer in that state."[25] James Strange
heard that "the Dr. had become quite steady in his habits; poor man I
fear it will be of short duration."[26]

Patsy de Graffenriedt was instrumental in having a tombstone put on
Phebe Kirkland McLester's grave. She requested Hines Holt, McLester's
executor, to do something about it, for although tombstones had been
provided for both McLester's grave in Savannah and his second wife's
grave in Columbus, none had been placed on Phebe's. In his cautious and
calculating way, Holt suggested to Ruffin that Maggie McLester might
wish to write an inscription and order a stone because he did not know
what to write and, furthermore, appropriate tombstones were not easily
obtained in Columbus. His real motive became clear when he suggested

that the stone could be paid for out of Maggie's funds. The eleven-year-old Maggie had no choice. Undoubtedly Ruffin, as her guardian, wrote the inscription and Maggie paid for the tombstone. At least she got the credit: "This tomb is erected by her only child Margaret A. McLester aged 11 years March 1854."[27]

As antebellum civilization neared its crest in the 1850s, economic conditions improved, the financial markets stabilized, and the weather was good for farmers. The Whig party reforms of the 1840s were beginning to be felt generally. Improvement and progress were noticeable in every facet of life. Most important economically to the state was the building of the North Carolina Railroad, which irrevocably changed the way people lived. It bridged regional gulfs and breached paralyzing isolation. It made markets accessible to thousands of farmers previously shut off from commerce by insurmountable problems of transportation. The apathy, sense of hopelessness, and depression of earlier decades were dissipated by optimism, even euphoria.

John Kirkland undoubtedly shared in the amendment of mood and commerce. The railroad, which would prove a blessing in so many ways, caused a contretemps, however, in the Kirkland family. John Kirkland saw an opportunity to secure a steady addition to his income and somewhat relieve his finances; he hoped to become secretary and treasurer of the railroad company, a job for which he was qualified by education and experience. William A. Graham recommended him to the officers, and he was offered the position. He was required to post bond for the performance of his duties and asked Ruffin to oblige him by signing the bond. Ruffin agreed to do so only with a number of stipulations, the nature of which can only be surmised because his letter has not survived. Ruffin understandably wished to protect himself from Kirkland's debts. Whatever the character of his conditions, however, John Kirkland found them humiliating, and he refused to accept them and declined the job. His letter to Ruffin made plain that Ruffin's lack of trust had hurt his pride. He had only his good name to leave to his children, and he meant to do all in his power to keep it unblemished.[28]

Immediately Ruffin was full of remorse and wrote back trying to soothe Kirkland's feelings and apologizing for the offense he had caused. He asked his wife to go see her brother and help make his peace with him. Kirkland accepted the apology but defended his wounded pride. Long pecuniary embarrassment, he explained, had made him hypersensitive to questions of probity; but he reiterated his keen sense of all Ruffin's past kindnesses to him. Kirkland's sense of injury must have been rekindled a few months later, however, when Peter Browne Ruffin, since 1844 a merchant established in William Kirkland's old store on lot 2, was made treasurer and secretary of the railroad. Thomas Ruffin had signed his son's bond for $80,000.[29]

Having failed to obtain the railroad position, John Kirkland accepted the job of cashier of the Hillsboro Savings Institution, a respectable post but not so remunerative as the railroad job would have been. He held the post until the bank was forced to close during the Civil War.[30]

Another Kirkland, however, found a livelihood in the railroad. After a short stint with Roulhac, Samuel Simpson Kirkland discovered that merchandising was unsuited to his talents and left his apprenticeship. Margaret Taylor gave Polly Burke an update on the Kirklands: "Susan and Mary Kirkland are well, John has a houseful of children, three grown: Sam is employed on the Rail Road, William is not at all promising; his father tries to keep him employ'd about his business; Annie is like Maria [Simpson] Hill. Phebe's little girl Mag goes to school to Mrs. Burwell. Maria made a short visit here this summer; she has lost a little girl two years old, has four children. Mr. and Mrs. Simpson continue there [sic] summer visits here yet, both much broken. Sarah [Simpson Manly] and five children are here now."[31]

For Betsy Kirkland, life in Orange County must have become ever more agreeable as her married sisters settled near her. Maria married Thomas Blount Hill in 1836 and had a fine house opposite Saint Matthew's Church. Mary married Henry Kollock Nash in 1838 and lived in town. Sarah still lived in New Bern, married to Matthias Manly, but, like her parents, spent much of the summer in Hillsborough.[32]

Despite Samuel Simpson's solid and continued prosperity, John Kirkland seems not to have drawn on him to any extent to meet his obligations. A debt to Simpson of about $600 is noted in one of Kirkland's store accounts and may have been repaid in merchandise. Simpson's will, proved in 1856, mentioned possible advances to Elizabeth Simpson Kirkland but no specific amounts. Simpson left his wife all his real estate—his home and brick store in New Bern, his house and lots in Hillsborough, slaves and furnishings and considerable bank stock—and to his four sons-in-law in trust for his daughters he also left bank stock. Elizabeth Kirkland was to receive for her "sole, separate, and exclusive use" twenty shares of the Bank of New York worth $500 a share. She was given the power to dispose of it in part or in whole and, if any residue remained at her death, to bequeath it to her children or grandchildren. Her father also added to her bequest any money advanced to her or money received as repayment, wording that suggests a gift of money to her. It could not have been a large amount; none of his daughters' shares exceeded $10,000 to $12,000, and if he had made a large advance to Betsy, it would have been reflected by a discrepancy in the amount of her bequest and her sisters'. A few years later he added a codicil to his will after a split in the New York bank stock replaced his original 40 shares with 200 new shares worth $100 each. He amended her bequest to 150 shares and added the remaining 50 shares to his wife's portion. Two years after Samuel Simpson's death in 1856, his widow died, leaving a will that divided her estate among her four sons-in-law in trust for her daughters. In the settlement of her mother's estate, Betsy Kirkland must have received a substantial addition to her separate wealth, and, unfortunately, just as likely must have had many occasions thereafter to draw on it.[33]

Vignettes of the Kirklands in the 1850s are limned in letters of friends and relations such as one from Alice Ruffin in the winter of 1855.

> I went down to see Uncle John this morning & regret to say that I found him very unwell; he looks badly, & has been confined to bed for more than a week. I had no idea of his situation, or I should certainly have gone to see him before. He suffers constant pain in his head day & night, & gets but little sleep. It is not headache, but a pain in the back of his head. Aunts Betsy & Mary think it rheumatism; Aunt Susan says it is neuralgia. He is a bad patient, you know, & will not call in a physician. He has a shocking cough, hard & dry, in fact has taken a very violent cold. He walked home from Dr. Strudwick's on a bitterly cold night week before last, without an overcoat, & has been sick ever since. He is very anxious to get some lemons, & there are none in town to be begged or bought.[34]

She asked her mother to send some lemons from her greenhouse and to visit him.

Comparatively few letters describe the Kirkland children or their emerging characters. One gives a glimpse of Samuel Kirkland in a role reminiscent of his father's courtship of Mary Ashe. Samuel Kirkland had fallen in love with Sally Jones, who seems to have spurned him after an on-again, off-again courtship of several years. James F. Cain, the author of the letter, recounting the outing of a large party of Hillsborough young people to a Virginia wedding, painted Sam and his sister in a flattering light.

> Sister Mary was exceedingly anxious to attend the wedding & I of course was compelled to become her escort. I was very unwilling to go having been absent from home so much & being at the time troubled with asthma—but Father insisted & she pouted & so I went. We were joined by Miss Sallie Jones, Miss Green, Mr. Cameron, S. Kirkland & John Webb (of course). We had a most delightful time both going & coming. More pleasant than while at Cascade [the Broadnaxes' plantation in Virginia]. Sam Kirkland, I am glad to say, acted towards Miss Sally with the greatest propriety, neither intruding nor yet retiring or distant so as to attract attention or remarks. She says, "she is glad to see that her manner has caused a change in Mr. K's bearing towards her." *I* thought she gave him every inducement to resume his addresses, but he, to his family's & friends' great satisfaction, shows no inclination to renew his attentions in that quarter. Annie Kirkland [Sam's sister] I think was most admired of all the ladies, and she is a beautiful & clever, in short a, "nice young lady."[35]

James Cain was not always so complimentary of his cousins. When his sister Mary Clack Cain became engaged to Thomas Ruffin, Jr., he wrote to Minerva, "Clack's affair is not known here to any one but Julia [his wife] & myself—but I presume will soon be as the Ruffins know it— when the Kirklands get it, it will be sown broadcast throughout the land—They mind other people's business as well as ever."[36]

At the end of the decade the first of John Kirkland's children married, but it was William Whedbee rather than Samuel Simpson. His bride was Susan A. Hardee, a niece of General William J. Hardee of Georgia, no doubt an auspicious choice for furthering his career, for William Whedbee Kirkland had early decided that he wished to go into the army. Possibly through Senator Willie P. Mangum, he had been able to get an appointment to West Point in 1852. An account of his life there reached his cousin Annie Roulhac. "I find that the North Carolinians here are very popular. Wheeler is universally beloved & he deserves it. My predecessor George Anderson [a grandson of Mary Cameron Anderson and later Confederate general] was very much, and I am glad to say that a great deal of that good feeling has fallen to me. So much for having a popular predecessor, it is a great advantage to a New Cadet."[37]

Unfortunately, Cadet Kirkland did not capitalize on his advantage and was expelled for infractions of the academy's numerous and strict rules. He was able to obtain a commission as a second lieutenant in the marines in 1855, however, and settled into a career that very soon won him glory. Soon after his marriage in 1859 he brought his bride to Hillsborough, where they were feted by his parents, the Thomas B. Hills, and the Camerons.[38] Later that year he wrote Ruffin, requesting help in transferring to the army and reviewed his career up to that date:

> I have always desired to be in the army. I deprived myself of this privilege by my improper course at West Point; but this is past. In 1855 I was commissioned in the 1st Regmt of Cavalry by Mr. [Jefferson] Davis—but owing to my having been a cadet, and my class being at the Point, at that time, I was not permitted to accept the appointment. To relieve my disappointment Mr. Dobbin [James C. Dobbin, William A. Graham's successor as secretary of the navy] gave me my present commission. I have now been in the Marine Corps three years and better and during that time have served in China two years. There I saw active service and was fortunate enough to receive a distinguished notice from my commanding officer. But I am anxious to return to the army to my old regiment if possible or to any regiment, but I would much prefer mounted service.[39]

Whether or not he succeeded at that time, his ambition was soon fulfilled, for the secession of the southern states and the establishment of the Confederate army at the outbreak of war gave him the opening he desired.

William Whedbee Kirkland's cousin William Alexander Kirkland may have been influenced by him or his own father's example at Captain Partridge's school to seek a career in the armed forces. Neither one could expect to pursue the life of a planter, and apparently neither had a taste for the professions or business. "Little Bill," as William Alexander Kirkland signed himself to his cousin Annie Roulhac, set his sights on the navy and at the age of fourteen was accepted at the Naval Academy at

Annapolis, in 1850 only five years old. William A. Graham, who became secretary of the navy in 1850, probably appointed Little Bill to the academy. Very much in the mold of his father, Alexander McKenzie Kirkland, both in appearance and disposition, Little Bill had difficulty accepting authority and disciplining himself to regulations. The style of his letters, even at fifteen—breezy, debonair, unabashed—shows the temper of the boy. He complained to Annie Roulhac of another cousin's neglect. "As for Annie Kirkland—she doesn't deserve to be treated with common Christianity. Just tell her from me that she is the very meanest white gal in all my extensive circle of acquaintance—and accordingly I don't value her—Shucks. No more'n I don't."[40]

He viewed the routine at the Naval Academy with humor which disguised the impatience he really felt. He described a typical day to Annie Roulhac:

> Being aroused at day break by the sound of a *drum*—that of course gives the awakening a *military air*—And then we are summoned to sweep out our rooms—ditto *drum*. After which, we are assembled, formed in two lines—answer to our names as they are called—and then marched to the Chapel—Where, the right Reverend Naval Chaplain attached to the Institution drawls out a prayer—At the expiration of which half the midn [midshipmen] have to be awakened before the order of retreat can be assumed—or before they can be stood up, and marched out—from the Chapel we march direct to the mess hall—with one or two Professors and Naval Lieuts (who act Police, to put down rebellion among the young gentlemen) hanging on the skirts of the force—ready to pick out any Rebellious person who shall be guilty of talking, laughing, or otherwise setting at nought the rules of the institution, for the formation of future Nelsons, Drakes, & Van Tromps—On arriving at the tables—over which one of the said Lieuts are keeping guard—we each stand behind the chair individually assigned until this August Personage deigns to give the order "Seats"—At the same time curling his moustaches and glancing his eyes rapidly around—to see that no disorder prevails—[41]

No more successful at first than his cousin William, Little Bill was perilously close to expulsion. In a letter to Graham written after he had been at Annapolis for eight months, he disarmingly described his situation: "My stay at the Academy is rendered extremely unpleasant by the number of my demerits, of which . . . I have a great many."[42] In another letter to Graham he explained, "I entered it [the Academy] under altogether mistaken ideas. I imagined that as a midshipman I could act in any manner I chose and without any danger of being dismissed."[43] Though he stood a poor chance of passing his examination and was likely to be dismissed, he was entirely dependent on succeeding. He had no alternatives.

His astonishing disregard of regulations was reckless, but it was balanced by so strong a desire and such pertinacious efforts to succeed that he carried the day. He was sent to sea for five years and taught the basic skills and discipline he needed. At the end of 1855, he returned to the academy and finished his course, after which he was again assigned to sea duty. While serving on a series of ships in the Brazilian squadron, in a flotilla that patrolled the South Atlantic waters, he met and married (around 1860) Consolación Gowland, the daughter of an Englishman and a native Uruguayan, residing in Montevideo.[44] The outbreak of the Civil War found Little Bill firmly entrenched in the United States Navy. It is difficult to know whether purely pragmatic dictates of his career kept him at his post or whether ideological shifts made him consciously choose the Union standard during the war. To some of his southern relations, however, his northern partisanship made him not only a maverick but a traitor.

A combination of differences, ideological and economic, exacerbated by firebrand politicians, alienated the North and South and eventually overcame the forces for reason and accommodation, in which many North Carolinians had long participated. Despite last-minute and urgent attempts to maintain peace, North Carolina was swept into the southern Confederacy, which proclaimed its independence, on the grounds of states' rights, from the United States, and civil war ensued. Inevitably the fate of the Kirklands, with all they lived for and by, was at stake. For them, geography had cast the die.

🍂 16 🍂

The End of the Line

WITH THE OUTBREAK of the Civil War in 1861, after valiant efforts of men like Ruffin and Graham to prevent secession had failed, four of John Kirkland's sons and their numerous cousins joined the Confederate forces. William Whedbee Kirkland became colonel of the Twenty-first North Carolina Regiment and made a name for himself and his brigade at Bristoe Station and Cold Harbor, in both of which actions he was wounded. He played a leading role in the battle of Winchester, where he was also wounded, taking a stone wall from the Union forces, and at the first battle of Bull Run. Before the war was over, he was made brigadier general, a responsibility he shouldered with honor. His battalion included the Eleventh, Twenty-sixth, Forty-fourth, Forty-seventh, and Fifty-second North Carolina regiments. After surviving unscathed at Cemetery Ridge in the battle of Gettysburg, the Wilderness, and the siege of Petersburg, he fought on to the bitter end at Bentonville.[1]

His brothers Samuel and Alexander volunteered in 1861 and John, Jr., in 1862. Samuel, who married Eliza Gaston, a granddaughter of William Gaston, in April 1861, was promoted to captain the same year but had to resign in 1862 for health reasons. Later he served as an aide to Generals Alfred M. Scales and William D. Pender. His last service was as quartermaster in Hillsborough. Alexander was an artillery officer in Company E, Third North Carolina Regiment, before transferring to a cavalry unit, Company E, Forty-first Regiment. In 1862 an injury to his foot from a horse's falling on it required a long recuperation before he rejoined the forces. He resigned in April 1864. In 1863 John Kirkland, Jr., was in Company A, Sixty-sixth Regiment, but he did not serve very long. His health was not good, and by early 1864 he was at Newberry Courthouse, South Carolina, where he married Fanny Harriet (Hattie) McLaren, a daughter of James and Sarah McLaren and a native of Charleston. A newspaper account of his wedding described him as "Captain John Kirkland, Jr., late of Maj. Gen. Early's Staff."[2] He wrote in the family Bible, "Owing to the state of the Country, our marriage was very quit [sic] & only a few friends were present to witness the happy union, which took place precisely at 11 o'clock A.M. After partaking of a hasty repast, we bid adieu to our friends and took the cars for Ayrmount, N.C. the home of my childhood."[3]

During the last year of the war, only General William Kirkland still remained with the fighting forces. "I think John Kirkland has but one son in the army now," Elizabeth A. Bingham wrote to Polly Burke in 1864; "3 others are in government employ. Wm., General Kirkland is a very brave officer. He is now suffering from wounds in Richmond. Mr. K. has several daughters grown—none married—they are highly spoken of. Mary and Susan still live with him. Are very much what they used to be. Mrs. Kirkland's health is delicate—Her sisters, Mrs. Hill & Mrs. Manly live in Hillsboro."[4] (She might have added the fourth sister, Mary Simpson Nash, who had inherited her father's house and lots in Hillsborough.) All four Kirkland sons came through the war with their lives, but ironically, the youngest son, Robert Roulhac, safe at home, died of an infection, possibly diphtheria.[5]

Another grandson of William Kirkland played a conspicuously gallant part in the Confederate army. Duncan Kirkland MacRae, whose career in law had been sidetracked by public service, again closed his books and took up his sword. He had been a representative in the General Assembly in 1842, United States district attorney in 1844, consul at Paris in 1853–57, and Whig candidate for governor in 1858. In 1861 he was appointed colonel of the Fifth North Carolina Regiment, which distinguished itself in the Peninsula Campaign, particularly at Williamsburg. He was twice wounded and forced to retire from active service, whereupon Governor Zebulon Vance sent him to Europe on a crucial search for badly needed supplies and markets for southern cotton and state bonds.[6]

Both of Alexander Kirkland's sons also served but on opposite sides of the conflict. Robert Strange Kirkland early volunteered in a company made up in South Carolina, where he was working at the time. During service in the Army of Northern Virginia, he was badly wounded in both legs at the battle of Gettysburg and left on the field for dead. He slowly recovered, gradually regaining the use of his legs.[7] His brother, William Alexander, having chosen to stick with the Union, quickly worked his way up the chain of command to the top. He was already a lieutenant commander in 1862 on the sloop *Jamestown*, posted at the China Station. In 1863–64 he was in the East India Squadron and in 1864–65 in the Western Gulf Blockading Squadron, commanding the ironclad *Winnebago*, the only assignment that pitted him against his kith and kin.[8]

For the families at home, the Civil War meant a continuous depletion of resources and supplies, and at its close, it left a population ill-clothed, ill-fed, thoroughly exhausted, and impoverished. Bright, if infrequent, moments of military success kept spirits high until almost the last year of the war. Hillsborough enjoyed a lift in mood one night in January 1863 when Confederate President Jefferson Davis, traveling from Virginia to Greensboro, North Carolina, got off the train at the station, was greeted by former Governor Graham as master of ceremonies, and made a heartening speech to the assembled people, telling them he saw peace ahead.[9] All assumed he meant peace through victory. Such expectations had faded, however, by the last year of the war, and almost everyone longed for peace at any price.

Oral tradition preserves a yarn about Ayr Mount in the closing days of the war, when General William T. Sherman was negotiating a surrender with General Joseph E. Johnston at the Bennett Place near Durham, not ten miles away. At the same time, General Wade Hampton had taken up quarters in the office at the Dickson farmstead, a mile southeast of Hillsborough, and there was consequently much movement of the bored and restless soldiery about the countryside while they awaited the outcome. The story goes that a group of Yankee soldiers came down the road past Ayr Mount and met its owner, an old man sitting by the roadside. They asked what place that was. After spitting out a bit of the reed he was chewing, he said he didn't know, that he never went near the place; it was for crazy folks. The soldiers went on by.[10] Thus Ayr Mount was saved from the proverbial looting by Union forces.

It was not the style of John Kirkland to play the sly hayseed, gulling Yankees, or to sit by the road under any circumstances, genteel and dignified man that he was. But folklore sacrifices truth to storytelling. As the years of hardship and struggle receded, remembered incidents evolved into anecdotes, shaped and altered in retelling until historical accuracy became almost irrelevant to psychological demand. That the Civil War generated so much lore is not surprising, for it was the most momentous event in southern experience. In it died not only shocking numbers of young men through disease and wounds but an economic system and a way of life that could never be revived.

Social changes were forced on the defeated population, not just by the Reconstruction government but by economic necessity. And emancipation of the slaves liberated the planters and their families, too. Women began to lose their shackles as they were no longer confined to the roles the old culture had assigned them. Paul Cameron had wise words for his children. He told them, "You will have to labour to live either by your head or your hands!"[11] It was a prophecy that affected John Kirkland's daughters as well as his sons. The stigma had been removed from work.

John U. Kirkland's daughter Susan Mary Kirkland, known as Sue May, put to use her gentility, the only capital she had. She seems to have taught music at Peace College in Raleigh, possibly in addition to other teaching or administrative responsibilities, for her experience and the success of her work there recommended her for a post in the new State Normal and Industrial School in Greensboro when it opened in 1892. Her title, lady principal (comparable to dean of women), comported well with her impressive presence. She was in charge of the social activities of the college, teaching the young ladies deportment and propriety and guarding their morals. She imparted to the institution the desired atmosphere of refinement and culture to which the young ladies, it was hoped, would aspire. Generations of them testified to the efficacy of her example. While proper and dignified, she was still sympathetic and warm. Her fashionable clothing, fine furniture from Ayr Mount, and well-trained servant—props for her setting—were matched by gracious manners, a discerning eye, understanding heart, and disciplined character. Many stories about her were recorded by grateful students, none more agreeable than her answer to a teacher who complained of two students sitting unchaperoned in a parlor with two young men. The teacher reminded Sue May that when *they* were young, *they* were not permitted to receive gentlemen without a chaperon, to which Miss Kirkland replied, "Yes, and see what it did for us."[12]

Maggie McLester, whose education and expectations of a financially secure life had not only matched but greatly exceeded Sue May's, found herself faced with the equally unpleasant alternatives of accepting the charity of her poor relations or finding a way to support herself. Thomas Ruffin had to tell her that her inheritance, entrusted to him, had turned to dust; he had exchanged the gilt-edged securities her father had invested in for Confederate bonds now not worth the paper they were printed on, a move he had also recommended to John U. Kirkland, who had followed his advice in respect to his wife's inheritance. All that was left to Maggie was $1,500. The sweetness and magnanimity of her character were patent in a letter to Ruffin. She had heard that he was troubled by her loss, but she urged him not to be; she was grateful to him and would not have wanted him to do otherwise.[13]

In 1866 she wrote again to tell him that she was engaged to be married to a Mr. Calder, who was as poor as she was but the noblest man alive. She joked that she would not be writing him any more begging letters. Calder's name, however, does not appear again in her letters. Instead of keeping her own house, Maggie offered her services to others. She spent at least one postwar year with General Kirkland's family in Baltimore, where he worked as an agent for a Savannah firm. From 1887 to June 1901 she was matron at Saint John's Hospital and, under its new organization, at Rex Hospital in Raleigh. From there she moved to the Odd Fellows Orphans' Home in Goldsboro, where she spent a miserable year. Probably one of her most congenial posts followed as companion and housekeeper to her aunts' elderly friend Maria Nash, who had been a principal of the Nash and Kollock School until old age overtook her. Close to home and friends and happy in a familiar setting, Maggie justified the affection and regard, won long before of Maria Nash's nephew Dr. William Strudwick and his wife, who had named a daughter for her.[14]

In 1905 she went to Wilson Sanatorium for less than a year before moving in 1906 to the family of a Mr. Briggs, also in Wilson, where she lived until 1912. Several more Wilson families employed her before she retired to Ayr Mount to live with the children of John U. Kirkland, Jr., whom she loved as her own. To their "Nannie," each of the daughters was "my precious child," and the youngest son signed his letters to her "your baby boy." In 1908 she had written in a diary, "I left my children for Wilson. Wish I could live with them but can't be dependent as long as I can work." She lived her last years at Ayr Mount, where her heart was, and died in 1921.[15]

The youngest daughter in John Kirkland's household, Maria Simpson, married in 1873, as her oldest sister, Annie, had done in 1865, so that only Margaret Jane, called Maggie J. to distinguish her from Maggie

McLester, remains unaccounted for. At first, she probably took short-term jobs in the households of relations and acquaintances when they needed assistance, but primarily she remained at home to help her parents as long as they lived. Thereafter, as letters from her to Maggie McLester show, she seems to have lived in Raleigh, at times in her sister Maria Crow's family, at others in housekeeping jobs like Maggie McLester's, until her death in 1895. In any case, she was not at Ayr Mount in December 1869. That year her father's Christmas letter to Maria, then visiting her aunt and uncle Manly in New Bern, describes how small the family had grown: "Instead of so many bright faces—bright & youthful & cheerful faces around our hearth to welcome its [Christmas's] advent as in former years there were but four sedate & solemn looking individuals long passed the meridian of life & two others of more tender age & no egg-nog. Upon the whole it was rather a dull time. We missed you & Maggie J. & the little children & Hattie & John to give life to our festivities."[16]

The four adults were, of course, John Kirkland, his wife, and two sisters; the two youngsters were his grandchildren, the children of Annie Ruffin Kirkland and Halbert G. Hill. Annie had died the previous year, and her children became permanent residents of Ayr Mount. A Nash daughter described to Polly Burke her old friends and pupils at this time: "I have not been to the Kirklands, but have seen both Mary & Susan, & they are in mature life, very much what they were as children."[17]

The years had all but severed John Kirkland's ties with the Kirklands abroad, but he heard of them once more through William A. Kirkland, whose adherence to the Union had not alienated his uncle. In the same Christmas letter to Maria, John Kirkland reported that William had lately been in London and tried to call on Sir John and Lady Kirkland, but both were in "wretched health." Possibly they had retired to their country house, the Priory, Rickmansworth, away from the bustle of London, for William did not see them.[18] This was the last news John Kirkland had of his cousins across the water.

His contact with William Alexander Kirkland shows that there were no hard feelings between John U. Kirkland and Alexander's sons. He must have taken pride and satisfaction, therefore, in William's professional rise. Far-flung service, ranging from the Far East to the South Atlantic, from commander of the Mediterranean Squadron to rear admiral of the European Squadron, did not change "El Rubio," as blond

Little Bill was called in South America, where he cut something of a heroic figure by his independent action in rescuing the American minister to Paraguay. (Charles A. Washburn's safety had become endangered because of his alleged participation in an assassination plot on the life of the Paraguaian dictator Francisco Lopez.) Through a long career he retained his sense of humor, irreverent manner, and independence, never entirely tempered to naval protocol. His promotion to vice admiral was barred, for example, despite Assistant Secretary of the Navy Theodore Roosevelt's support and recommendation, because of Kirkland's critical remarks about American missionaries in Turkey and other injudicious expressions of his opinions. Before these indiscretions occurred, however, in 1895, Rear Admiral William Kirkland was present with his flagship of the European Squadron for the ceremonies that inaugurated the Kiel Canal. The German emperor, Wilhelm II, whom Kirkland entertained aboard his ship, presented him as a memorial of the occasion with a gold snuffbox encrusted with diamonds—twenty-eight small and six large—the kind of present the kaiser was fond of dispensing and which the United States government allowed Kirkland to keep.[19] Unfortunately, John Kirkland did not live to see much of this heady success.

From Christmas 1869, John Kirkland's tenancy of Ayr Mount had less than a decade to run, the most difficult period financially that he had ever faced. He was already in his sixties, a venerable age in the nineteenth century, and physically weakening. Business was almost moribund, but he could not go where opportunity offered. Responsibilities tied him to Ayr Mount and Hillsborough. Savings, which he had invested in Confederate bonds, were gone, and land prices had plunged to a fraction of their former value. Selling the house and land would have yielded next to nothing even if a buyer could have been found. Paul Cameron knew the remedy and preached it persuasively to Tom Roulhac, one of Catherine's sons: "Be wide awake—be prudent—*and make your mark soon*—But my word for it, the *theatre*, in point of *action*, is the first consequence. . . . Had George E. Badger made his home in Boston or New York—his family would not now be in want and his professional reputation would have placed him in the front rank with Webster & Kent. Had Thomas Ruffin made his home in London, he would have sat on the bench with Lord Eldon. This is no extravagance. To be at the right place at the right time leads to fortune & to fame."[20] But John Kirkland, like the preacher himself, was too old for this advice.

During the war he had rented the tanyard and two slaves to James M. and John A. Turrentine for $650 a year. Tanning was still a profitable business, for leather was a crucial item in the war effort; armies moved on shoes. Steven, a skilled tanner and shoemaker, accounted for $150 of the charge; Ben, an old, diseased slave, was hired for only his board and keep. The contract specified that Ben was not to be put to any hard work. By a series of sales of real estate, John Kirkland contrived to survive during and after the war. In 1862 he had sold three town lots (126, 127, and 128) between Margaret Lane and King Street, possibly the three unspecified lots which William A. Graham had owned and which he had used as part payment for the acreage he purchased from John Kirkland in 1842. The sale of the three lots brought Kirkland $2,350.[21] In 1870 he sold his father's remaining town lot, number 44 (the hatter's shop) for $590. His last sale occurred in 1877, when he and Betsy parted with 209 acres for $1,000. They no longer needed the land, for they could no longer work it without help. John U. Kirkland's twenty-nine slaves enumerated in the 1850 census had undoubtedly increased significantly by 1865.[22] Their presence had made the plantation productive. Without them it was useless because he could not afford the labor to work it.

Nor did John Kirkland have the benefit of his sons' help. As his letter to Maria made plain, none of them lived at Ayr Mount. The Georgia connections of his wife had led William Whedbee Kirkland to settle in Savannah after the war. As a general of a vanquished army he could look for no future in his profession. He had to muddle through with civilian jobs of little moment and small remuneration. Samuel continued to find work with the engineering departments of railroad companies, his prewar experience standing him in good stead. Of Alexander's life after the war nothing is known. John Kirkland, Jr., apparently hoped to settle in Hillsborough, but circumstances temporarily decreed otherwise. A statement about him by William A. Graham suggests that he was forced to leave the state to avoid court action. "John Kirkland & family left yesterday evening," Graham wrote his wife, "to reside in Charleston. Your Brother writes me that the Judge declined to set aside the irregular judgements taken against him & Mr. Bond, as I had hoped."[23]

In the 1870s John Kirkland, Jr., was an agent for Carhart & Brother, a New York firm of importers and grocers, which did extensive business in the two Carolinas. Although the family Bible records the births of his three oldest children in South Carolina, the four youngest were born either in Hillsborough or at Ayr Mount. Sometime in 1872, the family apparently moved back to Hillsborough, where John Kirkland, Jr., continued in his job.[24]

Little is known of John Kirkland, Sr.'s, last decade. It must have seemed a succession of deaths, beginning in January 1870 with that of Thomas Ruffin, the redoubtable bulwark of the family. He had lived a life of unrelenting labor to support his enormous family in good style. The list of his property for taxation in 1861 showed how much wealth he had been able to accumulate despite his losses. He then owned close to two thousand acres and sixty-seven slaves, who, he calculated, were worth $23,450. He had investments worth $70,250 and $2,200 cash on hand. He was also the administrator for Joseph Roulhac's estate, worth $35,950, and had money in trust for his daughter Alice, $2,100, and his son Sterling, $4,333.33. Despite heavy losses through money invested in Confederate bonds, freed slaves, and plummeted land values, Ruffin was still well fixed and able to live a comfortable, untroubled domestic life in his retirement, an existence that his long years on the bench had precluded.[25]

Anne Kirkland Ruffin could at last enjoy her husband's company. Her health improved, free of the stresses imposed by plantation and family responsibilities, which she had shouldered alone. Ruffin was fully aware of her accomplishments and what he owed her. In a letter that can only be called a eulogy if not a love song, he wrote in his seventy-ninth year:

> With my wife I have lived nearly fifty-seven years, & from her I have derived nearly all the pleasures & enjoyment of life, my highest moral culture, my satisfaction with my employments & duties & the excitement to their performance, besides being indebted to her care & economy for the breeding of our children & the prosperity of my affairs & the serenity of my temper. She has been the whole world to me, & it has long been my prayer, that God may not leave me behind her—I should feel alone in the world without her & never be able to hold up my head, when I could no longer look on her face & get her counsels.[26]

After being pardoned by President Andrew Johnson (a humiliating requirement of every Confederate adherent with property worth more than $20,000), Ruffin was free but uncertain how to rebuild his life. The

question was settled for him by the gift from his son-in-law Paul Cameron of a house and lots in Hillsborough, later known as the Ruffin-
Roulhac place and now restored and used as the town hall.[27] It consisted
then of an entire block between Orange and North and Churton and
Cameron streets and encompassed, besides the main house, all the usual
outbuildings necessary to a well-run establishment. Ruffin named it Little Hawfields, memorializing his old home in the Hawfields. By the move
to town, he and Anne Kirkland Ruffin could enjoy the enlivening company of eight of their children and a crowd of grandchildren, as well as
the proximity of stores, church, medical attention, and railroad. Ruffin
also got his wish not to outlive his wife.

When he fell ill in early 1870 with a bad cold, it progressed, as his
colds always threatened to do, to pneumonia, and he died on January 15
at the age of eighty-two. Paul Cameron understood not only the importance of the man within his own family and place but also in his historical context. He therefore wrote a long letter to Bennehan Cameron, his
son, away at school, relating in detail Ruffin's illness, death, and burial
to impress on his son a sense of the occasion. He concluded:

> Thus my dear boy I have given you in a hurried way the particu-
> lars of your Grandfathers death, an event that has filled us all with
> deep & lasting sorrow. You & I will long remember his last Christ-
> mas dinner. He was so bright, so happy, so glad to have those that
> he had loved. His first toast was to Mama, who[m he] had loved &
> with whom he had lived for 60 years as man & wife—his next to
> Aunt Kate, his eldest born. His next "to all his children and grand-
> children—in Miss., Cal., old Virginia & Maryland." His next to
> "My big son Peter" & wishing him a new razor. His next to his
> grandson Bennehan Cameron with his promising young—mous-
> tache.[28]

Anne Ruffin survived her husband by five years. On her eightieth
birthday Paul Cameron sent her his love. Probably few mothers-in-law
have ever inspired such genuine affection.

> I now offer you the tender greetings of one who has known you
> long and loved you much. As I walked from your house I recalled
> the fact that our acquaintance commenced more than a half century
> ago at the dinner table when you occupied the unpretending cottage

yet standing in the yard. At that well spread (for I well remember the large head of yellow pickle cabbage) table sat yourself, your then rising and afterwards eminent husband and who had then been on the bench—and was then in the zenith of his fame as a laborious and successful advocate—who then had but just left the Court House at a late hour attended by your excellent Father and his old friends Dr. Umstead, Mr. Isaac Holt [Lettie Scott Holt's husband], and my uncle Mr. Thomas D. Bennehan. Of those that sat at that table you and I alone survive! But it was not the "yellow pickle" or the Judges kindness in making me go home with him & his old friends to dinner that first won my love for you. Subsequently [he meant "previously"] when I was a neglected school boy and boarding in the village with a large no. boys I happened at your house with my brother Thomas on a Saturday when you discovered *our condition* and with the tenderness and kindness of a good mother you spent a large part of that fore noon in combing our red heads. It was this act that first made me think you were "the salt of the earth." I have often told this of you and it ignited a spark in my heart that has never gone out. It is now 42 years since I entered your family as a son-in-law and during all that time I have never had cause to question your affection and confidence in me for one moment. And it is to me one of the most cherished pleasures of my life to call up my personal intercourse with that great man Judge Ruffin and know to what an extent I enjoyed his sympathy and personal confidence. And whilst I did not aspire "to the office" it is at least pleasant to me to know that I was entrusted by you and his children with the high duty of preparing *his* "monumental inscription" and the more so as it was so entirely approved by you. During all the 42 years that I have had your daughter & namesake for a wife I have shared with you many joys & sorrows. I shall continue to do it to [the] end.[29]

The year that began with Thomas Ruffin's death ended with Susan Kirkland's. Long deprived of her usefulness in the family by ill health but wrapped in the comfort of her religion, she died in November 1870. Anne Kirkland Ruffin was next in 1875, followed by Patsy de Graffenriedt in 1877 and John Kirkland in 1879. The last remaining child of William Kirkland, Mary, outlived John by only a year. Perhaps it is just as well that so few descriptions of them remain from their final years. Possibly Mary kept her good humor and laughter to the end. The only picture of John Kirkland to survive shows an elderly man with white hair and lusterless, sad eyes. Paul Cameron knew he had had little cause for joy for many years.

> Our old neighbor & friend Mr. Jno Kirkland passed away on Saturday morning about 6 o'clock as I am told with much suffering. I saw Dr. William Strudwick on yesterday who was with him at the last. He says he died at last with water on the heart. He will be buried this evening at 4 o'clock. He had lived as long as his friends could wish—Life had but little left to induce him to stay if he had any choice about it—He had made his 3 score & ten & life held out [to] him no sort of inducements to remain: he could contribute nothing to the maintenance of his large & dependent family. He dies I think in 75 year—the senior of Dr. Strudwick by 5 days. He is to be intered this afternoon at 4 o'clock.[30]

A slightly different version was given by Thomas R. Cain to his sister Minerva Caldwell: "I suppose you have already heard of the death of Uncle Jno Kirkland—his last moments were those of peace, quiet & consciousness—I have seen nothing & heard but little of the family since his death—none of the boys save John were here nor have been, though Sam has been expected for several days—"[31]

John Kirkland's last years had been embittered by family discord. Undoubtedly Thomas Cain and Paul Cameron, although they said nothing about it in their letters, were perfectly aware of the disturbing lawsuit Peter Browne Ruffin had brought against John Kirkland in the superior court in 1877, when Ruffin, as his mother's executor, was trying to settle her estate. The family harmony that Thomas Ruffin had wanted maintained was finally shattered. His will had bequeathed everything to his wife, directing that there be no division among his children until after her death, to assure her the greatest possible comfort. Only after her death, therefore, was the note uncovered that disclosed William Kirkland's still unpaid debt to Thomas Ruffin. Peter Browne Ruffin had no such tender scruples as his father about family solidarity. He felt legally bound to recover the debt to his mother's estate. With the consent of the other heirs and recognizing the slender means of his aging uncle, another nephew might have winked at the claim and written it off as a bad debt, but not all his brothers and sisters were as well fixed as Peter Browne Ruffin, and their claims had priority for him. Anne Ruffin's estate was worth something over $76,000, and the debt was $3,500 plus twenty-five years' interest.[32]

By the end of September 1877 John U. Kirkland, who had been summoned by the sheriff to answer the complaint, had returned no answer. The court ordered that Peter Browne Ruffin was entitled to recover the sum from the goods and effects in the hands of John U. Kirkland. Only little more than a year later, Kirkland was dead and more difficult problems were brought to light. Because he died intestate, Betsy Kirkland had to appeal to the court for her widow's dower and a year's support. The probate judge, Pride Jones (Peter Ruffin's brother-in-law), asked James Webb, Jr., and Thomas R. Cain to make an inventory of John Kirkland's personal possessions and from the total to allot to Betsy Kirkland the necessary household articles and supplies for her own use and that of the two grandchildren who lived with her. As a result, she received two bedsteads, a wardrobe, ten chairs "much worn," a dressing stand, a rocking chair, four tables, two sofas, a sideboard, a bureau, a wagon, and miscellaneous pots and pans. She was also allowed two mules, a steer, two cows and calves, and seven of John's ten shares of North Carolina Railroad stock. The total value of all this was $500.[33]

Augustus W. Graham, a son of William A. Graham, was granted the administration of John U. Kirkland's estate, and he soon discovered that no final settlement of William Kirkland's estate had ever taken place. The same probate court that awarded Betsy Kirkland her share of her husband's estate heard Graham's declarations concerning William Kirkland's estate. Probably because of this discovery, the Kirklands found themselves forced to make other living arrangements. In early December 1881, Thomas Cain told Minerva Caldwell, "Except John's family, all the Kirklands go to Raleigh the 1st Jan'y to remain till the first July. They are boarders in their own house. So report goes."[34] Presumably, Betsy Kirkland planned to join her daughters Maria Crow and Sue May Kirkland, who were established in Raleigh, taking her two grandchildren with her. John Kirkland, Jr., and his family would remain at Ayr Mount until some legal disposition could be made of the property. Why John's family was allowed to stay and Betsy's determined to leave is not clear. Betsy escaped this last humiliation: she died before the proposed move on December 30.[35]

Betsy Simpson Kirkland had had the good sense to make a will. In it she devised to her children sums of money which would be realized by the sale of the bank stock inherited from her father. To her unmarried daughters, Susan Mary and Margaret Jane, she left $4,000 each. To Maria Crow and Samuel Kirkland she left $3,000 each. She left to Samuel $2,000 in trust for her daughter-in-law, Hattie Kirkland, wife of her son John, Jr., to be used for Hattie's support and that of her children. (Presumably creditors still dogged the younger John's heels, and no money was safe in his keeping.) After Hattie's death the money was to be divided among Hattie's children. The residue of her estate she left to her sons William and Alexander and the two children of her daughter Anne Hill.[36]

The law's usual delays postponed until after Betsy's death the settlement of both John U.'s and William Kirkland's estates. Having finally determined what each one consisted of, Graham proceeded to sell the assets of both estates. John Kirkland's estate contained three shares of North Carolina Railroad stock, Confederate bonds worth $64, three town lots (213, 215, 216), 230 acres of land (later sold to John W. Graham), a few miscellaneous other tracts amounting to little over 100 acres, and one-half interest in the store building at Churton and King streets. Because of the depressed prices of real estate and the nature of the sale—at the courthouse door—all this property brought no more than $1,300. When the costs of administration, small bills, and the judgment to Ruffin were deducted, nothing was left.[37]

And what of William Kirkland's estate? In 1881, when Augustus Graham appeared before the probate court as the proper person to administer John U. Kirkland's estate, he swore that although William Kirkland died leaving a last will and testament, "his estate was not fully administered before the death of his executor," John U. Kirkland. Graham asked for and was granted the administration of that estate as well. He then swore under oath that William Kirkland's estate consisted of "His Home Tract, ½ Interest in Lot corner of King & Churton Street & Tan Yard Lot" worth about $3,000. Graham also testified that "Alexander Kirkland, Mary Kirkland, Susan Kirkland, Phebe McLester and Martha DeGraffenreid [sic] are the Devisees who are dead and their heirs are the parties entitled under said will to the said property subject to payments of the debts of testator."[38]

In due course, the tanyard lots were sold to Paul Cameron for $495, and the half interest in the store lot (no. 25) was sold to David Parks for $200. Jesse Miller, nephew of the old overseer, bought thirty-six acres for $366.61. Since by then the terms of Elizabeth Simpson Kirkland's will had also been executed, Samuel Simpson Kirkland, her oldest son, as trustee for John, Jr.'s, wife and children, was able to purchase Ayr Mount for $1,254. After administration costs were paid, $2,143.61 remained in William Kirkland's estate to be divided among the beneficiaries: the children of Patsy de Graffenriedt, Alexander Kirkland, and Phebe Kirkland.[39] William Kirkland's intentions and the letter of the law were to be fulfilled at last.

❦ *Afterword* ❦

AFTER THE FINAL settlement of William Kirkland's estate in 1885, another century was to pass with Kirklands living at Ayr Mount. In that century not a child first saw the light of day in the old house where so many had been born. The years went slowly but not kindly. Money became ever scarcer, and the last tenants were repeatedly forced to sell off acreage to keep going. At the end, on the remaining fifty-five acres, they built concrete block rental houses on small lots at the western border of the yard.

John Kirkland, Jr., Harriet, and their seven children, the last born in 1883, lived out their days as though under a spell. The two oldest sons tried to escape the inertia and accidie that enveloped the place by working in the North, where one married, but they made no mark in their careers as salesmen and left no children behind them. Those at home clung to the house and to each other, growing more protective and interdependent. When their mother died in 1908, title to Ayr Mount passed to six of her children. Gallantly, the four sons deeded their interest in the property to a trustee to be held for the benefit of their unmarried sisters Bessie and Hallie. At the sisters' deaths, the deed specified, the property would revert to any surviving sons.

Their sister Sadie McCready Kirkland was not mentioned either in the settlement of her mother's estate or in her brothers' deed of Ayr Mount to the trustee, yet Sadie lived until 1918, much of the time at Ayr Mount. A card sent to her from her brother Samuel, addressed to the State Hospital for the Insane at Morganton, gives the only clue to her exclusion from the legal documents. Later she was transferred to the Dix Hospital in Raleigh. Her only epitaph is a line written in the family Bible by Maggie McLester, then living out her years at Ayr Mount: "My darling child Sadie Kirkland died 5th April 1918 daughter of John & Harriet Kirkland."

Of the other two sons, one also became a salesman, traveling for a shoe company, even on the road his thoughts never far from home. The other farmed the dwindling acres, coaxing from the soil wheat and corn for market and, with his sisters' help, vegetables for the family. A few cows, calves, and pigs provided meat for the table, supplemented in season by game and fish. Though they were never actually in want and always proud, the quality of their lives was pinched, and they warmed themselves in the afterglow of a brighter past they had never known. Symbolic of the decline was the abuse of the Broadwood fortepiano: no longer played, its strings and weights were plundered for fishing line and sinkers.

One after another the brothers and sisters of the last generation died, and title to Ayr Mount was passed along till it rested in one surviving brother, Samuel Simpson Kirkland. His marriage late in life saved him from a solitary existence but could not save the line. A house that had been built as the cradle for a dynasty had become a vestibule to the tomb.

Although the Kirklands are gone from Ayr Mount, the splendor of William Kirkland's achievement—the house on its hill by the river—is in no whit diminished. If anything, it is enhanced by the restoration that took place in 1985–86. The concrete block rental properties have been removed. The clearing away of brush and trees crowding the structure has revealed the austere dignity of the architecture. A rebuilt porch in the original style, replacing a later porch across the width of the central section, has reestablished the proper dimensions. Largely invisible structural reinforcement and cosmetic repairs, respectful of the builder's intentions, have brought the house back to its pristine grandeur. Steep roofs, looming central section, clean profiles against the uncluttered skyline again compose a forthright, strong, and elegant monument to the dream of the man who built it.

"So go the landmarks," James Cain wrote when the Kirklands planned to move to Raleigh in 1881. But he was wrong. People go; landmarks remain.

~ *Appendixes* ~

Appendix A. William Kirkland's Purchases of Land in North Carolina

Description	Date	Source
Orange County		
Corner portion of lot 6, 33' by 65', Hillsborough	1795	1795 Tax List and Orange County Deed Book (OCDB) 5:463
346-acre tract on waters of Eno River (sold in 1802)	1796	OCDB 5:666
385-acre tract on Eno River, Kinchen's old place (later known as Ayr Mount)	1799	OCDB 8:251
118-acre tract adjoining the above tract	1799	OCDB 8:297
Tract of 5½ acres adjacent town (purchased with four others, sold in 1807)	1802	OCDB 13:3
200-acre tract on waters of Quaker Creek—with James Yarbrough (sold in 1804)	1802	OCDB 10:256, 11:202
300-acre tract on Little River (immediately resold)	1803	OCDB 12:12, 13
Deed of Trust on two tracts, 328 and 172 acres on Mountain Creek	1807	OCDB 13:303
Half of town lot 46—with James Phillips	1807	OCDB 13:110
A quarter of town lot 46—with James Phillips	1808	OCDB 13:109

Appendix A (continued)

Description	Date	Source
Town lots 2 and 44	1809	OCDB 14:160
217-acre tract on Cain Creek (immediately resold)	1809	OCDB 14:550, 553
Lot 6, Chapel Hill (sold in 1814)	1813	OCDB 17:204, 206
431-acre tract adjacent Estes et al. (McKerall tract)	1814	OCDB 15:376
325-acre tract on Little Creek of Eno River	1815	OCDB 15:178
217-acre tract on Eno River (Wm. Cabe tract)	1816	OCDB 16:349
Remaining portion of lot 46, Hillsborough—with James Webb and Thomas Ruffin	1818	OCDB 17:226
200-acre tract on waters of New Hope Creek	1820	OCDB 18:302
65-acre tract on Eno River, adjacent Ruffin, his own land, and Halifax Rd. (56 acres of this sold to W. M. Green and 5½ acres to Ruffin in 1827)	1821	OCDB 22:150, 416, 24:365
197-acre tract adjacent Cabe	1822	OCDB 26:240
Part of town lot 25, Hillsborough (Kirkland's corner)	1825	OCDB 22:153
Town lot 179, Hillsborough	[1825]	OCDB 22:155
Franklin County		
Part of town lot 4, Louisburg—with Henry Houze (sold 1819)	1818	Franklin County Deed Book (FCDB) 18:183, 149
Part of undesignated lot—with Henry Houze, possibly lot 41	1820	FCDB 19:179, 24:68

Appendix A (continued)

Description	Date	Source
215½ acres (Leghorn tract)	1825	FCDB 22:58 (purchase was not recorded; this is date and deed of sale)
365-acre tract on waters of Tar River (sold 1834)	1830	FCDB 26:240, 27:82
100-acre tract near Louisburg	1830	FCDB 26:240
House and lot, southwest corner of Main St. and courthouse square (Henry Y. Houze and Co.); possibly lots 29 and 40	1830	FCDB 24:68, 26:240
Cumberland County		
Lot 146′ × 25′, Mumford St., Fayetteville—with George McNeill	1818	Cumberland County Deed Book (CCDB) 33:8
Lot on Hay Street (150′ × 30′) in Fayetteville—with George McNeill (resold same year)	1819	CCDB 28:1026, 30:403
Lot on Hay Street (brick tenement)— with McNeill (sold 1829)	1819	CCDB 31:210, 38:330
Lot 20′ × 94′ (unidentified)—with McNeill (sold 1829)	1819	CCDB 32:220, 40:49
Part of lot (unidentified)—with McNeill	1819	CCDB 32:516
Lots on north side of Hay St. and north side of Bass St.—with McNeill from Baxter (portion sold in 1829)	1824	CCDB 36:290, 38:357
Exchange of storehouse lots—with John Clark	1825	CCDB 35:498, 36:388
Lot 153′ × 20′ (sold 1829)—from Richard Hackley	1826	CCDB 38:55, 479

Appendix A (continued)

Description	Date	Source
Lands of bankrupt Wm. McNeill bid in by Kirkland and McNeill	1827	CCDB 37:201, 203
Lot (unidentified)—with McNeill from Baker	1827	CCDB 37:320
Other lands of William McNeill	1827	CCDB 38:57
Town lot (unidentified) from George McNeill	1829	CCDB 38:238

Appendix B. Town Lots in Hillsborough, North Carolina, Owned by William and John U. Kirkland

(One acre in size when laid out and numbered, lots were often later subdivided and the parcels sold separately.)

Number or Letter	Size	Owner	Date of Purchase	Source
6	33′ × 65′	William Kirkland	1795	Tax List, OCDB 5:463
46	½ acre	William Kirkland (with James Phillips)	1807	OCDB 13:110
	¼ acre	William Kirkland (with James Phillips)	1808	OCDB 13:109
	¼ acre	William Kirkland (with James Phillips)	1818	OCDB 17:226
2	1 acre	William Kirkland	1809	OCDB 14:160
44	1 acre	William Kirkland	1809	OCDB 14:160
25	corner parcel ("Kirkland's Corner")	William Kirkland	1825	OCDB 22:153

Appendix B (continued)

Number or Letter	Size	Owner	Date of Purchase	Source
179	1 acre	William Kirkland	[1825]	OCDB 22:155
25	½ of his father's parcel	John U. Kirkland	1828	OCDB 23:257
A (not shown on map)	6 acres	John U. Kirkland	1835	OCDB 37:222
	9 acres when sold		1840	OCDB 37:223
6	his father's parcel	John U. Kirkland	1835	OCDB 34:138
126	1 acre	John U. Kirkland	sold 1862	OCDB 37:65*
127	1 acre	John U. Kirkland	sold 1862	OCDB 37:65*
128	1 acre	John U. Kirkland	sold 1862	OCDB 37:65*
108	1 acre	John U. Kirkland	sold 1837	OCDB 28:85
109	1 acre	John U. Kirkland	sold 1837	OCDB 28:85

* Lots 126, 127, and 128 may be those conveyed to John U. Kirkland by William A. Graham as part payment for 59 acres of the Ayr Mount tract in 1842. See OCDB 30:115.

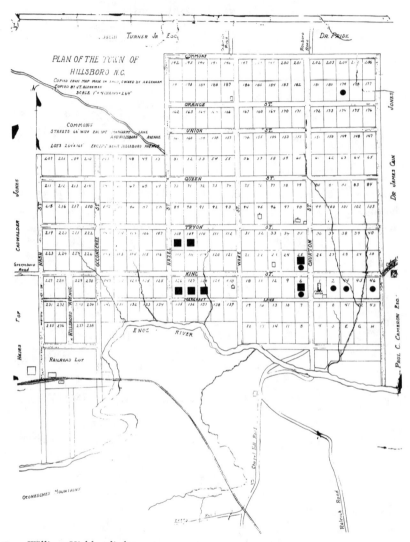

● = William Kirkland's lots
■ = John U. Kirkland's lots

Appendix C. Cemetery Records

The following is a list of Kirkland family members and their places of burial in or near Hillsborough, North Carolina. The names and dates listed here are not those inscribed on the tombstones. Instead, full names and dates adjudged to be accurate are given because the information on the tombstones is often partial or wrong.

Kirkland Family Cemetery at Ayr Mount

William Kirkland (1768–1836)
Margaret Blain Scott Kirkland (ca. 1773–1839)
Elizabeth Machen Kirkland McNeill (1796–1822)
William Kirkland McNeill (1815–17)
Mary Anderson Kirkland (1809–80)
Susannah Umstead Kirkland (1810–70)
John Umstead Kirkland (1802–79)
Elizabeth Adam Simpson Kirkland (1809–81)
Alexander McKenzie Kirkland (1807–43)
Anna McKenzie Cameron Kirkland (1817–90)
Margaret A. McLester (1842–1921)
John Umstead Kirkland, Jr. (1838–1914)
Fanny Harriet McLaren Kirkland (1844–1908)
Sadie McCready Kirkland (1875–1918)
Hallie McLaren Kirkland (1870–1926)
John Boswell Kirkland (1865–1938)
Robert Strange Kirkland (1877–1947)
Elizabeth Simpson Kirkland (1872–1948)
Samuel Simpson Kirkland (1883–1971)
Emily Davis Smith Kirkland (1912–89)

Also buried at Ayr Mount is Charles Manly (1855–56), son of Elizabeth Simpson
Kirkland's sister Sarah and Matthias Manly.

Unmarked burials at Ayr Mount

Elizabeth Simpson Kirkland, daughter of John U. and Elizabeth S. Kirkland
(1845–49)
Kenneth William Kirkland, son of John Kirkland of Glasgow, Scotland (?–1849)
Robert Roulhac Kirkland, son of John U. and Elizabeth S. Kirkland (1855–62)

Probable Unmarked Burials at Ayr Mount

Thomas Ruffin Kirkland, son of John U. and Elizabeth S. Kirkland (1839–42)
Child of John U. and Elizabeth S. Kirkland (ca. 1830)
Four infant sons of Margaret Scott and William Kirkland: William (1799), William (1801), James (1805), and David (1813).

Saint Matthew's Episcopal Church Cemetery*

Samuel Simpson Kirkland (1831–1904)
Eliza Gaston Kirkland (1841–77)
John Gaston Kirkland (1870–1940)
Anne McNabb Kirkland Ruffin (1794–1875)
Thomas Carter Ruffin (1787–1870)
Catherine Roane Ruffin Roulhac (1810–80)
Joseph Blount Gregoire Roulhac (1795–1856)
William Kirkland Ruffin (1812–80)
Anne Ruffin Cameron (1814–97)
Paul Carrington Cameron (1808–91)
Alice Roane Ruffin (1816–73)
Sterling Ruffin (1817–1908)
Jennie Lyman Hurton Ruffin (1843–1934)
Peter Browne Ruffin (1821–1900)
Mary Rebecca Jones Ruffin (1822–78)
Thomas Ruffin, Jr. (1824–89)
Mary Clack Cain Ruffin (1827–1908)
Jane Minerva Ruffin (1829–93)
Martha Phebe Ruffin (1831–96)
John Kirkland Ruffin (1834–1903)
Sarah Elizabeth Tayloe (1837–83)
Sally Nash Ruffin Gwynn (1836–79)

* Except for John Gaston Kirkland, no great-grandchildren or further generations of William Kirkland's descendants have been included in this list, although the graves of many lie in this cemetery.

Hillsborough Town Cemetery

James Whedbee Kirkland (1867–1943)
Catherine M. Dalton Kirkland** (1876–1959)

** Oral tradition says that because Catherine Dalton Kirkland was a Roman Catholic, she was not permitted to be buried at Ayr Mount. The same prohibition probably accounts for the burial of Samuel Simpson Kirkland and his Catholic wife, Eliza Gaston Kirkland, in the cemetery at Saint Matthew's Church.

❦ *Notes* ❦

Abbreviations Used in the Notes

OPR   Old Parochial Registers, General Register Office, New Register House, Edinburgh, Scotland.

OCDB   Orange County Deed Books, Register of Deeds Office, Hillsborough, North Carolina.

OCWB   Orange County Will Books, Office of the Clerk of the Court, Orange County Courthouse, Hillsborough, North Carolina.

Preface

1. Mark Girouard, *Life in the English Country House* (1978; rpt. New York, 1980), 3.

Chapter 1

1. Paterson, *History of Ayr*, 1:161, 183–84, 195–97, 2:524; Dunlop, *Royal Burgh of Ayr*, 53–55, 176; Graham, *Social Life of Scotland*, 146–200; Lenman, *Integration, Enlightenment, and Industrialization*, 1–4.

2. OPR, Ayr, Births, 1753–90.

3. OPR, Ayr, Marriages, 1687–1761. A tacksman was a middleman who held a lease on land from a freeholder and sublet it in smaller tracts to renters.

4. Graham, *Social Life of Scotland*, 152–68; Trevelyan, *English Social History*, 3:123–33. Two chapters of this volume of Trevelyan's history give a vivid and succinct description of life in eighteenth-century Scotland.

5. Trevelyan, *English Social History*, 3:131–34.

6. OPR, Ayr, Marriages, 1687–1761, Jan. 3 and 30, 1696.

7. OPR, Ayr, Marriages, 1687–1761, May 16, 1729. David Kirkland's birth and baptism are not registered, but his parentage may be deduced from the baptismal records of his children, in which the Smith granduncles are named and their relationship stated.

8. Graham, *Social Life of Scotland*, 159–60, 179–81; Trevelyan, *English Social History*, 3:132, 152.

9. Paterson, *History of Ayr*, 1:191–92; Graham, *Social Life of Scotland*, 4–17, 21–23.

10. Burgh Register, Craft Minute Book: Fleshers, Ayr, Mar. 14, 1748; Paterson, *History of Ayr*, 1:196–97.

11. Trevelyan, *English Social History*, 3:130, 150–57; Graham, *Social Life of Scotland*, 201–4.

12. Devine, "Glasgow Merchants and the Tobacco Trade," 50–74; Hook, *Scotland and America*, 8–10, 48; Nichol, *Glasgow and the Tobacco Lords*. Nichol's pamphlet, written for schoolchildren, admirably portrays the life-style of the tobacco lords and their trade connections with America.

13. Devine, "Glasgow Merchants and the Tobacco Trade"; Trevelyan, *English Social History*, 3:155–56; Nichol, *Glasgow and the Tobacco Lords*.

14. Strang, *Glasgow and Its Clubs*, 340. John Strang's brother Robert was a school fellow of John U. Kirkland in Glasgow and corresponded with him after the latter's return to America. This Strang family was related to that of Robert Strange (sic) of Fayetteville.

15. Bailyn, *Voyagers to the West*, 42, 114; Trevelyan, *English Social History*, 3:156.

16. Trevelyan, *English Social History*, 3:154, 156, 161; Dunlop, *Royal Burgh of Ayr*, 58–59, 179, 203, 221–23; Hook, *Scotland and America*, 91.

17. Dunlop, *Royal Burgh of Ayr*, 81; Paterson, *History of Ayr*, 1:161, 189–96; Snyder, *Life of Robert Burns*, 8, 19–26.

18. Paterson, *History of Ayr*, 1:161–62; Dunlop, *Royal Burgh of Ayr*, 70, 85.

19. James Boswell, trained for law but more interested in literature, wrote the now classic biography of his illustrious friend Samuel Johnson. John Galt wrote *Annals of the Parish* and other less well-known fiction of rural Scottish life. William McClure was born in Ayr, son of David and Ann Kennedy McClure (*Who Was Who in America 1607–1896*).

Chapter 2

1. OPR, Ayr, Births, 1721–53.

2. John Kirkland's education is inferred from his signature in the Fleshers' Minute Book and his leadership of the affairs of the corporation. See Burgh Register, Craft Minute Book, July 22, 1754, Oct. 3, 1765, and passim.

3. OPR, Ayr, Marriages, 1761–1819, Nov. 12, 1763 (the date on which they "gave in their names to be proclaimed in order for marriage"); John Kirkland,

Glasgow, to John U. Kirkland, Hillsborough, Sept. 9, 1824, in possession of May K. R. Reynolds. Dowie's wife was Sybilla Mackenzie Kirkland's sister.

4. Margaret Kirkland, Glasgow, to John U. Kirkland, Hillsborough, Apr. 19, 1822, Kirkland Family Papers, in the possession of Richard H. Jenrette. All references are to this collection except when designated Kirkland Family Papers (Duke University).

5. OPR, Ayr, Deaths, 1766–1819; Elizabeth Kirkland to William Kirkland, Sept. 13, 1810, Thomas Ruffin Papers; John Kirkland to John U. Kirkland, Sept. 9, 1824, in possession of May K. R. Reynolds; Sinclair, *Statistical Account of Scotland*, 89.

6. Galt, *Annals of the Parish*, 32–33.

7. Paterson, *History of Ayr*, 1:171–72; Robertson, *Ayrshire*, 1:3.

8. Paterson, *History of Ayr*, 1:189; Robertson, *Ayrshire*, 1:338–39; Dunlop, *Royal Burgh of Ayr*, 202–3; Bailyn, *Voyagers to the West*, 42.

9. Although William Kirkland does not appear on any Warren County tax list in 1789, in that year he signed several recorded deeds of Daniel Anderson's purchases of land and slaves, and with Scott he purchased two town lots. See Warren County Records, Warren County Deed Book 11:8, 9, 127; Warren County Will Book 5:85, 125.

10. William A. Kirkland, Jr., to John and Alice Kirkland Corbus, Feb. 4, 1958, William Alexander Kirkland Papers; Bute County Records, List of Taxables, 1771; Warren County Records, Tax Lists, 1781–1801.

11. Genealogy folder, Elizabeth Willis Anderson Papers; "Subscribers in Virginia, 1771–1772."

12. *Prince William*, 88–94.

13. Warren County Records, Tax Lists, 1781–1801; Warren County Deed Book 11:8, 9; Warren County Will Book 5:85, 125.

14. U.S. Department of Commerce, Bureau of the Census, *First Census, 1790: North Carolina*, 76, 78.

15. Warren County Records, Warren County Deed Book 11:127 (Apr. 23, 1790).

16. Warren County Records, Warren County Will Book 7:61, 249, 9:195, 10:325, 11:127; Accounts, Sept. 4, Nov. 4, 1793, James Webb Papers; Warren County Records, Warren County Will Book 7:61, 9:195, 10:325.

17. Orange County Records, Marriage Bonds, Dec. 24, 1792; Kirkland Family Papers, Kirkland Family Bible no. 1 records the actual marriage date as Dec. 25, 1792.

18. *Records of Dettingen Parish*, 14, 24, 25, 33; Bute County Records, Court Minutes, passim after 1768; Warren County Records, Warren County Deed Book A:110; Warren County Will Book 3:5; Bute County Records, Bute County

Marriage Bonds, George Tassie and Mary Armistead, Sept. 27, 1774; Warren County Records, Warren County Will Book 3:136.

Chapter 3

1. Robert Freeman's bill, Nov. 18, 1793, Cameron Family Papers; Messrs. William Kirkland and Co., Sept. 4, 1793, Webb's account with Kirkland, Nov. 7, 1813, James Webb Papers.

2. Orange County Records, Tax Lists, 1791–96; OCDB 5:463.

3. OCDB 5:463, 467, 666; William A. Kirkland, Jr., to John and Alice Corbus, Feb. 4, 1958, William A. Kirkland Papers.

4. OCDB 10:197; Henderson and Wooten, *Old Houses and Gardens*, Plate 54; Sheriff of Orange County to William Kirkland, OCDB 8:251. (The Kirklands' move to this tract at this time is inferred from Kirkland's sale of his former dwelling place and plantation in 1802.)

5. Land Grant from Lord Granville to Thomas Wiley, Book 12, no. 61, Secretary of State's Office; OCDB 3:456; Fruth, *Some Descendants of Richard Few*, 24–25, 59–60. Tryon's account reveals that he thought it just retribution to allow the militia horses and cattle to trample and destroy the crops of the Few plantation (William S. Powell, ed., *The Correspondence of William Tryon and Other Selected Papers*, 2 vols. [Raleigh, 1980], 2:729, 839). Few was later recompensed for these damages by the North Carolina General Assembly.

6. John Butler to Ralph McNair, OCDB 3:456; John Kinchen to William Courtney, OCDB 2:236–37; Few to Butler, OCDB 3:215–16; Sheriff to Kirkland, OCDB 8:251; Joseph Courtney to William Kirkland, OCDB 8:297. The estates papers of William Courtney, Jr., and Sr., have been confused in the North Carolina Archives. William Courtney, Jr., predeceased his father, probably about 1799; Courtney, Sr., lived until June 1803. See George Anderson to Duncan Cameron, June 3, 1803, Cameron Family Papers, which reports the elder Courtney's death.

7. Daniel Anderson to Duncan Cameron, Apr. 19, 1798, Cameron Family Papers.

8. William Kirkland to Duncan Cameron, Nov. 24, 1800, Kirkland's Agreement with Campbell and Bennehan, Sept. 9, 1802, Bennehan's tax list, folder 10–13 Aug. 1803, ibid.

9. OCDB 11:202–3, 13:109, 110, 14:160; Receipted bill, Oct. 7, 1802, Joseph Gibson Papers.

10. Orange County Records, copies of original censuses, Orange County, 1800:49, 1810:432.

11. OCDB 5:455, 8:183, 10:365. (James Kirkland witnessed and proved this last deed.) Orange County Records, Marriage Bonds: Holt and Scott, Apr. 30, 1795, Murphey and Scott, Nov. 5, 1801.

12. Lefler and Newsome, *North Carolina*, 328–33; obituary in *Fayetteville Observer*, Feb. 14, 1832.

13. Orange County Records, Marriage Bonds: Scott and Duffy, July 12, 1799; Sanders, *Cameron Plantation*, 36–40. Murphey named his second son for William Duffy, who died in 1810.

14. Carroll, *Francis Asbury in North Carolina*, 48, 62–63.

15. Journal, July 21, 1795, James Meacham Papers.

16. Loose paper in vol. 32, May 29, 1796, Cameron Family Papers.

17. Lefler and Wager, *Orange County*, 132–33; OCDB 13:3, 4.

18. Griffin, *Less Time for Meddling*, 3, 42, 47; Fries, *Records of the Moravians in North Carolina*, 6 (1793–1808): 2761, 2765. Anne McNabb Kirkland's name was originally spelled Ann. See her birth record in Kirkland Family Bible no. 1, Kirkland Family Papers.

19. Bible Records, Kirkland Family Papers.

20. James Webb to Duncan Cameron, June 12, 1803, Cameron Family Papers.

21. Rebecca Cameron to Thomas Bennehan, Dec. 6, 1806, ibid.

22. John A. Cameron to Rebecca Cameron, Sept. 20, 1808, Archibald Murphey to Duncan Cameron, Aug. 27, 1808, ibid.

23. Archibald Murphey to Thomas D. Bennehan, June 8, 1809, ibid.

24. *Cyclopedia of Eminent and Representative Men*, 2:40–45; Catherine Ruffin to Thomas Ruffin, July 14, 1827, Ruffin-Roulhac-Hamilton Papers.

25. Hoyt, *Papers of Archibald D. Murphey*, 2:40.

26. Thomas Ruffin to unknown, July 14, 1866, Thomas Ruffin Papers; John C. Pike to Duncan Cameron, Aug. 23, 1822, Cameron Family Papers; Mary Cameron Anderson to Catherine Ruffin, Nov. 23, 1824, Ruffin-Roulhac-Hamilton Papers; Bible Records, Kirkland Family Papers.

27. Invoices from Messrs. Gracie and Anderson, Sept. 4, Nov. 4, 1793, James Webb Papers; Daniel Anderson to Duncan Cameron, Aug. 8, 1806, Legal Papers, Dec. 1799, case of D. Campbell & Co. *vs* Jos. Williams & Co., Cameron Family Papers; "Notes on the Broadwood Grand Piano of 1797 to be used in the Sunday evening recital [Mar. 26, 1988] of chamber music 1988 SEHKS" (Southeastern Historical Keyboard Society), in possession of author.

28. Anderson, *Piedmont Plantation*, 18–19; Daniel Anderson to Duncan Cameron, Feb. 8, 1798, Cameron Family Papers.

Chapter 4

1. Kirkland's clerks often witnessed the deeds for his land purchases. James Kirkland was followed by John McLemore (George Anderson to Duncan Cameron, Sept. 14, 1805, Cameron Family Papers), William L. McNeill, a brother of George (OCDB 13:4), and George McNeill (OCDB 14:160, 550, 553; also Ruffin's account with William Kirkland and Company, Aug. 1811, Thomas Ruffin Papers). Later Kirkland employed George M. Johnston and Andrew Mickle.

2. No overseer's name is found until after William Kirkland's death, when John Miller's salary is noted in the executor's accounts (Thomas Ruffin Papers, vol. 37).

3. Elizabeth Kirkland to William Kirkland, Sept. 13, 1810, Thomas Ruffin Papers.

4. John Kirkland to William Kirkland, Sept. 22, 1810, ibid. "Auld Reekie" was an epithet more usually applied to Edinburgh and referred to the smog that overhung the town. John Kirkland seems to have used it to signify Scotland as a whole.

5. OPR, Ayr, Marriages, 1761–1819; Smith, *Alexander Mackenzie*, 5–9; MacDonald, *Lewis*, 165; Ruffin's analysis of Sybilla Mackenzie Kirkland's claim under the will of John McIver, Jan. 30, 1822, Thomas Ruffin Papers.

6. Smith, *Alexander Mackenzie*, 43–114.

7. Ibid., 148–49, 155, 169–71.

8. Elizabeth Kirkland to William Kirkland, Sept. 13, 1810, Thomas Ruffin Papers; *Bombay Almanac*, Part V, Bombay Civil Service List, 7; *Memorials of Old Haileybury College*; *Post-Office Annual Directory for 1829–30*, 153; *Robson's Improved London Directory*; *Thom's British Directory*, 272.

9. John Kirkland to William Kirkland, Sept. 22, 1810, Thomas Ruffin Papers.

10. Ibid., and Elizabeth Kirkland to William Kirkland, Sept. 13, 1810, ibid.

11. Murphey to Ruffin, July 30, 1811, ibid.; OCDB 13:612. Kirkland also registered the power of attorney with the clerk of court in OCWB D:318.

12. William Kirkland to Thomas Ruffin, Oct. 10, Dec. 17, 1811, John U. Kirkland to Thomas Ruffin, Apr. 19, 1812, Thomas Ruffin Papers; Invoice for china and castors, Oct. 29, 1811, Robert Strang to John U. Kirkland, Sept. 6, 1819, Aug. 30, 1831, Kirkland Family Papers.

13. Elizabeth Kirkland to William Kirkland, Sept. 13, 1810, Thomas Ruffin Papers; Bible Records, Kirkland Family Papers.

14. Contract of William Kirkland and George McNeill, June 15, 1812, Thomas Ruffin Papers.

15. Rose, *Thomas McNeill*, 61; Nott Mercantile Books, Vol. 1: Nott and Johnson Account Book, 1812.

16. OCDB 14:550, 553; 15:376; 17:204, 206.

17. William Kirkland to Thomas Ruffin, Dec. 3, 1815, Thomas Ruffin Papers. In 1812 William Collier had built the Eagle Hotel in Raleigh for Charles Parish (Murray, *Wake, Capital County*, 206).

18. Kirkland to Ruffin, Dec. 13, 1815, Thomas Ruffin Papers.

19. I am indebted to Catherine Bishir and Elizabeth Reid Murray for information on Briggs's career and family. Itemized accounts of the construction of Fairntosh, Feb. 9, Aug. 24, 1811, Dec. 17, 1812, Dec. 27, 1821, vol. 99, Thomas B. Littlejohn to Duncan Cameron, Aug. 7, 1817, Cameron Family Papers. The evidence that connects Briggs with Ayr Mount is found in the last noted letter and reads as follows: "I fear I shall not be able to settle with Mr. Briggs for running my staircase without getting from you or Mr. Kirkland the sums you paid for having your work done—my bargain with him was to pay the same price you and Mr. K. paid for the same kind of work—my passage is 12 feet wide—12 feet pitch, and the staircase (executed exactly like yours as Mr. Briggs informs me) has 23 steps—I think your passage is of the same width & pitch, and probably has the same number of steps—will you have the goodness to state to me.the price you gave for running the stair case, making wainscot, & the price of plain wainscot from the foot of the stair case to your parlour door, mentioning also the number of yards or feet in this last item. I hope you will pardon me giving you this trouble, but I fear I shall be unable to settle with Mr. Brigs [sic] without it—I understood you to say that your bargain was made with Mr. Fort, and the work executed by Mr. Brigs; but I understood Mr. Kirkland's bill was settled upon the same terms your work was done, and Mr. Brigs agreed with me to do my work upon the same terms."

20. Itemized accounts of the construction of Fairntosh, May 3, 1811, vol. 99, Cameron Family Papers; Wake County Records, Will of William Nutt; Henderson and Wooten, *Old Houses and Gardens*, 49.

21. Historical American Buildings Survey, Ayr Mount (NC/220), no. 1 of 20 sheets and unidentified newspaper clipping, June 25, 1953, Jane Dicks, "Hillsboro Home, Completed in 1800, Still Stands Sturdy and Beautiful," Kirkland Family Papers. The Dicks article is full of misinformation.

22. Phebe Kirkland to Catherine Ruffin, Mar. 18, 1825, Ruffin-Roulhac-Hamilton Papers.

23. Vol. 37, Thomas Ruffin Papers. Every planter had what seems today an overabundance of Windsor chairs. They reflect the amplitude of antebellum hospitality. Where they were kept has also been something of a mystery, but at Ayr Mount that problem was easily solved. Running along the inside wall of the long hall, which served as a sitting room as well as a passage, was a rail with many pegs on which, according to the last Kirkland owner, Samuel S. Kirkland, the chairs were hung. Unlike pegs for hanging clothing, these were positioned very

high on the wall. This rail was removed in the recent restoration.

24. Mary A. Kirkland to Eliza Bond, Jan. 30, 1828, Eliza Mary Bond Johnston Weissinger Papers.

Chapter 5

1. William Kirkland to Ruffin, Apr. 22, 1818, Jan. 1, 1820, Thomas Ruffin Papers; OCDB 17:226; *Fayetteville American*, Nov. 21, 1816; Bill to Cameron from Kirkland, Webb and Co., Nov. 22, 1816, Mar. 22, 1822, Cameron Family Papers; OCDB 17:226.

2. Franklin County Records, Franklin County Deed Book 18:149, 183; 19:17; Cumberland County Records, Cumberland County Deed Book 28:1026; 31:210; 32:220, 516; 33:8; 35:498; 36:290; 37:201, 203, 232, 320; 38:55, 57, 238; OCDB 15:178, 376; 16:349.

3. *Hillsborough Recorder*, Mar. 1, 1820.

4. OCDB 16:104.

5. Gifts of slaves, Aug. 1, 26, 1811, Anne Ruffin to Thomas Ruffin, Nov. 29, 1815, John MacRae to Ruffin, July 29, 1859, Thomas Ruffin Papers; Davis, *Revolution's Godchild*, 6, 7, 240, 241.

6. Anne K. Ruffin to Thomas Ruffin, Nov. 29, 1815, Thomas Ruffin Papers.

7. Sterling Ruffin to Anne K. Ruffin, Mar. 6, 1815, ibid.

8. Kirkland to Ruffin, Apr. 8, 1818, ibid.

9. Plat of Land, Nov. 28, 1818, ibid. In 1834 Paul C. Cameron bought Cain's house to make over for himself and Anne Ruffin Cameron. While the lot was being cleared and the vegetation burned, the house caught fire and burned down. He built Burnside on the same site. See Mary Cain to Catherine Ruffin, Jan. 15, 1834, Ruffin-Roulhac-Hamilton Papers; Rebecca Cameron to Alice Ruffin, Mar. 29, 1834, Cameron Family Papers; Paul C. Cameron to Thomas Ruffin, Jan. 22, 1834, Thomas Ruffin Papers.

10. George McNeill to Thomas Ruffin, Apr. 18, 1814, Robert H. Chapman to Ruffin, Sept. 21, 1816, Duncan Cameron to Ruffin, Sept. 24, 1816, Ruffin partnerships, Oct. 12, 1814, Jan. 4, 1817, Thomas Ruffin Papers (last two are in Oct.–Nov. 1815 folder); *Fayetteville Observer*, Sept. 23, 1824; OCDB 14:303, 20:321.

11. Records of Hillsborough Presbyterian Church.

12. Trevelyan, *English Social History*, 3:127.

13. Records of Hillsborough Presbyterian Church; William Kirkland to Thomas D. Bennehan, July 14, 1823, Mary Anderson to Duncan Cameron, Jan. 4, 1818, Cameron Family Papers: "Mr. Kirkland told me today in church." Mary Anderson, like her sons, was a devout Episcopalian.

14. MacRae, *The Descendants of Duncan and Ann (Cameron) MacRae*; *Fayetteville Observer*, Mar. 20, Sept. 4, 30, 1823, May 26, 1825, July 19, Nov. 1, Dec. 27, 1826, Feb. 21, 1827; William Kirkland's bond for John MacRae, Mar. 30, 1827, Thomas Ruffin Papers; Cumming, *North Carolina in Maps*, 25–27; Oates, *Story of Fayetteville*, 184, 322.

15. G. T. Bedell to John MacRae, Dec. 12, 1820, Thomas Ruffin to John MacRae, July 16, 1830, John MacRae Papers; John U. Kirkland to Anne K. Ruffin, Dec. 11, 1820, Ruffin to his wife, July 16, 1830, MacRae to Ruffin, Dec. 10, 1820, Thomas Ruffin Papers; MacRae, *Descendants of Duncan and Ann (Cameron) MacRae*, 5, 9.

16. MacRae, *Descendants of Duncan and Ann (Cameron) MacRae*, 9–12; MacRae to Ruffin, July 28, 1859, Thomas Ruffin Papers.

17. Bible Records and R. Strang to John U. Kirkland, Aug. 30, 1831, Kirkland Family Papers; John F. May to Ruffin, June 23, 1815, Strange to Ruffin, Jan. 10, 1853, Thomas Ruffin Papers; *Fayetteville Observer*, July 17, 1823, July 12, 1826, May 8, 1832, Feb. 18, 1962.

18. Orange County Records, Civil Action Papers, 1833; Lefler and Newsome, *North Carolina*, 347.

19. *Durham Herald*, Apr. 3, 1955. In 1960 McNally of Charlotte published a facsimile edition of *Eoneguski* with a foreword by Richard Walser.

20. *North Carolina Journal and Carolina Observer*, Special Edition, May 29, 1831; John Kirkland to John U. Kirkland, Sept. 9, 1824, in possession of May K. R. Reynolds.

21. The de Graffenried name was spelled in various ways: with or without a capital *d* in the particle, with or without a space between the particle and the name, with or without the final *t*, and with *ie*, *ei*, or *ea* in the last syllable. The name is also used with the particle *von*. Martha's husband, Edwin, spelled his name with the *t*. His descendants spelled theirs without the *t*. Bible Records, Kirkland Family Papers; de Graffenried, *History of the de Graffenried Family*; *Hillsborough Recorder*, Aug. 16, 1820; *Fayetteville Observer*, Aug. 12, 1824; John A. Cameron to Ruffin, Mar. 31, 1820, Thomas Ruffin Papers.

22. Polly Burke to Eliza Bond, Mar. 25, 1820, Weissinger Papers.

23. Martha K. de Graffenriedt to Polly Burke, Oct. 13, 1823, ibid.; William Kirkland to Thomas Ruffin, Nov. 15, 30, 1829, Thomas Ruffin Papers; Wright, *Burials and Deaths Reported in the Columbus [Georgia] Enquirer*, 120–21.

24. *Hillsborough Recorder*, Sept. 25, 1822; George McNeill to Thomas Ruffin, Oct. 13, 1825, Thomas Ruffin Papers; *Fayetteville Observer*, Feb. 18, 1962.

25. Junior Service League, *Guide to Historic Fayetteville*, 29, 48; R. Strange, Jr., to his sister Margaret, May 18, 1849, Benjamin R. Huske Papers.

26. Mary Anderson to Duncan Cameron, Jan. 4, 1818, Cameron Family Papers; John U. Kirkland to Anne K. Ruffin, Dec. 11, 1820, Duncan McFayden to

Ruffin, Oct. 22, 1823, Thomas Ruffin Papers; [R. Strang] to John U. Kirkland, Sept. 6, 1819, Kirkland Family Papers.

27. *Hillsborough Recorder*, Apr. 19, 1820; Mary Anderson to Duncan Cameron, May 7, 1820, Cameron Family Papers.

28. [R. Strang] to John U. Kirkland, Sept. 6, 1819, Kirkland Family Papers.

Chapter 6

1. Kirkland to Ruffin, Mar. 29, 1817, Thomas Ruffin Papers.

2. Estate of William Kirkland, vol. 37, p. 24, ibid.; OCWB B:290, Will of George Miller, D:94, Will of James Miller; Little River Presbyterian Church Cemetery; Markham, "Land Grants to Early Settlers"; Engstrom, "Early Quakers in the Eno River Valley," 8, 14.

3. Orange County Records, Orange County Censuses (microfilm), 1800: 493, 1810: 932, 1830: 269; Phebe Kirkland to Catherine Ruffin, Mar. 23, 1829, Ruffin-Roulhac-Hamilton Papers.

4. Vol. 37, pp. 1, 10, 15–16, Thomas Ruffin Papers.

5. Ibid., 15–16, 23, 24; Phebe Kirkland to John U. Kirkland, Nov. 28, [1839], Kirkland Family Papers.

6. Alexander M. Kirkland to Catherine Ruffin, Jan. 10, 1831, Ruffin-Roulhac-Hamilton Papers.

7. Susan Kirkland to Catherine Ruffin, Sept. 21, 1831, ibid.

8. Lefler and Newsome, *North Carolina*, 372.

9. Thomas Ruffin partnerships with Benjamin Chambers, Oct. 26, 1821, June 15, 1825, Will of Col. Benjamin Chambers, Nov. 28, 1826, Thomas Ruffin Papers.

10. Archibald Murphey to Ruffin, June 3, 1824, ibid.

11. Webb to Ruffin, Jan. 16, 1823, ibid.

12. Ruffin to his wife, Jan. 3, 1852, Patty Ruffin to Thomas Ruffin, Jan. 11, 1852, ibid.

13. Sally Ruffin to Thomas Ruffin, Jan. 17, 1852, Peter Browne Ruffin to Thomas Ruffin, Jan. 29, 1852, ibid.

14. Catherine Ruffin to Thomas Ruffin, Feb. 10, 1835, Ruffin-Roulhac-Hamilton Papers.

15. Orange County Records, Orange County Census (microfilm) 1850, Schedule 4, Products of Agriculture, 1183. John U. Kirkland seems to have been omitted from both the slave and agriculture schedules of the 1860 Orange County census.

16. Memo of William Kirkland, Dec. 1815, Kirkland to Ruffin, Mar. 18,

1818, Thomas Ruffin Papers; Kirkland to Bennehan, Apr. 27, 1818, Apr. 26, July 14, 1823, Cameron Family Papers.

17. James Webb to D. Cameron, Feb. 18, 1822, Kirkland to D. Cameron, July 14, 1823, Cameron Family Papers; Cotton gin accounts of Webb and Kirkland, June 1, 1825, Feb. 1, 1826, James Webb Papers; Kirkland to Ruffin, Nov. 18, 1830, Thomas Ruffin Papers.

18. Phebe Kirkland to Catherine Ruffin, Mar. 23, 1829, Ruffin-Roulhac-Hamilton Papers; Kirkland to D. Cameron, June 12, 1825, Cameron Family Papers.

Chapter 7

1. Thomas Ruffin to Catherine Ruffin, Apr. 23, 1824, William K. Ruffin to Catherine Ruffin, Nov. 14, 1824, A. M. Kirkland to Catherine Ruffin, Feb. 13, 1825, Ruffin-Roulhac-Hamilton Papers; Thomas Ruffin to Catherine Ruffin, Dec. 10, 1824, President of St. Mary's College to Thomas Ruffin, Dec. 26, 1824, Thomas Ruffin Papers.

2. Ruffin to Paul C. Cameron, Sept. 29, 1838, Cameron Family Papers; Thomas Ruffin to Joseph Roulhac, Mar. 17, 1838, Ruffin-Roulhac-Hamilton Papers; correspondence between Sept. 16 and Nov. 2, 1838, passim, Thomas Ruffin to Anne K. Ruffin, Jan. 2, 1846, Thomas Ruffin Papers.

3. Dialectic Society Minutes, Aug. 27, 1823, to Oct. 20, 1824, University of North Carolina Archives.

4. Alexander Kirkland to Catherine Ruffin, Apr. 17, 1825, Ruffin-Roulhac-Hamilton Papers. William Hooper, grandson of the signer of the Declaration of Independence, is probably meant. He was a tutor at the university before preparing for the Episcopal ministry. He was also a professor at the university for a short time before continuing his career in the Baptist ministry.

5. James Webb to D. Cameron, June 10, 1825, William Kirkland to D. Cameron, June 12, 1825, Cameron Family Papers.

6. Mary A. Kirkland to Catherine Ruffin, June 5, 1825, Ruffin-Roulhac-Hamilton Papers.

7. Aug. 30, 1825, ibid.

8. Webb to T. D. Bennehan, Dec. 27, 1826, Webb to D. Cameron, Jan. 11, 22, 1827, Cameron Family Papers. The alumni records of Norwich University, the institution into which Partridge's Academy evolved, show that Alexander entered in 1824 and graduated in 1828, but family letters make it clear that he did not go to Connecticut until January 1825 and returned in 1827.

9. Catherine Ruffin to Thomas Ruffin, Sept. 1827, Ruffin-Roulhac-Hamilton Papers.

10. Thomas Ruffin to Anne K. Ruffin, Sept. 29, 1827, Thomas Ruffin Papers.

11. *University of North Carolina, Chapel Hill, Alumni Directory*, 497.

12. Susan Kirkland to Catherine Ruffin, Aug. 30, 1825, Catherine Ruffin to Thomas Ruffin, Mar. 23, 1828, Ruffin-Roulhac-Hamilton Papers; F. Yarbrough to Eliza Bond, Dec. 29, 1829, Weissinger Papers.

13. Mary Bond to Eliza Bond, May 11, 1825, Weissinger Papers.

14. Fanny Yarbrough to Eliza Bond, Sept. 28, Oct. 6, 1825, ibid.

15. Fanny Yarbrough to Eliza Bond, Oct. 8, 1825, ibid.

16. Hamilton and Williams, *Papers of William A. Graham*, 1:160.

17. Mary Kirkland to Eliza Bond, Jan. 30, 1828, Weissinger Papers.

18. Paul C. Cameron to his sister, Oct. 25, 1828, Cameron Family Papers.

19. John U. Kirkland to Catherine Ruffin, July 8, 1827, Ruffin-Roulhac-Hamilton Papers.

20. Sarah Nash to Catherine Ruffin, May 1825, ibid. Mr. London has not been identified.

21. Maria Simpson to Mary A. Kirkland, Mar. 31, 1829, Kirkland Family Papers.

22. Cady (Caroline) Heartt to Eliza Bond, undated papers, Weissinger Papers.

23. Susan Kirkland to Catherine Ruffin, Aug. 30, 1825, ibid.

24. Smith to Kirkland, May 26, 1823, Thomas Ruffin Papers. Smith has either combined the names of two different medicinal plants, *Guaiacum Officinale*, commonly *lignum vitae*, wood of life, and *Rheum* or rhubarb, or he has used *lignum vitae* to describe rhubarb's beneficial properties. See George B. Wood and Franklin Bache, *The Dispensatory of the United States of America* (1833; rpt. Philadelphia, 1851), 370–72, 607–18.

25. Thomas Ruffin to Catherine Ruffin, Nov. 6, 1827, Catherine Ruffin to Thomas Ruffin, Oct. 30, 1827, Thomas Ruffin Papers.

26. Phebe Kirkland to Alice Ruffin, Jan. 30, [1839], Kirkland Family Papers.

27. Susan and Mary Kirkland to Phebe Kirkland, undated but probably May 1836, ibid.

28. Anne Ruffin to Catherine Ruffin, Nov. 19, 1829, Ruffin-Roulhac-Hamilton Papers.

29. Susan Kirkland to Catherine Ruffin, Aug. 30, 1825, ibid.

30. John Kirkland to John U. Kirkland, Sept. 9, 1824, in possession of May K. R. Reynolds; Susan Kirkland to Catherine Ruffin, Aug. 30, 1825, Ruffin-Roulhac-Hamilton Papers.

Chapter 8

1. Catherine Ruffin to Thomas Ruffin, Jan. 13, 1836, Phebe Kirkland to Catherine Ruffin, May 6, 1838, Ruffin to Joseph Roulhac, Oct. 6, 1852, Ruffin-Roulhac-Hamilton Papers; Martha de Graffenriedt to Anne K. Ruffin, Mar. 9, 1825, Alice Ruffin to Ruffin, Jan. 1836, Webb to Ruffin, Jan. 14, 1837, Thomas Ruffin Papers.

2. Veight, *Hysteria*; Showalter, *Female Malady*, 56, 132–40, 174, 190.

3. Thomas Ruffin to Catherine Ruffin, Mar. 5, 1836, Thomas Ruffin Papers.

4. William Kirkland to Thomas Ruffin, Nov. 30, 1829, ibid.

5. Ibid., John U. Kirkland to Ruffin, Feb. 1, 4, 1830, ibid.; Susan Nash to Catherine Ruffin, Jan. 30, 1830, Ruffin-Roulhac-Hamilton Papers.

6. John U. Kirkland to Ruffin, Feb. 11, 1830, William Kirkland to Ruffin, Mar. 29, Apr. 10, 1830, Thomas Ruffin Papers.

7. Anne Ruffin to Catherine Ruffin, May 31, 1830, Ruffin-Roulhac-Hamilton Papers. Anne probably meant by "Dr. C." Thomas Nash Cameron, who practiced in Fayetteville and the surrounding area; by "Dr. W." she undoubtedly meant Dr. James Webb.

8. William Kirkland to John U. Kirkland, June 10, 1830, William Kirkland to Ruffin, July 12, Aug. 2, Sept. 30, 1830, Thomas Ruffin Papers; Catherine Ruffin to Ruffin, June 21, 1830, Ruffin-Roulhac-Hamilton Papers.

9. Alexander Kirkland to Catherine Ruffin, June 10, 1831, Ruffin-Roulhac-Hamilton Papers.

10. Mary Anne Cameron to Duncan Cameron, Apr. 24, 1835, Cameron Family Papers; Margaret ? to Polly Burke, May 19, 1835, Weissinger Papers.

11. Margaret J. Taylor to Eliza Bond, Dec. 12, 1837, Weissinger Papers.

12. Thomas Ruffin to Anne K. Ruffin, July 27, 1845, Thomas Ruffin Papers.

13. Thomas D. Bennehan to Richard Bennehan, Aug. 24, 1825, Joseph Caldwell to Richard Bennehan, July 5, 1825, Cameron Family Papers.

14. Richard Bennehan to Thomas Bennehan, July 29, 1825, ibid.

15. A bill from Kirkland and Webb to Thos. D. Bennehan, Oct. 14, 1826, ibid.

16. Thomas Bennehan to Paul Cameron, Apr. 7, 1836, ibid.

17. James C. Turrentine to his wife, May 22, 1830, Michael H. Turrentine Papers.

18. To salivate a patient meant to dose with mercury to increase salivation. The excitation of the bodily secretions was sound medical practice in the nineteenth century.

Chapter 9

1. Kirkland to Ruffin, Feb. 22, 1834, Thomas Ruffin Papers.
2. Deed of Trust, Sept. 18, 1815, Murphey to Ruffin, Dec. 20, 1820, ibid.
3. Sale of Murphey's lands, Dec. 11, 1821, List of Murphey's debts, Dec. 29, 1821, James Webb Papers.
4. McNeill to Ruffin, Jan. 3, 1821, Thomas Ruffin Papers.
5. Thomas Ruffin to Solomon DeBow, Jan. 10, 1822, ibid.; OCDB 21:67.
6. OCDB 22:150, 26:240, 2:153; William Kirkland's surety for Houze and Yarbrough, Aug. 3, 1824, Bank of Cape Fear notices of directors, Jan. 7, 1825, Jan. 5, 1826, James Webb Papers.
7. *Fayetteville Observer*, Jan. 1, 1824; McNeill to Ruffin, Oct. 8, 13, 1825, Thomas Ruffin Papers.
8. *Fayetteville Observer*, Aug. 22, 1816; McNeill to Ruffin, Oct. 25, 1825, Mar. 9, 1829, deed of Kirkland to Ruffin, June 7, 1826, Ruffin to Dickins, Aug. 16, 1826, Feb. 19, 1827, Thomas Ruffin Papers.
9. Kirkland to Ruffin, Apr. 5, 14, 1827, McNeill to Ruffin, Apr. 6, 1827, Thomas Ruffin Papers.
10. William Kirkland's surety for Houze and Yarbrough, Aug. 3, 1824, James Webb Papers; William Kirkland to Thomas Ruffin, Feb. 13, 1829, Thomas Ruffin Papers; Franklin County Deed Book 22:58, 26:240.
11. OCDB 23:257; a bill of William Kirkland and Son dated Dec. 18, 1824, James Webb Papers, is the earliest evidence of the name change.
12. McNeill to Ruffin, Mar. 9, May 23, 1829, Thomas Ruffin Papers.
13. McNeill to Ruffin, May 23, 1829, ibid.
14. *Fayetteville Observer*, May 28, 1829; Irvin to Ruffin, June 15, 1829, Kirkland to Ruffin, June 18, 1829, Thomas Ruffin Papers.
15. McNeill to Ruffin, Sept. 30, 1829, May 3, 1831, Thomas Ruffin Papers; *North Carolina Journal and Carolina Observer*, Special Edition, May 29, 1831; Oates, *Story of Fayetteville*, 851.
16. Kirkland to Ruffin, June 29, 1829, Thomas Ruffin Papers.
17. Kirkland to Ruffin, Mar. 16, Aug. 19, Nov. 30, 1829, ibid.
18. Kirkland to Ruffin, Nov. 15, 1829, ibid.
19. Kirkland to Ruffin, Nov. 30, 1829, ibid.
20. Orange County Records, Will of William Kirkland; William Kirkland to D. Cameron, Dec. 29, 1829, Sept. 23, Dec. 10, 1830, Cameron Family Papers.
21. OCDB 24:155; obituary of Mrs. Jane Murphey, *Fayetteville Observer*, Apr. 23, 1829; *Hillsborough Recorder*, July 11, 1831; Kirkland to Ruffin, Nov. 30, 1829, Thomas Ruffin Papers.
22. Murphey to Gibson, July 20, 1829, Joseph Gibson Papers; Kirkland to Ruffin, June 18, 1829, Thomas Ruffin Papers.

23. Anne Ruffin to Catherine Ruffin, Feb. 3, 1832, Ruffin-Roulhac-Hamilton Papers; Walker Anderson to D. Cameron, Feb. 1, 1832, Cameron Family Papers.
24. Thomas Ruffin to Anne K. Ruffin, Feb. 3, 1832, Thomas Ruffin Papers.
25. Lefler and Newsome, *North Carolina*, 314–26.

Chapter 10

1. Rebecca Cameron to Paul C. Cameron, Nov. 25, 1839, Cameron Family Papers; Jane de Graffenried and Phebe Kirkland to John U. Kirkland, Nov. 25, [1839], Kirkland Family Papers.
2. Phebe Kirkland to John U. Kirkland, Nov. 25, [1839], Kirkland Family Papers.
3. Alice Ruffin to Catherine Ruffin, Jan. 26, 1840, Ruffin-Roulhac-Hamilton Papers; Margaret J. Taylor to Polly Burke, Nov. 2, 1840, Weissinger Papers.
4. Mary McL. Bryant to Mildred Cameron, Sept. 18, 1841, Cameron Family Papers.
5. Phebe McLester to Polly Burke, Oct. 2, 1842, Weissinger Papers.
6. John U. Kirkland to Anne K. Ruffin, May 1844, Thomas Ruffin Papers.
7. Dr. James Webb to Mary Burke, Mar. 8, 1845, Margaret J. Taylor to Mary Burke, Oct. 5, 1835, Weissinger Papers; John U. Kirkland to Ruffin, Aug. 15, 1850, Ruffin to his wife, July 4, 1852, Estate of Nelson McLester, Mar. 4, 1859, Thomas Ruffin Papers; Wright, *Burials and Deaths Reported in the Columbus [Georgia] Enquirer*, 304.
8. John U. Kirkland to Ruffin, Jan. 17, 1853, Maggie McLester to Ruffin, May 18, 1857, Oct. 10, 1859, Ruffin to Anne K. Ruffin, Dec. 24, 1857, Sept. 15, 1858, Thomas Ruffin Papers.
9. Catherine Ruffin to John Kirkland, July 8, 1827, Ruffin-Roulhac-Hamilton Papers.
10. John U. Kirkland to Catherine Ruffin, Oct. 16, 1828, ibid.
11. Allcott, "Robert Donaldson," 333–66.
12. John U. Kirkland to Catherine Ruffin, Oct. 16, 1828, Sarah K. Nash to Catherine Ruffin, Aug. 8, 1824, Ruffin-Roulhac-Hamilton Papers.
13. Betsy Simpson to Catherine Ruffin, Nov. 26, 1828, ibid.
14. Matthias Manly to William A. Graham, Dec. 23, [1828], William A. Graham Papers.
15. John U. Kirkland to Ruffin, Dec. 24, 1828, Ruffin to Anne K. Ruffin, Dec. 28, 1828, Thomas Ruffin Papers; Catherine Ruffin to Ruffin, Jan. 4, [1829], misdated 1828, Ruffin-Roulhac-Hamilton Papers.
16. William Kirkland to Ruffin, Nov. 15, 1829, Thomas Ruffin Papers; John

U. Kirkland to Catherine Ruffin, Dec. 17, 1829, Ruffin-Roulhac-Hamilton Papers.

17. OCDB 24:148; *Hillsborough Recorder*, Oct. 21, 1829; Margaret J. Taylor to Eliza Johnston, Dec. 12, 1837, Weissinger Papers.

18. OCDB 24:365; Alice Ruffin to Catherine Ruffin, Mar. 20, 1838, Phebe Kirkland to Catherine Ruffin, May 6, 1838, Ruffin-Roulhac-Hamilton Papers. The Green tract, which John U. Kirkland bought, is now known as Montrose, the name given it by the William A. Graham family, to whom John Kirkland sold the tract in 1842.

19. OCWB E:182; John U. Kirkland to Catherine Ruffin, Dec. 17, 1829, Ruffin-Roulhac-Hamilton Papers.

20. Maria Simpson to Catherine Ruffin, Oct. 22, 1829, Ruffin-Roulhac-Hamilton Papers; John U. Kirkland to Ruffin, Feb. 11, 1830, Thomas Ruffin Papers.

21. H. B. Elliott to George M. Johnston, Mar. 3, [1829], misfiled as 1823, Weissinger Papers.

22. Victor Moreau Murphey to Graham, Aug. 6, 1835, William A. Graham Papers.

Chapter 11

1. Mary A. Kirkland to Catherine Ruffin, June 17, 1825, Ruffin-Roulhac-Hamilton Papers.

2. William A. Kirkland, Jr., to John and Alice Corbus, Feb. 4, 1958, William Alexander Kirkland Papers.

3. Clinton to Johnston, Feb. 18, 1830, Weissinger Papers.

4. Alexander Kirkland to Catherine Ruffin, Nov. 17, 1830, Ruffin-Roulhac-Hamilton Papers.

5. John U. Kirkland Account Books, vol. 2, Cain and Kirkland, 1831–33; bills from Cain and Kirkland, Oct. 27, 1834, Apr. 19, 1836, Cameron Family Papers.

6. Paul C. Cameron to D. Cameron, Oct. 21, 1834, V. M. Murphey to Paul C. Cameron, May 2, 1836, Cameron Family Papers; Murphey to Catherine Ruffin, Dec. 26, 1834, Ruffin-Roulhac-Hamilton Papers.

7. Murphey to Paul C. Cameron, June 7, 1836, May 3, 1861, Cameron Family Papers.

8. Murphey to Cameron, Jan. 18, [1837], ibid.

9. *Hillsborough Recorder*, Mar. 17, 1837.

10. Alexander Kirkland to Catherine Ruffin, Mar. 6, 1832, Ruffin-Roulhac-Hamilton Papers.

11. Murphey to Catherine Ruffin, July 18, 1833, ibid.

12. Paul Cameron to Rebecca Cameron, Jan. 6, 1835, Cameron Family Papers.

13. OCDB 28:148, 23:132–35; Mary Anderson to D. Cameron, Mar. 25, 1828, Cameron Family Papers; Margaret A. R. Burwell to Mary A. Kirkland, Jan. 17, 1846, Susan Mary Kirkland File, Burwell School Records Room.

14. Phebe Kirkland to Eliza Johnston, undated, Weissinger Papers.

15. Anne Owen Cameron to D. Cameron, Mar. 4, 1835, Cameron Family Papers.

16. Ibid.; OCDB 32:443.

17. Mary E. A. Cameron to Catherine Ruffin, Mar. 12, 1835, Phebe Kirkland to C. Ruffin, Mar. 19, 1835, Ruffin-Roulhac-Hamilton Papers.

18. Susan Kirkland to Eliza Johnston, undated, Weissinger Papers.

19. Catherine Ruffin to Anne K. Ruffin, Mar. 19, 1836, Ruffin-Roulhac-Hamilton Papers.

20. Catherine Ruffin to Anne K. Ruffin, Mar. 24, 1836, ibid.

21. Ibid.

22. Genealogical charts, William Alexander Kirkland Papers; OCDB 28:363; Catherine Roulhac to Joseph Roulhac, Sept. 30, 1839, Ruffin-Roulhac-Hamilton Papers.

23. Lizzie Cameron to Mildred Cameron, May 3, 1842, Cameron Family Papers.

24. John Kirkland to Mary A. Kirkland, May 10, 1843, Kirkland Family Papers (Duke University).

25. Thomas Ruffin to Catherine Ruffin, May 6, 1843, Ruffin-Roulhac-Hamilton Papers.

26. William A. Kirkland, Jr., to John and Alice Corbus, Feb. 4, 1958, William Alexander Kirkland Papers.

27. Alice Ruffin to Catherine Roulhac, June 17, 1843, Ruffin-Roulhac-Hamilton Papers; Thomas Ruffin to Anne K. Ruffin, Jan. 5, 1846, Thomas Ruffin Papers; Margaret A. R. Burwell to Mary A. Kirkland, Jan. 17, 1846, Susan Mary Kirkland File; Francis T. Stubbins to John Cameron, Feb. 18, 1846, Anna Cameron to Margaret Cameron, Sept. 11, 1846, Cameron Family Papers.

28. Ruffin to his wife, Jan. 21, 1846, Thomas Ruffin Papers; Margaret A. R. Burwell to Mary A. Kirkland, Jan. 17, 1846, Susan Mary Kirkland File; Stubbins to J. Cameron, Feb. 18, 1846, Cameron Family Papers.

29. Anna Kirkland to D. Cameron, June 23, 1846, Cameron Family Papers. The *Hillsborough Recorder*, January 27, 1848, carried an advertisement for Anna Kirkland's school.

30. William A. Kirkland to Thomas Ruffin, Dec. 13, 1855, Robert S. Kirkland to Thomas Ruffin, May 25, 1857, Feb. 2, 1859, Thomas Ruffin Papers.

31. Robert S. Kirkland to Ruffin, Oct. 5, 1862, ibid.; William A. Kirkland, Jr.,

to John and Alice Corbus, Feb. 4, 1958, William A. Kirkland Papers.

32. Paul C. Cameron to Pauline Cameron Shepard, Feb. 12, 1890, Cameron Family Papers.

Chapter 12

1. Catherine Roulhac to Joseph Roulhac, Oct. 22, 1840, Ruffin-Roulhac-Hamilton Papers.

2. Thomas Ruffin to Catherine Ruffin, Nov. 6, 1827, ibid.

3. Mary Kirkland to Catherine Ruffin, June 17, 1825, ibid.

4. Anne K. Ruffin to Thomas Ruffin, Sept. 30, 1827, Thomas Ruffin Papers.

5. Patty Ruffin to Thomas Ruffin, Jan. 11, 1852, ibid.

6. William K. Ruffin to Catherine Ruffin, Nov. 14, 1824, Alexander Kirkland to Catherine Ruffin, Feb. 13, Apr. 17, 1825, Ruffin-Roulhac-Hamilton Papers.

7. Alexander Kirkland to Catherine Ruffin, Feb. 13, 1825, ibid.

8. Sophia Witherspoon to William A. Graham, Apr. 14, 1828, William A. Graham Papers.

9. James Graham to William A. Graham, Mar. 21, 1827, ibid.

10. Mary Morrison to William A. Graham, Jan. 7, 1829, ibid.

11. Mary Anne Cameron to Paul C. Cameron, Feb. 19, 1828, Cameron Family Papers.

12. Anne Ruffin to Anne K. Ruffin, 1829 (in folder Nov. 16–30, 1829), Thomas Ruffin Papers.

13. Anne Ruffin to Catherine Ruffin, Dec. 7, 1829, Ruffin-Roulhac-Hamilton Papers.

14. John Kirkland to Catherine Ruffin, Dec. 17, 1829, ibid.

15. Ruffin to Anne K. Ruffin, July 30, 1830, Thomas Ruffin Papers.

16. Jane Strange to Catherine Ruffin, Mar. 23, 1829, Ruffin-Roulhac-Hamilton Papers.

17. Ruffin to Anne K. Ruffin, Jan. 31, 1832, Thomas Ruffin Papers.

18. Sarah K. Nash to Catherine Ruffin, June 17, 1831, ibid.

19. Catherine Ruffin to Paul C. Cameron, Apr. 24, 1833, Cameron Family Papers.

20. Paul C. Cameron to Catherine Ruffin, May 3, 1833, Ruffin-Roulhac-Hamilton Papers.

21. Paul C. Cameron to Catherine Ruffin, Mar. 26, 1836, ibid.

22. Catherine Ruffin to Thomas Ruffin, Feb. 23, 1832, ibid.

23. Eliza Gaston to William Gaston, Aug. 4, 1837, William Gaston Papers.

24. Ruffin to D. Cameron, Oct. 10, 1837, Ruffin to his wife, June 22, 1844, Thomas Ruffin Papers; Donnelly, "North Carolina Deaths and Marriages," 223.

25. Alice Ruffin to Catherine Ruffin, Mar. 29, 1832, May 18, 1834, Sarah K. Nash to Catherine Ruffin, June 23, 1832, Mar. 20, 1834, James H. Ruffin to Catherine Ruffin, Mar. 1, 1833, Ruffin-Roulhac-Hamilton Papers.

26. Catherine Ruffin to Thomas Ruffin, Jan. 27, 1833 (misdated by Catherine, the letter was written in 1834), Thomas Ruffin to Catherine Ruffin, Jan. 20, 1834, ibid.; Anne K. Ruffin to Ruffin, Jan. 1834, Ruffin to Green, June 18, 1834, Green to Ruffin, June 23, 1834, Thomas Ruffin Papers.

27. Sarah Nash to Catherine Ruffin, Jan. 25, 1834, Ruffin-Roulhac-Hamilton Papers.

28. Mary R. Cain to Catherine Ruffin, Jan. 15, 1834, ibid.

29. Maria Spear to Catherine Ruffin, June 16, 1834, ibid.

30. Eleanor Boylan to Catherine Ruffin, Feb. 21, 1834, ibid.; Minutes of the Vestry Proceedings of St. Matthew's Church, Apr. 23, 1838; Lefler and Wager, *Orange County*, 329.

31. Ruffin to Catherine Ruffin, Mar. 5, 1836, Thomas Ruffin Papers; Catherine Ruffin to Thomas Ruffin, July 5, 1836, Ruffin-Roulhac-Hamilton Papers. Dr. Hays was a pioneer in eye surgery and in the study of color blindness and astigmatism; he was a founder of the Franklin Institute and the American Medical Association (*Who Was Who in America: Historical Volume, 1607–1896* [Chicago, 1967], 312).

32. *Raleigh Register*, Jan. 30, 1856; Joseph Roulhac to Catherine Ruffin, Nov. 8, 1836, Catherine Ruffin to Thomas Ruffin, July 5, 1836, Ruffin-Roulhac-Hamilton Papers.

33. Obituary of Joseph Roulhac, *Raleigh Register*, Jan. 30, 1856.

34. Joseph Roulhac to Catherine Ruffin, Sept. 27, 1836, Ruffin-Roulhac-Hamilton Papers.

35. Mary Anderson to Catherine Ruffin, Oct. 27, 1836, ibid.; Margaret J. Taylor to Eliza Johnston, Nov. 19, [1836], filed with undated papers, Weissinger Papers.

36. Orange County Records, Marriage Bonds; *Hillsborough Recorder*, Dec. 16, 1836.

37. Ruffin to Anne K. Ruffin, June 22, 1844, Mar. 16, 1853, July 8, 1852, Thomas Ruffin Papers; Jane Ruffin to Catherine Roulhac, May 9, 1846, unnamed newspaper clipping, Mar. 22, 1853, John U. Kirkland to Joseph Roulhac, Nov. 30, 1849, Ruffin to Joseph Roulhac, Dec. 26, 1841, Ruffin to Catherine Ruffin Roulhac, Dec. 7, 1846, Ruffin-Roulhac-Hamilton Papers. The Roulhac children were Anne Ruffin, Frances Gray, Sarah Jane, Joseph, Thomas Ruffin, John, and William Sterling.

38. Thomas Ruffin to Joseph Roulhac, Jan. 3, 1853, Thomas Ruffin Papers.

39. Catherine Roulhac to Joseph Roulhac, July 14, 1837, Ruffin-Roulhac-Hamilton Papers.

40. *Raleigh Register* (semiweekly), Jan. 26, 1856; Pride Jones to Ruffin, Nov. 17, 1856, Thomas Ruffin Papers.

Chapter 13

1. Temin, *Jacksonian Economy*, 54–155.

2. William Kirkland to Ruffin, Sept. 30, 1830, Thomas Ruffin Papers.

3. Information from Eva Mickle Stevens, Bandera, Texas, sent to Roger Foushee, Chapel Hill Historical Society, now in Kirkland Family Papers.

4. Orange County Records, Estates: William Kirkland.

5. William Kirkland to Ruffin, Feb. 3, 1836, Thomas Ruffin Papers; Margaret J. Taylor to Eliza Johnston, Dec. 12, 1837, Walker Anderson to George Johnston, undated papers, Weissinger Papers; Walker Anderson to D. Cameron, Feb. 17, 1827, Cameron Family Papers; Robina Hogg to Jane Tillinghast, Dec. 18, 1839, Tillinghast Family Papers. The *Fayetteville Observer*, April 30, 1818, ran an advertisement by one Andrew Mickle, a tailor, looking for journeymen tailors to assist him. This may have been young Andrew's father.

6. J. S. Mulhollan to George Johnston, May 31, 1831, Weissinger Papers.

7. Herndon Haralson to Archibald Murphey, June 20, 1831, Thomas Ruffin Papers.

8. Kirkland to Ruffin, June 26, 1831, ibid.

9. William Kirkland to Ruffin, Aug. 2, Oct. 18, 1831, John U. Kirkland to Ruffin, May 29, Oct. 31, 1831, ibid.; John U. Kirkland to D. Cameron, June 29, 1831, John U. Kirkland to Bennehan, Oct. 22, 1831, Cameron Family Papers.

10. Paul C. Cameron to Ruffin, July 21, 1833, Thomas Ruffin Papers; Anderson, *Piedmont Plantation*, 46–47.

11. William Kirkland to Ruffin, Aug. 4, 1833, Thomas Ruffin Papers.

12. William Kirkland to Ruffin, Apr. 10, May 18, 1830, William Kirkland to Tom, Betty, and Susan Mary Ruffin, Mar. 11, 1832, ibid.; William Kirkland to Thomas Ruffin, Jr., Aug. 8, 1834, Moreau Murphey to Catherine Ruffin, Dec. 8, 1833, Ruffin-Roulhac-Hamilton Papers.

13. William Kirkland to Thomas, Jr., and Betty Ruffin, Oct. 4, 1831, Ruffin-Roulhac-Hamilton Papers.

14. William Kirkland to Ruffin, July 30, 1832, Thomas Ruffin Papers; Paul C. Cameron to D. Cameron, July 16, 1835, Mary Anne Cameron to D. Cameron, Apr. 24, 1835, Cameron Family Papers.

15. John Kirkland to John U. Kirkland, Nov. 10, 1830, Cameron Family Papers.

16. Ibid.; *Thom's British Directory*, 272. The names of John Kirkland's wives

given in this handbook are incorrect. See genealogical chart I.

17. John Kirkland to John U. Kirkland, Nov. 10, 1830, Cameron Family Papers.

18. Ibid. John Kirkland gave his address as Springbog near Glasgow.

19. William Kirkland to Ruffin, Feb. 22, 1834, Thomas Ruffin Papers.

20. Paul C. Cameron to Duncan Cameron, July 16, 1835, Cameron Family Papers.

21. William Kirkland to Thomas D. Bennehan, Sept. 30, 1835, ibid.

22. Paul C. Cameron to Duncan Cameron, Feb. 8, 1836, ibid.

23. Paul C. Cameron to Duncan Cameron, May 21, 1836, ibid.

24. Susan Kirkland to Phebe Kirkland, undated papers, Thomas Ruffin Papers.

25. John U. Kirkland to Ruffin, June 17, 1836, ibid.

26. William Ruffin to Thomas Ruffin, June 20, 1836, ibid.

27. Vol. 37, estate of William Kirkland, ibid. Errors in dates on tombstones are common.

28. Duncan Cameron to Paul C. Cameron, June 24, 1836, Cameron Family Papers.

29. *Fayetteville Observer*, June 30, 1836.

30. John Cameron to William A. Graham, July 8, 1836, William A. Graham Papers.

31. Anne Ruffin Cameron to Paul C. Cameron, June 30, 1836, Cameron Family Papers.

32. Paul C. Cameron to D. Cameron, May 21, 1836, ibid.; Susan Kirkland to Phebe Kirkland, undated papers, Thomas Ruffin Papers.

33. Catherine Ruffin to Thomas Ruffin, July 5, 1836, Ruffin-Roulhac-Hamilton Papers.

34. Mary Anderson to Catherine Ruffin, Jan. 13, 1835, ibid.

35. Mary Anderson to Duncan Cameron, Jan. 27, 1817, Cameron Family Papers.

36. Anna Webb to Polly Burke, Aug. 23, 1836, Weissinger Papers.

37. V. M. Murphey to Paul C. Cameron, May 3, 1861, Cameron Family Papers.

Chapter 14

1. John U. Kirkland to Ruffin, June 29, 1836, Thomas Ruffin Papers.

2. Orange County Records, Estates: William Kirkland.

3. Paul C. Cameron to Thomas D. Bennehan, June 28, 1836, Cameron Family Papers.

4. John U. Kirkland to Thomas Ruffin, June 29, 1836, Thomas Ruffin Papers. Ruffin's draft of the will, though dated June 1829, is filed under the date of John U. Kirkland's letter: June 29, 1836.

5. Orange County Records, Wills: William Kirkland.

6. John U. Kirkland to Thomas Ruffin, June 29, 1836, Thomas Ruffin Papers.

7. Orange County Records, Estates: William Kirkland, "Orange County, Court of Equity, Fall Term 1843, Answer of John U. Kirkland to the Bill of Complaint of Edwin L. DeGraffenreidt [sic] etc.," "A List of Debts Outstanding for which the estate of William Kirkland is liable in whole or in part"; John U. Kirkland to Duncan Cameron, Sept. 14, 1836, Cameron Family Papers. The estate accounts show only $6,000 owing to Cameron, but John Kirkland's letter to Cameron specifically accounts for $10,000.

8. "Inventory of all the effects Real and Personal belonging to the late William Kirkland deceased of which he died possessed both in North Carolina and elsewhere taken 1836," William A. Graham Papers.

9. Anna Webb to Polly Burke, Aug. 23, 1836, Weissinger Papers.

10. Margaret J. Taylor to Eliza Johnston, Sept. 26, 1836, ibid.

11. Thomas Ruffin to Paul C. Cameron, Oct. 30, 1836, Cameron Family Papers.

12. Margaret J. Taylor to Eliza Johnston, Nov. 19, [1836], filed among undated papers, Weissinger Papers.

13. Thomas Scott to Duncan Cameron, Dec. 28, 1821, Cameron Family Papers: "In offering my services as the Sheriff I am induced solely by the consideration of supporting my family; having lately been deprived of the means of doing so by Mr. Murphey's failure."

14. Thomas Ruffin to Paul C. Cameron, Oct. 30, 1836, Cameron Family Papers; Anne R. Cameron to Catherine Ruffin, July 29, 1836, Thomas Ruffin to Catherine Ruffin, Jan. 19, 1837, Ruffin-Roulhac-Hamilton Papers.

15. John U. Kirkland to Duncan Cameron, Sept. 14, 1836, Cameron Family Papers; vol. 37, pp. 1–8, Thomas Ruffin Papers.

16. John U. Kirkland to Ruffin, Mar. 9, 1837, Thomas Ruffin Papers.

17. Joseph Roulhac to Catherine Roulhac, Apr. 7, 1837, Ruffin-Roulhac-Hamilton Papers.

18. OCDB 22:416, 24:365, 27:571 (McKerall tract), 28:124 (Cook tract), 28:182 (Cabe tract); Franklin County Records, Franklin County Deed Book 27:319; Alice Ruffin to Catherine Ruffin, Mar. 20, 1838, Ruffin-Roulhac-Hamilton Papers.

19. Robert H. Morrison to Graham, May 10, 1836, William A. Graham Papers; Margaret J. Taylor to Eliza Johnston, Dec. 12, 1837, Weissinger Papers.

20. Margaret J. Taylor to Eliza Johnston, Dec. 12, 1837, Weissinger Papers.

21. Thomas Ruffin to Joseph Roulhac, Feb. 20, 1838, Feb. 5, 1839, Mar. 17,

1838, Ruffin-Roulhac-Hamilton Papers; Thomas Ruffin to Paul C. Cameron, Sept. 29, 1838, Cameron Family Papers; Alice Ruffin to Thomas Ruffin, Sept. 16, Nov. 2, 1838, Thomas Ruffin Papers.

22. Alice Ruffin to Catherine Roulhac, Mar. 20, 1838, Ruffin-Roulhac-Hamilton Papers.

23. Robina Hogg Norwood to Jane Tillinghast, Oct. 16, 1838, Tillinghast Family Papers.

24. Vol. 37, p. 23, Thomas Ruffin Papers.

25. Catherine Roulhac to Thomas Ruffin, Sept. 28, 1827, Susan Kirkland to Catherine Ruffin, undated papers, Phebe Kirkland to Catherine Ruffin, Mar. 18, 1825, Mary Kirkland to Catherine Ruffin, June 17, 1825, Ruffin-Roulhac-Hamilton Papers; Margaret J. Taylor wrote to Polly Burke that "Mary and Susan are large and fat" (Oct. 5, 1845, Weissinger Papers).

26. Mary Kirkland to Catherine Ruffin, Nov. 14, 1829, Ruffin-Roulhac-Hamilton Papers.

27. Margaret J. Taylor to Polly Burke, Nov. 30, 1850, Weissinger Papers.

28. Susan Kirkland to Catherine Ruffin, May 21, 1834, Ruffin-Roulhac-Hamilton Papers.

29. William Cain to Minerva Cain, Feb. 27, 1837, Tod R. Caldwell Papers.

30. Maria Simpson to Catherine Ruffin, Oct. 22, 1829, Ruffin-Roulhac-Hamilton Papers; Phebe Kirkland to Alice Ruffin, undated papers, Anne Ruffin to Ruffin, July 2, 1839, undated papers, Thomas Ruffin Papers; *Hillsborough Recorder*, July 11, 1839.

31. Ruffin to Roulhac, Nov. 14, 1839, Ruffin-Roulhac-Hamilton Papers.

32. Paul C. Cameron to Duncan Cameron, Nov. 28, 1839, Cameron Family Papers.

33. Vol. 37, pp. 11–20, 29, also items 81, 82, 83–91, Thomas Ruffin Papers.

34. Vol. 37, items 10, 12, 14, 15, 19, 28, 33, 42, 45, 60, 61, 75, 112, 140, ibid.

35. Orange County Records, Estates: William Kirkland, "Orange County, Court of Equity, Fall Term 1843: The Answer of John U. Kirkland etc.," pp. 6–7; vol. 37, pp. 21–22, Thomas Ruffin Papers.

36. Vol. 37, pp. 21–22, Thomas Ruffin Papers; OCDB 34:12.

37. Margaret J. Taylor to Eliza Johnston, Mar. 24, 1840, Weissinger Papers.

38. OCDB 30:115 (Nov. 22, 1842), the sale of land from John U. Kirkland to William A. Graham. Documentation for John U. Kirkland's purchase of Green's property comes only from Alice Ruffin's letter to Catherine Roulhac, Mar. 20, 1838, Ruffin-Roulhac-Hamilton Papers: "Uncle John has bought Mr. Green's house."

39. Samuel E. Brietz to Ruffin, Apr. 25, 1842, John U. Kirkland to Ruffin, Apr. 30, 1842, vol. 37, pp. 23–28, Thomas Ruffin Papers.

40. Orange County Records, Estates: William Kirkland.

41. E. L. de Graffenriedt to Thomas Ruffin, Feb. 3, 1840, Thomas Ruffin to E. L. de Graffenriedt, Feb. 11, 1840, Thomas Ruffin Papers.

42. Orange County Records, Estates: William Kirkland, "Account Sales of Personal Property sold 1839."

43. "Orange County, Court of Equity, Fall Term 1843, Answer of John U. Kirkland etc.," and "A List of debts outstanding for which the estate of William Kirkland is liable in whole or in part," ibid.

44. Vol. 37, pp. 23–28, Thomas Ruffin Papers.

Chapter 15

1. John U. Kirkland Account Books, vol. 8, Mar. 1, 1844, and passim.

2. Lefler and Wager, *Orange County*, 181, 346, 367; Orange County Records, "Book of Proceedings, the Court of the Wardens of the Poor"; Blackwelder, *Age of Orange*, 13.

3. Blackwelder, *Age of Orange*, 23; Thomas Ruffin to Sterling Ruffin, Aug. 1, 1856, Thomas Ruffin Papers ("Your Uncle John is not at home, having gone to Chapel Hill . . . to attend the tax-gatherings; pretty clear evidence of earnest electioneering!"); Hamilton and Williams, *Papers of William A. Graham*, 6:473–74, Samuel F. Phillips to William A. Graham, Dec. 28, 1865.

Phillips became solicitor general of the United States in President Ulysses S. Grant's administration.

4. Russell, *The Woman Who Rang the Bell*, 28; Lefler and Wager, *Orange County*, 193, 358.

5. Margaret J. Taylor to Polly Burke, July 24, 1847, Weissinger Papers.

6. Taylor to Burke, Dec. 9, 1848, ibid.

7. Catherine Roulhac to Joseph Roulhac, Oct. 6, 1844, Susan Nash to Catherine Roulhac, Mar. 10, 1845, Ruffin-Roulhac-Hamilton Papers.

8. Thomas Ruffin to Catherine Roulhac, Jan. 15, 1840, Thomas Ruffin to Joseph Roulhac, Nov. 7, 1844, ibid.

9. *Hillsborough Recorder*, Jan. 28, 1847. John Scott, Lewis Mitchell Scott, and Nancy Scott Brachen were Thomas Scott's children. See John Scott to Catherine Roulhac, Oct. 27, 1832, and Lewis M. Scott to Catherine Ruffin, July 16, 1833, Ruffin-Roulhac-Hamilton Papers.

10. *Hillsborough Recorder*, Oct. 30, 1845; Margaret J. Taylor to Polly Burke, Oct. 5, Dec. 1, 1845, Weissinger Papers.

11. Robert Strange to Catherine Roulhac, June 2, 1846, Ruffin-Roulhac-Hamilton Papers.

12. J. W. Strange to Robert Strange, Dec. 22, 1852, Robert Strange, Jr., Papers;

John U. Kirkland to Ruffin, Feb. 16, 1851, Ruffin to Anne K. Ruffin, Jan. 9, 1842, Thomas Ruffin Papers.

13. Robert Strange to Ruffin, Jan. 10, 1853, Thomas Ruffin Papers.

14. Joseph Roulhac to Ruffin, July 28, 1853, J. W. Strange to Ruffin, Feb. 21, Mar. 23, 1854, ibid.; Cumberland County Records, Wills: Robert Strange. Strange's second wife was Mrs. Margaret Nelson of Raleigh.

15. John U. Kirkland to Ruffin, Jan. 18, 1849, Thomas Ruffin Papers.

16. *Hillsborough Recorder*, Jan. 31, 1849.

17. J. W. Strange to Robert Strange, Jr., Jan. 19, 1849, Robert Strange, Jr., Papers.

18. *Hillsborough Recorder*, Jan. 31, 1849. Among the silhouettes cut by Augustin Edouart in Glasgow in 1832 was that of K. W. Kirkland of St. George's Road. This was probably Kenneth William Kirkland. See Jackson, *Ancestors in Silhouette*, 146. I am grateful to John Patrick Manley, Market Lavington, Wiltshire, England, for bringing this book to my attention.

19. Robina Norwood to Polly Burke, Apr. 16, 1849, Weissinger Papers.

20. Sir John Kirkland to John U. Kirkland, Mar. 8, 1849, Ruffin-Roulhac-Hamilton Papers.

21. Ibid.; Shaw, *Knights of England*, 2:340. Sir John Kirkland died in 1871. His son, John Agmondisham Vesey Kirkland was educated at Harrow before joining the army and ultimately became a brigadier general. He died March 24, 1896, in Fordel, Glenfarg, Perthshire, Scotland (*London Times*, Jan. 16, 1871, Mar. 27, 1896).

22. Thomas Ruffin to Joseph Roulhac, Nov. 12, 1849, John U. Kirkland to Roulhac, Nov. 30, 1849, Ruffin-Roulhac-Hamilton Papers.

23. Margaret J. Taylor to Polly Burke, Dec. 25, 1849, Dec. 15, 1853, Weissinger Papers.

24. Jane Ruffin to Catherine Roulhac, May 9, 1846, Ruffin-Roulhac-Hamilton Papers; Mary Moses to Polly Burke, Mar. 6, 1851, Weissinger Papers.

25. Hines Holt to Ruffin, Apr. 25, 1854, Thomas Ruffin Papers.

26. James W. Strange to Catherine Roulhac, Mar. 13, 1845, Ruffin-Roulhac-Hamilton Papers.

27. Hines Holt to Ruffin, Dec. 17, 1853, Thomas Ruffin Papers. I am grateful to Clason Kyle of Columbus, Georgia, a de Graffenried descendant, for sending me the tombstone inscription.

28. John U. Kirkland to Ruffin, July 15, 20, 1850, Thomas Ruffin Papers.

29. John U. Kirkland to Ruffin, Aug. 15, 1850, Ruffin to Anne K. Ruffin, Aug. 18, 1850, Peter B. Ruffin to Ruffin, Oct. 16, 1850, ibid.

30. Lefler and Wager, *Orange County*, 274; John U. Kirkland to Ruffin, Feb. 24, 1863, Thomas Ruffin Papers.

31. Margaret J. Taylor to Polly Burke, Sept. 21, 1851, Weissinger Papers; John K. Ruffin to Ruffin, Mar. 20, 1854, Thomas Ruffin Papers.

32. Paul C. Cameron to Rebecca B. Cameron, Sept. 16, 1836, Cameron Family Papers; *Hillsborough Recorder*, Oct. 25, 1838; Ruffin to Anne K. Ruffin, June 22, 1844, Thomas Ruffin Papers. The only son in the Simpson family committed suicide in late 1831 or early 1832. See Elizabeth S. Kirkland to Catherine Ruffin, May 26, 1832, Ruffin-Roulhac-Hamilton Papers.

33. John U. Kirkland Account Books, vol. 7, p. 490; Craven County Records, Wills: Samuel Simpson, Elizabeth Simpson.

34. Alice Ruffin to Anne K. Ruffin, Feb. 15, 1855, Thomas Ruffin Papers.

35. Thomas R. Cain to Minerva Caldwell, Jan. 12, 1854, James F. Cain to Minerva Caldwell, Nov. 30, 1856, Tod R. Caldwell Papers.

36. James F. Cain to Minerva Caldwell, Jan. 5, 1857, ibid.

37. Ruffin to Anne K. Ruffin, Jan. 23, 1859, Thomas Ruffin Papers; William W. Kirkland to Annie Roulhac, July 19, 1852, Ruffin-Roulhac-Hamilton Papers.

38. Hamilton and Williams, *Papers of William A. Graham* 5:97, Graham to William A. Graham, Jr., Mar. 3, 1859.

39. W. W. Kirkland to Ruffin, Apr. 2, 1859, Thomas Ruffin Papers; Hamilton and Williams, *Papers of William A. Graham*, 5:52n.

40. W. A. Kirkland to Annie Roulhac, Sept. 5, 1852, Ruffin-Roulhac-Hamilton Papers; Hamilton and Williams, *Papers of William A. Graham*, 4:50, W. A. Kirkland to William A. Graham, Mar. 3, 1851.

41. W. A. Kirkland to [Annie Roulhac], Nov. 21, 1855, Ruffin-Roulhac-Hamilton Papers.

42. Hamilton and Williams, *Papers of William A. Graham*, 4:50, W. A. Kirkland to Graham, Mar. 3, 1851.

43. Ibid., pp. 212–13, Kirkland to Graham, Oct. 30, 1851.

44. William A. Kirkland to Annie Roulhac, Nov. 21, 1855, Ruffin-Roulhac-Hamilton Papers; William A. Kirkland, Jr., to Alice and John Corbus, Feb. 4, 1958, also family charts, William Alexander Kirkland Papers; W. A. Kirkland to Ruffin, June 30, 1856, Thomas Ruffin Papers.

Chapter 16

1. Freeman, *Lee's Lieutenants*, 1:448, 3:237, 243–46, 546; Hamilton and Williams, *Papers of William A. Graham*, 3:375n–376n, 6:49.

2. Hamilton and Williams, *Papers of William A. Graham*, 5:371, 407; Paul C. Cameron to Sterling Ruffin, July 4, 1862, Thomas Ruffin Papers; Kirkland Family Bible no. 2, Kirkland Family Papers; Manarin and Jordan, *North Carolina Troops*, 1:585, 4:270–71, 5:251.

3. Kirkland Family Bible no. 2, Kirkland Family Papers.

4. Elizabeth A. Bingham to Polly Burke, June 15, 1864, Weissinger Papers.

5. Craven County Records, Wills: Samuel Simpson; James F. Cain to Ruffin, Jan. 15, 1862, Thomas Ruffin Papers.

6. MacRae, *The Descendants of Duncan and Ann (Cameron) MacRae,* 9–10.

7. William A. Kirkland, Jr., to Alice and John Corbus, Feb. 4, 1958, William Alexander Kirkland Papers; Robert S. Kirkland to Ruffin, Oct. 5, 1862, Thomas Ruffin Papers.

8. William A. Kirkland, Jr., to Alice and John Corbus, Feb. 4, 1958, William Alexander Kirkland Papers.

9. Paul C. Cameron to Ruffin, Jan. 5, 1863, Thomas Ruffin Papers.

10. Newspaper clipping, Jane D. Dicks, "Former Smithfieldian Restores Ayrmount," *Smithfield Herald,* Feb. 23, 1954, Kirkland Family Papers.

11. Paul C. Cameron to his son Duncan, Sept. 27, 1865, Cameron Family Papers.

12. Delta Kappa Gamma Society, *Some Pioneer Women Teachers,* 114–16; Bowles, *Good Beginning,* 9–10, 19–20, 36–37, 82, 173. A dormitory built in 1914 was named Kirkland for Susan Mary. It was demolished in 1964.

13. Maggie McLester to Ruffin, June 13, 1865, Thomas Ruffin Papers.

14. Maggie McLester to Thomas Ruffin, Oct. 18, 1866, ibid. Paul C. Cameron to Thomas R. Roulhac, Nov. 17, 1869, Ruffin-Roulhac-Hamilton Papers; Nash, *Ladies in the Making,* 130–31, 140; two little books belonging to Maggie McLester: "Souvenir Album," and *Daily Light and Strength* (New York, 1897), containing Maggie McLester's marginal jottings, and two newspaper clippings: E. J. Parkins, "From Hospital to College to Parking Lot," *Raleigh Times,* Nov. 11, 1964, and an unidentified and undated newspaper clipping, Kirkland Family Papers.

In Maggie McLester's "Souvenir Album" are the names of Willie and R. E. Calder, one of whom was probably the man she hoped to marry.

15. Marginal jottings by Maggie McLester in *Daily Light and Strength,* Hallie Kirkland and Samuel Kirkland to Maggie McLester, Jan. 4, 1913, Kirkland Family Papers.

Other Wilson employers of Maggie McLester were Herbert Rountree and R. P. Watson.

16. Maggie J. Kirkland to Maggie McLester, May 29, 1884, Aug. 25, 1886, Kirkland Family Papers; John U. Kirkland to "My very Dear Daughter," Dec. [29], 1869, letter in possession of May K. R. Reynolds.

17. Susan M. Read to Polly Burke, Feb. 22, 1868, Weissinger Papers.

18. John U. Kirkland to "My very Dear Daughter," Dec. [29], 1869, letter in possession of May K. R. Reynolds; *Thom's British Directory,* 656.

19. William A. Kirkland, Jr., to Alice and John Corbus, Feb. 4, 1958, H. A.

Hubert, Sec'ty of the Navy, to Admiral W. A. Kirkland, July 11, 1895, William Alexander Kirkland Papers. Powell, *Dictionary of North Carolina Biography*, 3:370–71.

20. Paul C. Cameron to Thomas R. Roulhac, Dec. 27, 1868, Ruffin-Roulhac-Hamilton Papers. Cameron's references to Webster and Kent are to Daniel Webster, lawyer, orator, and statesman, and to James Kent, jurist and professor of law. Lord Eldon was John Scott, for many years a jurist and lord chancellor.

21. OCDB 36:417, 37:65.

22. OCDB 40:59, 45:45; United States Census 1850: Orange County, Slave Schedule, microfilm, p. 101.

23. W. R. King to Samuel S. Kirkland, June 30, 1876, Samuel S. Kirkland to Eliza G. Kirkland, Aug. 23, 1876, Kirkland Family Papers; Hamilton and Williams, *Papers of William A. Graham*, 7:552, William A. Graham to Susan W. Graham, May 22, 1868; William W. Kirkland to Anne K. Ruffin, Jan. 31, 1870, Thomas Ruffin Papers.

In later life General Kirkland had a post office job. He died in Washington, D.C., in a home for old soldiers and was buried at Elmwood Cemetery, Shenandoah Junction, West Virginia, in the family plot of his son-in-law Rezin Davis Shepherd (William H. Dean to Craig Mathews, May 29, 1952, Kirkland Family Papers). Shepherd was a well-known Shakespearean actor. Under her stage name, Odette Tyler, Elizabeth Lee Kirkland Shepherd also had a successful career in the theater and toured in her husband's company. She turned to literature as a second career and wrote plays, short stories, and novels, among them *Boss, A Story of Virginia Life* and *Between Two Angels*. I thank May K. R. Reynolds for this information about Elizabeth Kirkland.

24. Copy of item from *Raleigh Sentinel*, Mar. 9, 1873, Kirkland Family Papers.

25. "Property for Taxation by Confederate States, [Jan.] 1861," Petition for pardon, undated but probably summer 1865, Thomas Ruffin Papers.

26. Ruffin to unknown, July 14, 1866, ibid.

27. Paul C. Cameron to Ruffin, [Dec. 1865], ibid.; Lefler and Newsome, *North Carolina*, 484.

28. Paul C. Cameron to Bennehan Cameron, Jan. 18, 1869 (misdated but filed under same date in 1870), Bennehan Cameron Papers.

29. Paul C. Cameron to Anne K. Ruffin, May 22, 1874, Thomas Ruffin Papers.

30. Family Bible Records, Kirkland Family Papers; information from Patsy de Graffenriedt's tombstone, copied by Clason Kyle, and obtained through the courtesy of John L. Sanders; Paul C. Cameron to his sisters, Jan. 26, 1879, Cameron Family Papers.

31. Thomas R. Cain to Minerva Caldwell, Feb. 14, 1879, Tod R. Caldwell Papers.

32. Orange County Records, Wills: Thomas Ruffin, Estates: William Kirkland, Anne K. Ruffin.

33. Ibid., Estates: John U. Kirkland.

34. Ibid., Estates: William Kirkland; Thomas Cain to Minerva Caldwell, Dec. 26, 1881, Tod. R. Caldwell Papers.

35. Kirkland Family Bible no. 1, Kirkland Family Papers.

36. OCWB H:307. When Betsy Kirkland's New York Bank stock had risen to par value, John U. Kirkland had sold it and invested the proceeds in the Raleigh National Bank stock, which made up her estate at her death (Orange County Records, Estates: E[lizabeth] A. Kirkland). All that Betsy had inherited from her mother's estate had probably been lost in the war or spent for the family's support in the intervening years.

37. Ibid., Estates: John U. Kirkland; OCDB 48:273 (one-half interest in tanyard), 47:508 (one-half interest in lot 25), 48:92 (74 acres), 50:403 (18 acres).

38. Orange County Records, Estates: John U. Kirkland, William Kirkland.

39. OCDB 47:482 (tanyard lots), 47:563 (85 acres), 49:469 (Ayr Mount); Orange County Records, Estates: William Kirkland.

❦ *Bibliography* ❦

Primary Sources

Chapel Hill, North Carolina
  Southern Historical Collection, University of North Carolina Library
    Elizabeth Willis Anderson Papers
    John L. Bailey Papers
    Tod R. Caldwell Papers
    Bennehan Cameron Papers
    Cameron Family Papers
    Sarah Rebecca Cameron Papers
    1816 Direct Tax List of Orange County, North Carolina
    William Gaston Papers
    Joseph Gibson Papers
    de Graffenried Family Papers
    William A. Graham Papers
    Benjamin R. Huske Papers
    John U. Kirkland Account Books
    John MacRae Papers
    Archibald Debow Murphey Papers
    Nott Mercantile Books
    Ruffin-Roulhac-Hamilton Papers
    Thomas Ruffin Papers
    Robert Strange, Jr., Papers
    University of North Carolina Archives
    James Webb Papers
    Eliza Mary Bond Johnston Weissinger Papers
Durham, North Carolina
  Duke University Manuscript Department, William R. Perkins Library
    Kirkland Family Papers
    James Meacham Papers
    Tillinghast Family Papers
    Michael H. Turrentine Papers
Edinburgh, Scotland
  General Register Office, New Register House

Burgh Register, Craft Minute Book: Fleshers, Ayr, 1661–1794. Microfilm, Genealogical Library, Church of Jesus Christ of Latter-Day Saints,
Raleigh, North Carolina

Old Parochial Registers, County of Ayrshire, Parish of Ayr, Births: 1721–
53, 1753–90, Marriages: 1687–1761, 1761–1819, Deaths: 1766–1819.
Microfilm, Genealogical Library, Church of Jesus Christ of Latter-Day
Saints, Raleigh, North Carolina

Greenville, North Carolina
  East Carolina University Manuscript Collection
    William Alexander Kirkland Papers

Hillsborough, North Carolina
  Burwell School Records Room
    Susan Mary Kirkland File
  Hillsborough Presbyterian Church
    Records of Hillsborough Presbyterian Church
  Office of the Clerk of the Court, Orange County Courthouse
    Orange County Will Books
  Register of Deeds Office, Court Street Annex
    Orange County Deed Books
  Saint Matthew's Episcopal Church
    Minutes of the Vestry Proceedings of St. Matthew's Church, Hillsboro,
      Orange Co., North Carolina

Northfield, Vermont
  Norwich University Archives
    Alumni Records

Private Papers
  Kirkland Family Papers in possession of Richard H. Jenrette, New York,
    New York
  Kirkland letters in possession of May Kirkland Robertson Reynolds, Mount
    Pleasant, South Carolina

Raleigh, North Carolina
  North Carolina Division of Archives and History
    Bute County Records: List of Taxables, 1771; Marriage Bonds, Court
      Minutes
    Craven County Records: Wills
    Cumberland County Records: Deed Books (microfilm), Wills
    Franklin County Records: Deed Books (microfilm)
    Orange County Records: "Book of Proceedings, the Court of the War-
      dens of the Poor"; Civil Action Papers; Census Records, 1800–1850
      (manuscript); Estates; Marriage Bonds; Court Minutes; Superior

    Court Minutes; Tax Lists, 1791–96; Wills
  Wake County Records: Wills
  Warren County Records: Deed Books (microfilm), Marriage Bonds;
    Court Minutes; Tax Lists, 1781–1801; Wills, Will Books (microfilm)
Secretary of State's Office
  Lord Granville Land Grants
  North Carolina Land Grants

Secondary Sources

Allcott, John V. "Robert Donaldson, the First North Carolinian to Become
  Prominent in the Arts." *North Carolina Historical Review* 52 (Autumn
  1975): 333–66.
Anderson, Jean Bradley. *Piedmont Plantation: The Bennehan-Cameron Family
  and Lands in North Carolina.* Durham, 1985.
Bailyn, Bernard. *Voyagers to the West: A Passage in the Peopling of America on
  the Eve of the Revolution.* New York, 1986.
Blackwelder, Ruth. *The Age of Orange.* Charlotte, N.C., 1961.
The Bombay Almanac, Directory, and Register. Bombay, 1841.
The Bombay Calendar and Register, 1823. Bombay, 1823.
Bowles, Elisabeth Ann. *A Good Beginning: The First Four Decades of the Uni-
  versity of North Carolina at Greensboro.* Chapel Hill, 1967.
*Boyle's Fashionable Court and Country Guide and Town Visiting Directory,
  January, 1847.* London, [1847].
Carroll, Grady L. E. *Francis Asbury in North Carolina.* Nashville, 1964.
Cumming, William P. *North Carolina in Maps.* Raleigh, 1966.
Cyclopedia of Eminent and Representative Men of the Carolinas. 2 vols. Madi-
  son, Wisc., 1892.
Davis, Curtis C. *Revolution's Godchild.* Chapel Hill, 1976.
Delta Kappa Gamma Society Committee on Pioneer Women in Education. *Some
  Pioneer Women Teachers of North Carolina.* N.p., 1955.
Devine, T. M. "Glasgow Merchants and the Collapse of the Tobacco Trade,
  1775–1783." *Scottish Historical Review* 52–53 (1973–74): 50–74.
Donaldson Academy and Manual Labor School. Fayetteville, 1834.
Donnelly, Ralph W., comp. "North Carolina Deaths and Marriages from the
  United States Catholic Miscellany, June 1822–July 1852." *North Carolina
  Genealogical Journal* 12 (November 1986): 220–27.
Dunlop, Annie I., ed. *The Royal Burgh of Ayr.* Edinburgh, 1953.
Engstrom, Mary Claire. "Early Quakers in the Eno River Valley, *ca.* 1750–

1847." *Eno* 7, no. 2 [1989]: 1–73.

Freeman, Douglas Southall. *Lee's Lieutenants: A Study in Command*. 3 vols. New York, 1942–44.

Fries, Adelaide, et al., eds. *Records of the Moravians in North Carolina*. 11 vols. Raleigh, 1922-69.

Fruth, Florence Knight. *Some Descendants of Richard Few of Chester County, Pennsylvania, and Allied Lines, 1682–1976*. Beaver Falls, Pa., 1977.

Galt, John. *Annals of the Parish*. Edinburgh, 1821. Reprint. New York, 1972.

The Glasgow Directory Containing a List of the Merchants, Manufacturers, Traders, etc. in the City and Suburbs. Glasgow, 1820.

de Graffenried, Thomas P. *History of the de Graffenried Family*. N.p., 1925.

Graham, Henry Grey. *The Social Life of Scotland in the Eighteenth Century*. London, 1928.

Griffen, Francis. *Less Time for Meddling: A History of Salem Academy and College, 1772–1866*. Winston-Salem, 1979.

Hamilton, J. G. de Roulhac, and Max R. Williams, eds. *The Papers of William A. Graham*. 7 vols. Raleigh, 1957–84.

Henderson, Archibald, and Bayard Wooten. *Old Houses and Gardens of North Carolina*. Chapel Hill, 1939.

Hoyt, William Henry. *The Papers of Archibald D. Murphey*. 2 vols. Raleigh, 1914.

Hook, Andrew. *Scotland and America: A Study of Cultural Relations, 1750–1835*. Glasgow, 1975.

Jackson, Mrs. F. Neville. *Ancestors in Silhouette*. London, 1921.

Junior Service League. *A Guide to Historic Fayetteville and Cumberland County*. Fayetteville, 1975.

Lamb, W. Kaye, ed. *The Journal and Letters of Sir Alexander Mackenzie*. Cambridge, Eng., 1970.

Lane, Mills. *Architecture of the Old South: North Carolina*. Savannah, 1985.

Lefler, Hugh T., and Albert R. Newsome. *North Carolina: The History of a Southern State*. Chapel Hill, 1954.

Lefler, Hugh T., and Paul Wager. *Orange County, 1752–1952*. Chapel Hill, 1953.

Lenman, Bruce. *Integration, Enlightenment, and Industrialization: Scotland, 1746–1832*. Toronto, 1981.

MacDonald, Donald. *Lewis: A History of the Island*. Edinburgh, 1978.

MacRae, Lawrence. *The Descendants of Duncan and Ann (Cameron) MacRae of Scotland and North Carolina*. (Copy in North Carolina Collection, University of North Carolina, lacks title page with place and date of publication.)

Manarin, Louis H., and Weymouth T. Jordan, Jr., eds. *North Carolina Troops, 1861–1865: A Roster*. 11 vols. to date. Raleigh, 1966–.

Markham, Allan B. "Land Grants to Early Settlers in Old Orange County, North Carolina." 1973. Map.

Memorials of Old Haileybury College. Westminster, 1904.

Merrens, Harry Roy. *Colonial North Carolina in the Eighteenth Century.* Chapel Hill, 1964.

Murray, Elizabeth Reid. *Wake, Capital County of North Carolina.* Raleigh, 1983.

Musgrave, Sir William, comp. *Obituaries prior to 1800.* London, 1899.

Nash, Ann Strudwick. *Ladies in the Making.* Hillsborough, 1964.

Nichol, Norman. *Glasgow and the Tobacco Lords.* London, 1966.

Oates, John A. *The Story of Fayetteville and the Upper Cape Fear.* Fayetteville, 1950.

Paterson, James. *History of the County of Ayr.* 2 vols. Edinburgh, 1847–52.

The Post-Office Annual Directory for 1829–30. Glasgow, 1829.

The Post-Office London Directory for 1833. London, [1833].

Powell, William S., ed. *Dictionary of North Carolina Biography.* 3 vols. to date. Chapel Hill, 1979–.

Preminger, Erik Lee. *Gypsy and Me.* Boston, 1984.

Prince William: The Story of Its People and Its Places. Manassas, Va., 1961.

Records of Dettingen Parish, Prince William County, Virginia. Dumfries, Va., 1976.

Robertson, William. *Ayrshire: Its History and Historic Families.* 2 vols. Kilmarnock, Scotland, 1908.

Robson's Improved London Directory, Street Guide, and Carriers' List for 1820. London, 1820.

Rose, Ben L. *Thomas McNeill of Caswell County, North Carolina, His Forebears and Descendants.* Richmond, 1984.

Royal Kalendar and Court and City Register for England, Scotland, Ireland, and the Colonies for the Year 1837. London, 1837.

Russell, Phillips. *The Woman Who Rang the Bell.* Chapel Hill, 1949.

Sanders, Charles Richard. *The Cameron Plantation in Central North Carolina (1776–1973) and Its Founder Richard Bennehan.* Durham, 1974.

Shaw, William A. *The Knights of England.* 2 vols. 1906. Reprint. Baltimore, 1971.

Showalter, Elaine. *The Female Malady.* New York, 1985.

Sinclair, Sir John. *A Statistical Account of Scotland.* Edinburgh, 1792.

Smith, James K. *Alexander Mackenzie, Explorer: The Hero Who Failed.* Toronto, 1973.

Snyder, Franklyn B. *The Life of Robert Burns.* New York, 1932.

Strang, John. *Glasgow and Its Clubs.* London, 1856.

"Subscribers in Virginia to Blackstone's *Commentaries on the Laws of England,*

Philadelphia, 1771–1772." *William and Mary Quarterly* 2d ser., 1 (1921):183.

Temin, Peter. *The Jacksonian Economy.* New York, 1969.

Thom's British Directory and Official Hand-book of the United Kingdom, 1862. London, 1862.

Trevelyan, George M. *Illustrated English Social History.* 3 vols. New York, 1942.

U.S., Department of Commerce, Bureau of the Census. *Heads of Families at the First Census of the United States Taken in the Year 1790: North Carolina.* Washington, D.C., 1908.

The University of North Carolina, Chapel Hill, Alumni Directory. Chapel Hill, 1954.

Veight, Ilza. *Hysteria: The History of a Disease.* Chicago, 1965.

Who Was Who in America, 1607–1896. Chicago, 1963.

Wright, Buster W., comp. *Burials and Deaths Reported in the Columbus [Georgia] Enquirer, 1832–1872.* N.p., 1984.

Newspapers

Fayetteville American
Fayetteville Observer
Hillsborough Recorder
North Carolina Journal and Carolina Observer
Raleigh Register

ꙮ *Index* ꙮ

Adam, Robert, 30
Allison, John, 16
Alves, Walter, 20–21
American Literary, Scientific, and
  Military Academy. *See* Norwich
  University
American Revolution, 20, 27, 114;
  and tobacco trade, 5, 6, 11, 13
Amis, John D., 111
Anderson, Daniel, 12–13, 18, 22, 23–
  24, 59, 80, 193 (n. 9)
Anderson, Daniel, and Company, 13
Anderson, George, 80, 122
Anderson, Gen. George B., 160
Anderson, Mary Cameron, 23, 24, 59,
  97, 117, 124, 130–31, 160
Anderson, Walker, 59, 69, 96, 97,
  102, 117, 121
Anderson, William, 59
Armistead, Mary, 14
Asbury, Bishop Francis, 20
Ashe, Mary. *See* Moses, Mary Ashe
Aykroyd, James, 64
Ayr, Scotland, 1, 3–4, 6–8, 9–11, 13,
  28, 29
Ayr Mount (Airmount), 41, 91, 92,
  120, 137, 167, 168; location and
  description of, vii, 124; and William
  Kirkland, vii, viii, 31, 37, 148; as
  plantation, viii, 26, 49–50, 53–55,
  77, 141; furnishings of, viii–ix, 36–
  37, 138, 142–43, 166, 180; land title of, 16–17; construction of, 31–
  37; grandchildren at, 43, 61, 99,

114, 124; visitors at, 62–63, 86,
  92, 96–97, 116, 123–26, 164; attempted sales of, 80–81, 85, 142–
  43, 144, 147, 175, 177; burials at,
  100, 105, 129, 152–53, 187–88;
  and William Kirkland's heirs, 139,
  147–48, 149, 167, 171, 175; Civil
  War anecdote about, 165; last Kirklands at, 179–80
Ayrshire, Scotland, 1–2, 3–4, 6–8, 10,
  11

Badger, George E., 169
Bagge, Charles F., 80, 136, 139, 144–
  45, 146, 147
Bain, Nathaniel D., 132, 133
Bank of Cape Fear, 77, 136, 138
Bank of the State of North Carolina,
  124, 127, 136
Barringer, Daniel, 112
Battle, William H., 59
Ben (Kirkland slave), 170
Bennehan, Richard, 18, 23, 61, 71–72
Bennehan, Thomas Dudley, 22, 152,
  173; friendship with Kirklands, 23,
  61, 71–72, 96, 123, 124, 128; busi-
  ness with Kirklands, 54–55, 122;
  and Catherine Ruffin, 110–11
Berry, John, 143, 149
Berry and Kirkland, firm of, 149
Betsy (Kirkland slave), 50
Bingham, Elizabeth A., 164
Bingham, Phoebe. *See* Kirkland,
  Phoebe Bingham

Bingham, William, 21
Bingham, William J., 21, 51
Bingham School, 21
Birch, Mary, 90
Bishop, Louisa. *See* Kirkland, Louisa
  Bishop
Blacknall, Dr. Richard, 73
Bland, J. H., 41
Bond, Eliza. *See* Johnston, Eliza Bond
Bond, Thomas, 57
Borland, Andrew, 98
Boswell, James, 7, 192 (n. 19)
Boylan, Eleanor, 95, 114, 115, 125
Boylan, James, 124
Brainerd, Miss (teacher), 64
Branch, William, 60
Brazier, Robert H. B., 42
Briggs, James, 34
Briggs, John Joyner, 33–34, 197
  (n. 19)
Briggs, Thomas H., 34
Broadnax, Susan Mary Ruffin, 125
Brown and Kirkland, firm of, 98
Brown[e], Peter, 72
Brownsville, Tenn.: Kirkland land
  near, 121, 122
Bryant, Mary McLean, 86, 111, 116
Buchanan, George, 5
Buchanan, Hastie and Company, 5
Burgwin, Eliza, 107
Burgwin, George, 107
Burgwin, Julia, 64, 107
Burgwin, [Margaret] Mag, 107
Burke, Mary (Polly), 59, 60, 71, 87,
  132; and Dr. de Graffenriedt, 45–
  46; school of, 56, 70, 142; move to
  Alabama, 95, 97
Burke, Gov. Thomas, 15, 45, 56
Burns, Robert, 7, 9
Burnside (Hillsborough), 198 (n. 9)

Burwell, Margaret Anna R., 102, 137,
  157
Burwell, Rev. Robert, 102
Burwell School, 88, 96
Butler, John, 17

Cain, Dr. James F., 159, 180
Cain, Julia E. Tate, 159
Cain, Mary Clack. *See* Ruffin, Mary
  Clack Cain
Cain, Mary Ruffin, 40, 56, 113, 115,
  130
Cain, Minerva. *See* Caldwell, Minerva
  Cain
Cain, Thomas R., 174, 175
Cain, William, 21, 41, 55
Cain, William, Jr., 40, 47, 94, 98,
  142, 143, 159, 198 (n. 9)
Cain and Kirkland, firm of, 94, 95,
  119
Calder, R. E., 217 (n. 14)
Calder, Willie, 217 (n. 14)
Caldwell, Rev. Joseph, 64, 71
Caldwell, Minerva Cain, 142, 159,
  174
Call, Daniel, 96, 102
Cameron, Anna (Nancy) Call, 96, 98,
  102, 104, 147
Cameron, Anna McKenzie. *See*
  Kirkland, Anna McKenzie Cameron
Cameron, Anne Owen, 96–97
Cameron, Anne Ruffin, 82, 111, 132,
  141; and aunts, 63, 69–70, 73; and
  Paul C. Cameron, 96, 109–10, 122,
  173; childbirth troubles of, 130,
  138
Cameron, Bennehan, 172
Cameron, Duncan, 19, 22, 42, 59, 61,
  117; business with Kirklands, 16,
  18, 21, 24, 81, 136, 139; friendship

with Kirklands, 21, 24, 57, 122–24,
129; house of, 32, 34; children of,
66, 86, 109; and Anna Kirkland,
96–97, 102–4
Cameron, Jean Syme, 97
Cameron, John, 100, 101, 102, 104,
129
Cameron, John A., 45
Cameron, Lizzie, 99
Cameron, Margaret B., 97
Cameron, Mary, 97
Cameron, Mary Anne, 109, 126
Cameron, Paul Carrington, 72, 94,
159; and Alexander Kirkland, 57,
95–96; and John Kirkland, 60, 174,
176; and Catherine Ruffin, 109–10,
111–12, 117; and Anne Ruffin,
109–10, 111, 122, 173; and Wil-
liam Kirkland, 126, 127, 128, 133,
143; advice of, 166, 169; relations
with wife's parents, 172–74; home
in Hillsborough, 198 (n. 9)
Cameron, Rebecca Bennehan (wife of
Duncan Cameron), 22, 110, 123
Cameron, Rebecca Bennehan (daugh-
ter of Duncan Cameron), 97, 123,
124
Cameron, Thomas Amis Dudley, 57,
96, 173
Cameron, Dr. Thomas Nash, 69, 203
(n. 7)
Cameron, William E., 96, 104
Cameron, William E., Jr., 95, 102,
104, 114
Campbell, Alexander, 5
Campbell, Catlett, 18, 143
Campbell, Daniel, 5
Cascade plantation, 159
Castlehill (Ayr, Scotland), 2, 3, 9
Cathcart, Hon. Charles, 7

Chambers, Benjamin, 52, 77
Chany (Kirkland slave), 50
Charity (Kirkland slave), 50, 143
Churton, William, 15
Civil War, 149, 150, 157, 162, 163–
66
Clark, Louisa, 90
Clifton, William, 47
Clinton, Richard S., 93
Collier, William, 32–33
Collin (Kirkland slave), 50
Colonial Inn (Hillsborough), 143
Colquhoun, Robert and Walter, firm
of, 17, 18
Columbus, Ga.: de Graffenriedts in,
46, 80–81, 85–88, 145, 146, 155
Courtney, William, 16, 17, 20
Courtney, William, Jr., 17
Crow, Maria S. Kirkland, 167, 168,
175, 176
Cumberland County, N.C.: Kirkland
property in, 39
Cunningham, William, 5
Cupid (Ruffin slave), 40

Davis, Jefferson, 160, 165
DeBow, Dr. Solomon, 77
De Graffenried, Edwin Louis, Jr., 155
De Graffenried, Jane. *See* Thompson,
Jane de Graffenried
De Graffenried, Victoria, 155
De Graffenried, William Kirkland, 46
De Graffenriedt, Dr. Edwin Louis, 45,
46, 80–81, 86, 145, 155
De Graffenriedt, Dr. John, 45
De Graffenriedt, Martha (Patsy)
Shepperd Kirkland, 94, 130, 135,
137; birth of, 22; marriage and
family of, 45–46, 80–81, 85, 86,
155; health of, 66, 137; and father's

Index

Hogg, James, 15, 30, 39, 153
Hogg, John, 30
Holloway, John, 38
Holt, Dr. Archibald Murphey, 121
Holt, Hines, 155
Holt, Isaac, 19, 173
Holt, Jane Lockhart, 19
Holt, Letitia Wale Scott (Letty or Lettie), 19, 138, 173
Holt, Michael, 19
Hooper, William, 15
Hooper, Rev. William, 57, 201 (n. 4)
Houze, Henry Y., 38, 79, 147
Houze and Yarbrough, firm of, 77
Hudson, Cephus, 52
Huntingdon, Roswell, 95
Huske, Rev. Joseph Caldwell, 153
Huske, Margaret Strange, 46, 153
Hutchison, George, 3
Hutchison, Jane (Jean). *See* Kirkland, Jane Hutchison
Hutchison, Jenet McLure, 3
Hybart, Thomas L., 45
Hysteria, x, 66–71, 73, 85

Irvin, Thomas, and Company, 79

Jeany (Kirkland slave, sold to Edmund Strudwick), 50
Jeany (Kirkland slave), 50
Jenny (Kirkland slave), 86, 143
Jenrette, Richard Hampton, vii, viii
Jerry (Murphey slave), 76
Jesse (Ruffin slave), 125
Joe (Kirkland slave), 50
Johnston, Charles W., 98
Johnston, Eliza Bond, 59, 92, 94, 97
Johnston, George Mulholland, 59, 92, 93, 94, 121, 196 (n. 1)
Johnston, Gen. Joseph E., 165
Johnston, William, 15

Jones, Mrs. Edward. *See* Jones, Mary Curtis Mallett
Jones, Mary Curtis Mallett, 56, 106
Jones, Pride, 175
Jones, Sally, 159
Jones, Capt. William, 34
Jones, Willie, 111
Judy (Kirkland slave), 50

Kinchen, John, 16, 17
Kinnion, Paul, 41
Kinnion, Paul, and Co., 41
Kirkland, Alexander McKenzie, 70, 119, 120, 127, 154; birth and upbringing of, 22, 29, 57–58, 93; and Catherine Ruffin, 51, 56, 89, 94, 95, 107, 108–9; description of, 58, 93, 97, 99, 103; career and marriage of, 93–94, 95–99, 139; death of, 99–101, 103, 146; and father's estate, 135, 137, 138, 145, 176, heirs of, 147, 177
Kirkland, Alexander Mackenzie (son of John Kirkland, grocer), 28, 127
Kirkland, Alexander McKenzie (son of John Umstead Kirkland), 163, 170, 176
Kirkland, Ann (sister of William Kirkland), 28
Kirkland, Ann (daughter of John Kirkland, grocer), 127
Kirkland, Ann (daughter of Nugent Kirkland), 28, 127
Kirkland, Anna McKenzie Cameron, 119, 129, 142; family background of, 95–96; marriage and children of, 96–99, 101, 114, 130, 137; insanity of, 102–5, 155
Kirkland, Anne McNabb. *See* Ruffin, Anne McNabb Kirkland
Kirkland, Annie Ruffin. *See* Hill, An-

planter establishment, ix, 24–25, 31–32, 37, 39, 41; Scottish origins of, 1–12; and Daniel Anderson, 12–14, 18, 22, 23–24; partnerships of, 13, 18, 30, 38, 55, 79; marriage and family of, 14, 18–19, 21–22, 30; and Duncan Cameron, 16, 18, 21, 24, 81, 122–24, 129; slaves of, 16, 18, 40, 42, 49–50, 86, 142, 143; and Hillsborough stores of, 16, 38, 39, 79, 82, 130, 132; acquisition of property by, 16–17, 18, 31, 38–39, 76, 77, 181–86; clerks of, 17, 26, 38–39, 92, 120–21, 132, 196 (n. 1); tanyard of, 18, 38, 140–41, 144, 147, 170, 176; and religion, 20, 41–42, 47; and education, 20–21, 29–30, 47, 56, 57, 64; and daughters, 20–21, 40, 46, 68–70, 85; sociability of, 22–23, 62–63, 71–72, 96–97, 122–25, 173; visit to Scotland, 26, 29–30; as planter, 26, 49–50, 53–55; Fayetteville store of, 30, 41, 47, 78, 79; and Thomas Ruffin, 39, 40, 75–78, 80, 133–36, 174; financial difficulties of, 75–84, 119–20, 127–28; will and estate settlement of, 81, 132–39, 142–48, 174–75, 176–77; trip to Tennessee, 120, 121–22; illness and death of, 126, 128–31

Kirkland, William, and Company, 16, 17, 23

Kirkland, William, and Son, 79, 89, 98, 122, 146

Kirkland, William (infant son of William Kirkland, b. 1799), 22

Kirkland, William (infant son of William Kirkland, b. 1801), 22

Kirkland, Adm. William Alexander,

98, 105, 114, 147, 160–62, 164–65, 168–69

Kirkland, Gen. William Whedbee, 150, 157, 159–60, 163, 164, 167, 170, 176, 218 (n. 23)

Kirkland and Houze, firm of, 79

Kirkland and Webb, firm of, 122

Kirkland's corner (lot 25), 79, 98

Kirkwood, Anne, 29

Kirkwood, Jean Kirkland (Jane) (sister of William Kirkland), 29

LaGrange, Tenn.: William Kirkland visit to, 122

Laws, George, 50

Lea, Anness. *See* McNeill, Anness Lea

Lenox Castle (Rockingham County), 71, 76

Lewis (Kirkland slave), 50

Little Hawfields (Hillsborough), 172

Littlejohn, Thomas B., 34

Little River Presbyterian Church, 20, 49

Lochiel plantation, 97

Lockhart, Jane. *See* Holt, Jane Lockhart

Louisburg, N.C.: William Kirkland property in, 38, 79, 144

McAdam, John L., 7

McClure, William, 7–8

Machen, Betty. *See* Scott, Elizabeth Machen

Machen, George Wale, 14

Machen, Henry, 14

Machen, John, 14

Machen, Letty, 14

Machen, Thomas, 14

Machen, Thomas, Jr., 14

McIntee, Mary Machen, 14

Moravian Boarding School for Girls, 21

Moravians, 21

Morrison, Mary Graham, 109

Moses, Mary Ashe, 60, 89, 155, 158

Muirhouse, Scotland, 9

Mulhollan[d], J. S., 121

Murphey, Archibald DeBow, 31, 121, 128; description of, 19; and Kirklands, 19, 23, 29, 75–77, 82, 120, 146; and Thomas Ruffin, 23, 52, 75–77, 81; financial debacle of, 75–77, 81–82, 138; death of, 82–83

Murphey, Jane Armistead Scott, 19, 76, 138

Murphey, Dr. Victor Moreau, 94, 95, 112, 113, 114, 124, 131

Murphey and Kirkland, firm of, 94, 98

Myrtle Hill plantation, 46–47, 69

Nash, Ann. *See* Strudwick, Ann Nash

Nash, Gen. Francis, 15

Nash, Chief Justice Frederick, 61, 123

Nash, Henry Kollock, 59, 157

Nash, Maria, 61, 167

Nash, Mary Simpson, 157, 164

Nash, Sarah Kollock (Sally), 61, 90, 111, 113

Nash, Susan. *See* Read, Susan Nash

Nash and Kollock School, 167

Nashville, Tenn.: William Kirkland visit to, 121

Newfields, Ayrshire, 9

New Hope Presbyterian Church, 20

Noah (Ruffin slave), 52–53

Norfleet, Anna, 21

Norfleet, Felicia, 21

North Carolina Railroad, 156, 157

Norwich University, 57, 93, 160

Norwood, Helen Mary, 121

Norwood, Jane. *See* Tillinghast, Jane Norwood

Norwood, Joseph, 121

Norwood, Robina Hogg, 140, 153

Norwood, Judge William, 51, 121, 123

Nugent, Capt. Lawrence, 7

Nutt, Elhannon, 34

Nutt, William, 34

Odd Fellows Orphans' Home, 167

Odend'hal, Jean, 143

Old Indian Trading Path, 15, 16, 17

Orange County, N.C.: William Kirkland's move to, 14; William Kirkland's land in, 16–17, 24, 39, 181–85

Orange Hotel (Hillsborough), 143

Osborn (Kirkland slave), 50

Parish, Charles, 32, 33, 197 (n. 17)

Parker, Harrison, 143

Parks, David, 177

Parmy (Ruffin slave), 40

Partridge, Capt. Alden, 57

Partridge's Academy. *See* Norwich University

Patsy (Kirkland slave), 50

Peace College, 166

Phil (slave, tanner), 38

Phillips, James, 18

Phillips, Capt. James, 40

Phillips, Polly, 21

Phillips, Samuel F., 150

Pike, John C., 23

Plummer, Lucy, 59

Plummer, William, 59

Pollock, Cullen, 39

Polly (Kirkland slave), 98

borough, 17, 35. *See also* illustrations following p. 73

Scotland: in eighteenth century, 1–8

Scott, Elizabeth Machen (Betty), 14, 76, 82, 94, 125, 137, 138, 141

Scott, Jane Armistead. *See* Murphey, Jane Armistead Scott

Scott, John, ix, 12, 13, 14, 19, 22, 24

Scott, John (son of Thomas Scott), 151, 214 (n. 9)

Scott, Letitia (Letty). *See* Holt, Letitia Wale Scott

Scott, Lewis Mitchell, 151, 214 (n. 9)

Scott, Margaret Blain. *See* Kirkland, Margaret Blain Scott

Scott, Maria Duffy, 19, 23

Scott, Nancy, 151, 214 (n. 9)

Scott, Thomas, 23, 128, 141; business of, 18, 31, 76, 138; wife and family of, 19, 151, 214 (n. 9); illness and death of, 150, 151; as candidate for sheriff, 212 (n. 13)

Scott, Thomas, and Company, 76

Scott and Kirkland, firm of, 13, 14, 18

Shepherd, Elizabeth Lee Kirkland, 218 (n. 23)

Shepherd, Rezin Davis, 218 (n. 23)

Sherman, Gen. William T., 165

Shocco Springs (Warren County, N.C.), 71, 110

Simpson, Elizabeth Adam (Betsy). *See* Kirkland, Elizabeth Adam Simpson

Simpson, Maria. *See* Hill, Maria Simpson

Simpson, Samuel, 90, 91, 92, 144, 157, 158

Simpson, Mrs. Samuel, 157, 158

Simpson, Sarah. *See* Manly, Sarah Simpson

Slaves, 98, 123, 132, 149; of John Scott, 12, 13; of Kirklands, 16, 49, 50, 86, 134, 142, 143, 170; of Ruffins, 40, 51–53, 76; feared insurrection of, 51; of Archibald Murphey, 76

Smith, Andrew, 62–63

Smith, Mrs. Andrew, 62, 64

Smith, Elizabeth. *See* Kirkland, Elizabeth Smith

Smith, Dr. James S., 68, 82

Smith, Rachel, 63

Society of Improvers of Knowledge of Agriculture, The, 4

Spear, Maria, 113

Spencer, Isaiah, 143

Stagville plantation, 54–55, 113

State Bank of North Carolina, 78

State Hospital for the Insane (Morganton, N.C.), 179

State Normal and Industrial School (Greensboro, N.C.), 166

Steven (Kirkland slave), 170

Strang, John, 45

Strang, Robert, 30, 44, 45, 47–48

Strange, Alexander, 151–52

Strange, French, 151, 152

Strange, James (father of Robert Strange), 44

Strange, James W., 63, 151, 152, 153, 155

Strange, Jane Rebecca Kirkland, 56, 62, 63, 69; birth of, 22; marriage and family of, 44, 151, 152; homes of, 46; ill health and death of, 66, 137, 151; and Catherine Ruffin, 110, 117

Strange, John, 151–52

Strange, Margaret. *See* Huske, Margaret Strange

76; character of, 52, 137; and Polly
 Burke's school, 56
Webb, James, Jr., 175
Webb, John, 159
Webb and Kirkland, firm of, 81
White Sulphur Springs, W.Va., 71,
 123
Whitted, William, 21
Wiley [Wylie], Thomas, 16
Wilhelm II, Kaiser, 169
William (Kirkland slave), 50
Williamson, George, 41

Wilson Sanatorium, 167
Windsor (Bertie County, N.C.), 114,
 116
Witherspoon, Rev. John, 21, 41, 47
Witherspoon, Sophia Graham, 109

Yarbrough, David, 76, 80, 134, 135,
 136
Yarbrough, Fanny, 59
Yarbrough, James, 18, 79
Yarbrough and Kirkland, firm of, 55